MIND
MATTERS

MICHAEL S. GAZZANIGA

MIND MATTERS

How Mind and Brain Interact to Create Our Conscious Lives

Houghton Mifflin Company   Boston

Published in association with the MIT Press, Bradford Books

Library of Congress Cataloging-in-Publication Data
Gazzaniga, Michael S.
Mind matters.
"Bradford books."
Bibliography: p.
Includes index.
1. Neuropsychology—Popular works.   2. Psychology,
Pathological—Popular works.   I. Title.   [DNLM:
1. Mental Disorders—popular works.   2. Neuropsychology
—popular works.   WL 103 G291m]
QP360.G39   1988   152   87-26246
ISBN 0-395-42159-4
ISBN 0-395-50095-8 (pbk.)

Printed in the United States of America

S 10 9 8 7 6 5 4 3 2 1

Book design by Victoria Hartman

The author is grateful for permission to quote
from the following works:
New Perspectives in Abnormal Psychology by Alan
E. Kazdin, Alan S. Bellack, and Michael Hersen.
Copyright © 1980 by Oxford University Press, Inc.
Reprinted by permission.
"Vermin" by E. B. White. Reprinted by permission; © 1944, 1972
by E. B. White. Originally published in The New Yorker.

For my mother
ALICE MARIE GAZZANIGA
Gallant, loving, and enduring

Contents

Foreword

by Robert Bazell

The science of the brain is characterized best by its enormous potential. This book offers an excellent path to explore that potential and appreciate the extent to which it is being realized.

I met the author when I set out to prepare a feature report for the *NBC Nightly News* on the implications of split-brain research. Reading a few articles and talking to other scientists, I learned quickly that Michael Gazzaniga was pre-eminent, the one whose work should be featured. So I called for an appointment. But I was wary. An encounter between a brain scientist and a journalist carries risks that experience has taught me not to ignore.

Those who study the brain work in a field where so little is known compared to other sciences that the researchers are free to theorize and experiment with far fewer constraints than those toiling in the more "mature" sciences such as physics and chemistry. The results they achieve have much greater appeal to the public than most science. The physicist who discovers a new subatomic particle of matter will see his name on the front page of newspapers for a day and might win a Nobel prize, but few nonscientists will know or care what he has achieved. An endocrinologist who finds a means of preventing some gall bladder disease will bring great joy to those who fear they might suffer the affliction, and that is likely to be no small number. But let an experimental psychologist or brain chemist say he has elicited a truth about the nature of pain, intelligence, love, or stress (to name a few of the subjects in this book), and the audience will be massive indeed.

This relative freedom and popular appeal allow a few individuals to thrive in brain research who, at least at a given time, might be regarded as producing results that do not stand up to the accepted rigors of the scientific method. In other words, they are flakes, and most often with no shortage of hubris. But that is inevitable for a field so open to new ideas and approaches. To avoid accusations that they are less than scientific, certain brain researchers strictly confine their experiments and their interpretations of them. They manage to produce work that is scientifically sound, boring, and meaningless. What a shame. For one of the great attractions of brain science is the variety of the ideas to be considered. At a gathering of brain researchers, one may be discussing the implications of quantum mechanics and religion for theories of consciousness while another describes experiments measuring the transmission of electrical signals through the nerve cells of a squid. And the two discussions can merge! The possibilities for studying our brain are no more limited than its capabilities.

In the first seconds of our first conversation, I realized that Gazzaniga was as far as possible from the flakes. His research is sound. His methods are the best. His long list of publications and professional honors attests to that. More important, I was struck by the logic and clarity of his work. We know Gazzaniga's results are correct from the usual proofs of science, but his research has the additional attribute that we know intuitively it is so from our experience of ourselves and others. Such findings are rare in any field of research, including brain science. In addition, Gazzaniga cannot be counted among the timid. He is willing to propose theories, to suggest connections, and to call on as many as possible of the intellectual resources available for the study of the brain, including (and this is rare indeed) a sense of humor.

All this he brings to *Mind Matters*. Here is a summary of what is current in brain research, from the chemistry of molecules that carry information among neurons, to the anatomy of those neurons, to studies of the way the mind forms ideas. But this is no dry textbook. Its organization under headings of everyday states of mind holds our interest. It may seem uninspiring to read about a molecule; it is another matter to consider the molecule's role in sexual arousal, addiction, and anxiety.

Although this book is not about Gazzaniga's research, the reader should keep it in mind. Often he uses his work as a platform to observe the research of others. In his own studies, Gazzaniga has examined people whose brains have been cut in half. To treat intractable epilepsy, for example, a surgeon might sever the main bundle of nerve fibers connecting the right and left hemispheres. The patients then have, in effect, two brains operating independently. Other scientists have inferred a great deal of simplistic and often nonsensical popular psychology from Gazzaniga's work with split-brain patients. Anyone even slightly familiar with those assertions will be interested in reading what the actual experiments revealed. Gazzaniga details some of them in this book and more in earlier books devoted entirely to split-brain research.

This is not to say that Gazzaniga's results are boring. When we videotaped him working with split-brain patients, the interactions proved fascinating to a wide audience.

One of the main conclusions of the research is that different parts of the human brain operate independently of one another. Often one part of a person's brain will cause a certain behavior, and he will not know why he is acting that way. When that happens, another part of the brain, what Gazzaniga calls the "left-brain interpreter," steps in and offers an explanation or rationalization, no matter how far-fetched, to explain the behav-

ior. Gazzaniga postulates a role for the interpreter for each of
the mind states he describes. It is an intriguing set of conclusions
that offer each of us a new way of considering our own behavior.

Gazzaniga also invokes the left-brain interpreter as part of
his argument against the idea, fashionable among many scientists, that there is no mind at all. There is, the argument goes,
only a glob of matter, containing cells and chemicals, called
the brain, and if we understood its parts well enough, we would
understand consciousness and all the other aspects of thought
that we consider precious. This biological determination was
expressed by Carl Sagan in his popular book *The Dragons of
Eden*. "My fundamental premise about the brain," Sagan wrote,
"is that its workings—what we sometimes call 'mind'—are a
consequence of its anatomy and physiology and nothing more."

In one sense, what Sagan asserts has to be true. Obviously,
our thoughts originate in our brain. But saying that certainly
does not help us much to understand our brain or our behavior.
At this point, science has as much chance of understanding
the brain solely through the study of cells and molecules as
one would have of appreciating the beauty of a Mozart sym-
phony by learning how a piano string works.

Gazzaniga's view, backed amply by his research and that of
others, is that "mind affects brain and brain affects mind." He
makes his case forcefully and offers some profound insights
into the way we do and should consider behavior. Because of
his ability to appreciate both the profound new discoveries in
the molecular biology of the brain as well as the studies in his
own area, cognitive psychology, Gazzaniga offers us a refresh-
ing and comprehensive survey of a field of science that never
fails to fascinate.

Preface

For years, I have studiously avoided writing about most of the topics covered in this book. My interests have centered on how the human brain is built and how that architecture supports normal human cognition, human beliefs, human consciousness. Believe it or not, compared to the subjects in this book, those are pretty clean and straightforward. By staying with them, I felt fairly safe and also aloof from the stuff of most of our life, the hard properties of our existence such as pain, love, depression, craziness, and so on.

One evening, sitting in the Rainbow Room high above Rockefeller Center, a friend suggested that I ought to write a practical book about drugs for the general public and that it would pay a lot of money. I said—with an ear to the money part—I'd do it. I go to bed at night seeing bursar's bills in my dreams, burdened with what is apparently the endless task of paying college tuition fees for my gang of daughters. But I said a practical or "how-to" book wouldn't be half as interesting as a "what-do-we-know" book about various mental states. This assertion covered my then considerable ignorance about such matters of mind.

The bravado over drinks soon had to be translated into action, and I became leery. Learning about these matters has been invigorating for me. It forced me to read a new literature and to discover that my previous work on the brain had prepared me for much of what can be said about mental states. More importantly, the exercise revealed the many ways mind and brain interact over a wide variety of everyday psychological states. It also showed me how discussing neurobiological information in the absence of a psychological context was as empty as discussing states of mind without bringing into play the new knowledge of brain states. The luxury of remaining ignorant about one or the other area is no longer available to the contemporary student of human nature. This book is my effort to bring general readers into these fascinating topics and to show them the links between mind and brain. But there is more.

It is impossible for someone who has spent his life in one type of brain research not to see relations that might well exist in another type of research. The aphrodisiac of the scientist is the hypothesis, a statement about what may be going on when given a body of information to consider. I am no different, and herein I invite both the professional and the curious reader to consider how certain ideas derived from my kind of brain research, research on patients with divided brains, might apply to the common problems of everyday as well as pathological mental states. The framework suggested here serves as a bridge between the psychologist interested in behavior and the neurobiologist who struggles to determine the wholly physical characteristics of the brain. Bridges are needed and this is mine.

There are dozens of people to thank for helping me complete this book. They range from the supercritical to the supportive. Bill Hirst gave his critical and editorial best, as did Joseph Le Doux. Ira Black was tough on me in the early going and offered sage suggestions. Jerome Posner, who is my nominee for the best physician in the world, weighed in with much good advice. Finally, there is Leon Festinger, who can find the loophole in a Supreme Court brief. I was highly encouraged by the fact that he kept on reading, although I burned his criticisms. No one can deal with the profound level on which he treats all matters. My appreciation goes to many others, including Julie Eilenberg and Susan Buros—also my wonderful daughters and my wife, who spent hours in the library pulling out the relevant papers for me to read and typing and retyping the manuscript. It is always appropriate to thank one's editor, as a matter of course. In this case, Austin Olney deserves far more than I can say. He saw a man who needed help with language and supplied it with an unmatched zeal and verve. Many thanks to all.

Introduction
Mind Facts, Brain Facts

It is old hat to say that the brain is responsible for our mental activity. Such a claim may annoy the likes of Jerry Falwell or the Ayatollah, but it is more or less the common assumption of educated people in the twentieth century. Ever since the scientific revolution, the guiding view of most scientists has been that knowledge about the brain, its cells, and its chemistry will explain mental states. However, believing that the brain supports behavior is the easy part; explaining how is quite another. This challenging topic has been, to a great extent, divided into two disciplines. On the one hand, there are scientists who study the brain and are concerned first and foremost with its functioning. They are like computer scientists who are interested in the hardware of a computer. They want to know how the cells of the brain are organized and how they work. On the other hand, there are those scientists interested in studying mental behavior. They are like computer scientists who analyze the software programs of a computer. They realize that functional software depends on functional hardware, but they concentrate on understanding the processes necessary to elicit behavior, not necessarily on the way the hardware carries out these processes.

In the past two decades, advances in thinking about how

brain and mind operate separately have been richly rewarding. More important, scientists are now beginning to understand how the brain and mind interact. Until recently, the brain scientists could not imagine how to talk to the mind scientists, just as the mind scientists have avoided discussion with the brain scientists. In the past, each has laid undue claim to understanding the mind-brain functions from his own perspective alone. Let's say you have a delusional friend who thinks he is the King of Siam. The conventional brain scientist says the problem with your friend is biochemical, and the conventional mind scientist notes something about a traumatic childhood. Both ideas, or, more accurately, dispositions, miss the mark of an adequate explanation by a mile.

The challenge for mind and brain scientists has been to come up with a conceptual framework that can tie together abnormalities of brain tissue, or, more commonly, normal variations in brain chemistry, with the personal, psychological reality of our individual minds. Until recently, it has been possible only to say that states of mind *must* relate to brain states. Now, because of a startling set of findings in brain chemistry, it is possible to identify specific malfunctions in brain metabolism and chemistry and to associate them with a wide variety of mind states ranging from memory capacity to feelings of love. However, that is only half the story. The other half is made possible because of developments in mind science that are beginning to reveal how humans interpret and respond to felt changes in body chemistry. When the two developments are put together, a framework appears that goes a long way toward explaining our states of mind in straightforward, mechanistic terms. For the first time, an explanatory picture that builds on both brain research and mind research emerges. Either one alone does not do the trick. This book is about that framework and about how it helps us to understand a wide variety of very personal mind states we all experience at one time or another.

The model is simple but powerful. Let's say a brain change

occurs in Harry. This may be due to an over- or underproduction of a certain chemical. Such happenings are now known to occur frequently in all of us—as a reaction to environmental stimuli, the reaction of a previously silent brain structure, or for no discernible reason. The brain change produces a different feeling in Harry, a feeling that must be interpreted. The human mind seems intent on interpreting everything as a matter of course, and thus it is a part of Harry's psychology to find a cause for his changed state. He assesses his outside environment, his inside thoughts, and comes up with a theory as to why he has this unfamiliar feeling.

The human mind does not say, "I feel this way because of brain chemistry." It speeds right past that account and goes on to identify a cause. That interpretation itself becomes an event in Harry's life, and as such it becomes a memory. Harry's brain is working normally when it comes to memory, so Harry stores this information. His interpretation becomes a part of his life experience.

Let's say Harry stored the idea that being in crowds makes him nervous. He developed that idea because when he was in a crowd before, his brain state changed and he suddenly felt anxious. Scientists now know what biochemical events occur that suddenly unleash that feeling. But even though Harry may know about such things at an academic level, his internal interpreter asks "Why?" Looking around, he deduces that the cause must be crowds. Eventually, Harry develops a phobia for crowds, since he does not like feeling anxious.

Harry then goes to a doctor who diagnoses the problem as endogenous anxiety. The doctor explains to him that there are chemicals in his brain that malfunction on occasion and give rise to the feeling of anxiety. This is easily countered by a drug. When he takes the drug, Harry no longer has anxiety attacks. The medication's effectiveness suggests that Harry's problem was essentially biochemical in nature. But what about the phobias and other distorted views of life he developed during the attacks? The drug does not work for those problems, because there is a psychological as well as a biochemical dimension to them. His phobias and other theories are now normally established memories, which have their own existence in his brain. They continue to govern areas of his life. Harry may no longer feel anxious in crowds, but he still avoids them. His memory of past anxiety attacks is too vivid. So, to deal with psychological problems, drugs will not do. One must deal with Harry's view of the world—a job for a psychiatrist or psychologist, not a pharmacologist.

This example underscores how brain (the fluctuating physical-chemical state) interacts with mind (the interpretative state). It also shows how activities at one level influence processes at the other. The chemical state provoked a change in Harry's mental state about crowds. His changed mental state fed back to and changed his brain state. Harry's case suggests that understanding how people come to think about themselves and others can be greatly influenced by learning how closely brain mechanics are tied to our seemingly highly personal mind mechanics.

In what follows we will attempt to uncover certain key relationships between brain and mind, drawing upon both psychological and neurobiological research and presenting it in the mind–brain framework just described.

Brain Science

Modern research about the brain and about the psychological nature of humans is not conceptually taxing in the way a topic is in physics, such as statistical mechanics. In fact, most of current brain and mind science is built on a few simple principles.

There are two main levels to most current research on the brain. The first involves events within individual cells, and the second is concerned with how large groups of cells are organized in such a way that they produce human conscious experience.

The first level is by far the easier of the two to learn about.

The brain is made up of different kinds of cells, and the ones of most interest for students of behavior are neurons. Neurons come in all shapes and sizes and are the basic building blocks of the nervous system. Neurons are complex things. They must accept messages from other neurons, decide whether or not to pass on the information (which makes them consummate bureaucrats), and then, having made the decision to send it, must do so in an efficient manner. Whether or not the neuron decides to pass on the information it receives depends not only on its original state but also on what other neurons are saying to it. In hundredths of a second, any particular neuron may adjudicate up to hundreds of messages by other neurons as to what each of them suggests it should do. It is estimated that there are one hundred billion neurons in the human brain, and each of them is busy most of the time.

The part of the neuron that receives information is a gangly mesh of sensitive tissue called the dendrite. The dendrite is a wonderfully complex system that is sensitive to various sets of chemicals constantly being released in its local environment, and even to chemicals released at some distance and brought to it through the blood. The dendrites recognize these chemicals through a receptor mechanism. It is the discovery of the special brain receptors that has allowed us to understand how specific chemicals cause a neuron to trigger itself to pass on information by sending a tiny electrical signal down its long output pathway, which is called the axon. The action takes place in the neuronal membrane that surrounds the neuron like the skin of a hot dog.

It is this straightforward series of events that finds a neuron receiving a message and responding. The neuron takes into account all of the electrical impulses it is receiving by way of its many dendrites, and if a threshold is reached, it fires. This is the receiving, or input, side of the story. Once the neuron fires, we no longer think of it as a receiving system. Suddenly, it becomes a sending system, as it now tries to influence all the neurons it is connected to. First it's a catcher, then it's a batter.

Along the axon there is a torrent of activity in the comings and goings of small, electrically charged ions that play a crucial role in sending the message along its way. Then an important event occurs at the axon's terminal. The electrical message signals the release of a chemical called a neurotransmitter, which will energize the dendritic membranes of neighboring neurons so that they too will send electrical impulses. Once the neurotransmitter has been discharged and sent on its way, the neuron stops being a batter and gets itself ready once again to be a catcher and to accept the next set of neurotransmitters thrown to it by nearby neurons. This process continues incessantly, while we are asleep or awake.

The chemical decision as to whether or not a neuron will trigger is made at the synapse, which is the linking place between neurons where much of the fundamental business of brain activity is carried out. It needs a closer look.

Imagine that neuron A has fired. The discharge activates structures at its tip called synaptic boutons. The boutons quickly secrete the neurotransmitter into the synaptic cleft (the space between synapses where two neurons communicate). Most neurons secrete only one kind of transmitter, but some secrete many. There are twenty-six known neurotransmitters. One of the most common is acetylcholine. When released into the cleft, some of this transmitter will find a receptor on neuron B, which, logically enough, is called a postsynaptic neuron. Some of it will be split apart into other chemicals and pumped back for reuse into the cell from which it came. That is called reuptake. The molecules that find their way out of neuron A to a receptor on neuron B will try to change neuron B's membrane so that it too will discharge. But remember, neuron A merely contributes to the decision neuron B must make about firing. Neuron B is listening to many other neurons at the same time, and some may be telling it not to fire. The neuron, like any good congressman, is listening to all its constituents before casting its vote to fire.

As a general rule, the greater the amount of excitatory neurotransmitter there is in a cleft, the higher the probability that neural transmission will occur. And the more receptors a neuron has, the more likely it is to fire when the correct transmitter is present in the cleft. Clearly, the chemical events that take place at the synapse determine whether or not neural communication continues.

The brain would stop functioning if there were no neurotransmitters to pass messages between neurons. Because of this critical role, they have become a central preoccupation for researchers in brain science. The vast majority of work done in the field of psychopharmacology is in examining the biochemical conditions under which neurons will transmit a message. Scientists have learned how some diseases occur when certain neurons do not get enough or, alternatively, get too much of a neurotransmitter, and then either try to get more of the needed neurotransmitter or, conversely, try to find a chemical way of blocking the effect of having too much. In either case, the neuron is restoring the balance and, if successful, should once again function normally.

The much discussed and prevalent neurological disorder Parkinson's disease illustrates the basic process. The disorder results from the death of nerve cells in a particular part of the brain. These cells are active in producing a neurotransmitter called dopamine and are part of a brain circuit that is heavily involved in managing our ability to move and walk. Parkinsonian patients lose control of muscular activity. They tremble and have trouble with fine motor movements. It was first thought that if more dopamine was made available to the whole brain, the impoverished area might benefit in some way. It doesn't work that way. If patients were given huge doses of this chemical, it would be to no avail, since it is known that the chemical has the wrong shape to get across something called the blood-brain barrier, a special system the brain has to keep out unwanted body chemicals.

The search continued. Scientists knew some nerve cells could still be living in the zone of death afflicted by the disease, and perhaps if they could be made to produce more dopamine, all would be well. In order to by-pass the blood–brain barrier problem, researchers injected patients with L-dopa, a very small molecule that could sneak through the barrier. L-dopa is a precursor of dopamine, the desired chemical. With more of the precursor available to the remaining neurons, they could make more than their normal quota of dopamine. In effect, the remaining neurons, by working harder, could cover for their dead companions. L-dopa worked! Patients with debilitating Parkinsonism found that they again had control over their muscles and could move normally. The Parkinson's disease story is truly remarkable. Theory and practice came together.

There are other tricks psychopharmacologists have developed to help manipulate the chemical activity at the synapse. For example, they can manufacture chemicals called agonists. Some agonists mimic the action of particular neurotransmitters and will trigger the same receptors the neurotransmitter triggers. They can also manufacture chemicals called antagonists, which block the action of neurotransmitters by tying up the receptors to which the neurotransmitter normally attaches.

The second level of analysis of brain function moves beyond the event in any single connection between neurons to the larger pattern of those nerve connections. In computers, different electrical circuits produce different machines with different capacities. The same appears to be true for the brain. Most brain scientists assume that the actual pattern of connections in a particular brain is vastly important to understanding the patterns of behavior associated with that brain. While the general anatomical relations are the same for all human brains—for example, the nerves from the eyes project to specific regions of the brain— the details of projection vary from one person to another. The possibilities for variation in what is called the association cortex, the part of the human brain believed to be most active in the production of thought, are enormous. When you recall that over one hundred billion neurons are somehow tied together in a network, it seems highly unlikely there could be anything but variation at the cell-to-cell level. A major challenge has been to demonstrate how these variations in neural patterns reflect psychological patterns. To date, however, we can demonstrate only that variations in cell-to-cell organization *can* occur and can be produced by changing the milieu of the developing brain.

Another important factor in understanding how brains work is the role of inheritance. It is well established that the process for hooking up one hundred billion neurons in an orderly way is largely a function of the messages read from the genes. In addition to controlling the wiring pattern of the neurons, genes also influence the degree to which certain cells will react to particular neurotransmitters. That is, genetic influences can be evident at the synapses, making them more or less efficient, as the case may be. In short, genes can affect the performance of brain networks.

Mind Science

With an awareness about brain chemicals, nerve networks, and genes, we move on to the final and highest level of analysis, the mind. Again using the computer analogy, we turn now from the hardware to the programs. The mind has its own realities and its own characteristics. Just as water has properties that differ from those of its component elements, hydrogen and oxygen, the mind has properties that can be described at the level of function. Since the mind is derived from brain tissue, the state of brain tissue ought to affect mind. And since the mind resides in brain tissue, the state of mind ought to have effects on brain.

It is important to realize here that I am not suggesting that mind is something other than what derives from brain, something that floats around, as it were, independent of brain but making frequent visits upon it to try to influence it. Recognizing that there are two distinct levels of analysis does not imply that mind is not part of brain. "Mind" is used here in the sense that a physical system can have emergent properties that become active in guiding the workings of the physical system that gave rise to them. Just as the water molecule is in dynamic equilibrium with the elements hydrogen and oxygen, the mind is in some kind of dynamic equilibrium with the cellular and network aspects of the brain. Clearly, the properties of water are quite different from the properties of the elements that make it up. Compare the simple equilibrium of a water molecule with the complex equilibrium that must exist among billions of nerve cells and their product and you have a notion of the magnitude and density of mind-brain interactions. More important, the emergent properties of brain, the operating rules of the system we call mind, can push information around in such a fashion that the actual functioning of the nerves can be influenced by what the mind does.

Scientists studying brains learn how the mind is altered by brain changes. When they study patients with brain lesions of one kind or another, they discern how, and to some extent where, certain psychological functions are carried out in the brain. The effort is founded on the tried and true principle that studying broken systems helps to understand normal ones. Careful consideration of these studies leads to insights about how information from the physical environment and from the prior history of the organism can affect the generation of our mental life.

According to the prevailing view, the mind has a modular organization. Dozens, perhaps hundreds, of discrete and rather specific subsystems in the mind actively contribute to our capacity to think, feel, and move. These modules can work in parallel, which means their activities can all go on at the same time; one module does not have to wait for another to finish. Many of the modules carry out their work outside the realm of conscious awareness.

Functioning mental modules must have a physical reality, but the brain sciences are not yet able to specify the nature of the actual neural networks involved. What *is* known is that the modules can express themselves to the motor system, the neurons that produce action, and thereby produce behavior and thought. Catching up with what the brain is doing seems to be a function of an interpretative module. Watching this "interpreter" work under strict experimental conditions is most dramatic, and the concept is essential to understanding how our mind and brain are intertwined.

Special tests given to patients who have had the hemispheres of their brain disconnected were the key to discovering the interpreter module. This is a surgical procedure carried out on select patients who have otherwise uncontrollable epilepsy. The human brain has two halves. By and large, the left half of the brain is dominant for language and speech. It also controls and senses the right side of the body's surface. The right half of the brain is also specialized, but for other and fewer functions than the left. It controls the left half of the body and senses its surface. The two halves are interconnected by a huge nerve fiber system called the corpus callosum. This system keeps each half brain up to date on what is going on in the other. After split-brain surgery, patients experience nowhere near the same number of convulsions they had suffered prior to their operation. Clearly, they are much better off, but ironically, it is not clear why the surgery works.

The operation gives scientists an opportunity to study each half brain working more or less independently of influences from the other. This situation is made possible because of the way the visual system is organized in the human brain. Information, such as a picture or a word, presented to the left of a fixed point is projected to the right half brain, while information presented to the right of that point is projected to the left half brain. In the normal, intact brain, information presented to either side is quickly named because of the presence of the communicating nerve bundle, the corpus callosum. In the split-brain patient, however, quite a different story emerges. A picture presented to the right of the point is quickly named, just like in a normal person, because the information is projected to the normally dominant left half brain, the seat of language and speech. The left brain sees the picture and easily describes it. When the picture is presented to the left of the fixed point, however, the split-brain patient is unable to identify it. The image is projected to the right brain and remains isolated in that nondominant hemisphere as a consequence of the discon- necting callosal surgery. The right brain cannot talk; only the left can. As a result, the patient says (this is the left brain talking), "I didn't see anything." And this is true: the left brain didn't see anything. The only way the right brain can indicate it knows something about the stimulus is to point to a matching or related picture. If a picture of an apple had been flashed to the right brain, the patient, while not being able to talk about it, could pick out another apple picture from a group of pictures. Using that strategy, one can test the perceptual and other cognitive functions of the silent right hemisphere. What is important for our current story, however, is how the left brain deals with the behaviors independently generated by the right brain. A simple experiment tells the tale.

The patient is shown two pictures, one exclusively to the left hemisphere and one exclusively to the right, and is asked to choose, from an array of pictures in full view, the one associ- ated with the pictures presented to the left and right brain. In one classic example of this kind of test, a picture of a chicken claw was flashed to the left hemisphere and a picture of a snow scene to the right hemisphere. Of the array of pictures, the obviously correct association was a chicken for the chicken claw and a shovel for the snow scene. In this experiment the patient responded by choosing the shovel with the left hand and the chicken with the right. When asked why he chose these items, he (actually his left hemisphere) replied, "Oh, that's simple. The chicken claw goes with the chicken, and you need a shovel to clean out the chicken shed." Here the left brain, observing the left hand's response, interpreted that response in a context consistent with its sphere of knowledge—one that did not include information about the snow scene.

Another example of this phenomenon of the left brain interpreting actions produced by the disconnected right brain involved sending a written command, "laugh," to the right hemisphere by quickly flashing it to the left visual field. After the word was presented the patient laughed, and when asked why, said, "You guys come up and test us every month. What a way to make a living!" In still another instance, when the command "walk" was flashed to the right hemisphere, the patient stood up from his chair and began to leave the testing van. When asked where he was going, his left brain said, "I'm going into the house to get a Coke." The examples are rich and are easy to elicit in these patients.

There are many ways to influence the interpretative system. As already mentioned, we wanted to know whether or not the emotional response to pictures presented to one half brain would have an effect on the emotional system of the other half brain. In this particular study, we showed the right hemisphere a series of film vignettes that included either violent or calm sequences. We used a device that permits prolonged exposure of visual pictures to the right hemisphere while the eyes remain fixed on a point. The computer-based system keeps careful track of the position of the eyes, so that if they move from the fixed point, the movie sequence is electronically turned off. For example, in one test a film depicting one person throwing another into a fire was shown to the patient's right hemisphere. She responded, "I don't really know what I saw; I think just a white flash. Maybe some trees, red trees like in the fall. I don't know why, but I feel kind of scared. I feel jumpy. I don't like this room, or maybe it's you getting me nervous." As an aside to a colleague, she then said, "I know I like Dr. Gazzaniga, but right now I'm scared of him for some reason." Clearly, the emotional tone associated with the movie had crossed over from the right to the left hemisphere. The left hemisphere was unaware of the content of the movie that produced the emotional change, but it experienced the emotion and had to deal with it. The left-brain interpreter responded by making up a story that explained the newly felt state of mind.

The kinds of things we see in these special patients and under these laboratory conditions can be related to many everyday experiences. Consider how often we go to bed in a good frame of mind only to awake feeling depressed and cranky (or the other way around). The facts about our life haven't changed during the night; why the change in mood? Could it be that a set of memories in a particular mental module have become activated and unleashed biochemical mechanisms that give rise to a specific mood? The idea here is that the left hemisphere, which articulates our thoughts, would then try to interpret these feelings, and might well, somewhat gratuitously, attribute their cause to otherwise innocent events also happening at the same time.

My cursory outline of brain mechanisms should be sufficient to begin exploring mind states and how they interact with brain states. As the story unfolds, it will become apparent how intertwined these processes are. A thought can change brain chemistry, just as a physical event in the brain can change a thought. As I said at the beginning, this is not a new idea; it is the assumption of most twentieth-century scientists. What is new, however, is the realization that we can spell out the implications of this reality for a variety of mental states.

This model of consciousness should provide us with a deep

respect for how our life experiences shape the quality of our mind and how the genetically endowed brain works with its available inheritance—to produce, if not the good life, at least the best life possible under the circumstances. Our adventure starts by considering the basic, "hard" states of brain and mind that are responsible for so much of our life. We all experience pain, memory loss, and limited intellect. And we all fear losing our mind. In the subsequent chapters we will explore these and the more mercurial states dealing with our moods and passions, such as love, anxiety, obsessions, depression, and addictions. Finally, we will discover how brain and mind are inextricably linked to our bodily health and well-being.

Pain

Pain and the mind? How could they be related? Pain is like a reflex, it is commonly argued. It results from information gathered through a large network in the body that tells the brain when to withdraw from things like hot and cold surfaces. It tells us when muscles have been exerted beyond normal capacity. It tells us all kinds of valuable things that enable the body to survive. Yes, pain is unpleasant, but like the IRS, it is necessary because we live in an imperfect world.

Nevertheless, the interpretation of pain information can involve the mind, and the interpretation adopted by someone can feed back and influence the nerve cells that gave rise to the pain information. The psychological component is actually huge—and apparent to any astute observer of behavior—but it has been a hard battle to establish that fact in a scientific setting. The key to the pain-mind connection is the existence of many people who suffer chronic pain in what appears to be the absence of a simple physical explanation. Such people suffer in the worst way and seem outside the realm of help. Their story and the story about how we interpret our body's pain messages are the stuff of mind-brain interactions.

The consideration of whether something is painful varies at different times in an individual, among individuals, and in different cultures. Physicians and many others in our society have a tough time accepting that. We have a big industry that profits by trying to alleviate pain, and it is difficult to mass-market pain pills if it is generally believed that a lot of pain is in the mind of the beholder. Yet there is ample evidence for this view.

Paradoxes of Pain

As scientists have studied the many different circumstances of pain, they have encountered puzzling situations that a purely physical theory of pain cannot explain. For instance, there are patients who experience no pain. The most famous of these cases is that of Miss C., who was examined in Montreal in 1950. She bit her tongue, burned her skin, never gagged—in short, never responded to any noxious stimuli. Such a state of affairs was not good. As a consequence of Miss C.'s failure to feel pain, she never moved while sleeping, never shifted her weight while standing, and never avoided certain inadvisable postures. As a result, her joints became malformed and diseased, which led to infection and ultimately to her death. At autopsy, the pathologists were shocked to discover what could only be described as a perfectly normal nervous system. She appeared to have all the cells needed to relay pain and discomfort information to the brain. The case seemed to make no sense then, nor does it now.

Then there are patients who feel pain when there is no injury. Sufferers of Lesch–Nyhan disease, which afflicts young children, respond to the slightest touch by mutilating their own bodies. For example, they will bite their arm if their skin is barely touched. When their brains come to autopsy, they too look completely normal. Researchers do know that such patients are extremely sensitive to drugs like caffeine, but the significance of this is not understood. They also know that Lesch–Nyhan disease is inherited. In fact, it results from a deficiency in one of the millions of genes in the body. Because of the deficiency, the liver does not produce a certain enzyme. Scientists do not yet understand the connection between the missing enzyme and the drastically exaggerated perception of pain, which leads to their bizarre biting behavior.

There is also the mystery of kidney stone pain, which can be excruciating. It occurs when small pieces of crystallized substances, the "stones," move from the kidney into the ureter on the way to the bladder. The ureter has only a very few nerve receptors, far fewer than an equivalent area on the surface of the skin. Yet, mysteriously, the pain of passing a stone is second to none, although it vanishes the minute the stone enters the bladder, with no apparent damage to any parts of the pathway.

Finally, there is the story of phantom-limb pain, the pain that strangely occurs in a member that no longer exists. This well-recognized clinical syndrome supplies many clues about the nature of brain organization. It supports the notion that the brain has established maps of our body surfaces. The loss of a limb does not remove the map of that limb, which had been drawn over the course of a lifetime. Somehow, a stimulus activates one sector of the map and creates the illusion that something painful is happening to the nonexistent arm or leg.

These are the puzzles, the freak cases that underline some of the great individual variations in the experience of pain, variations that seem to have little or nothing to do with human psychology. But is it possible that at least some aspect of these perceptions of pain could be attributed to a mental rather than a physical state? As we will see, there are many instances where the psychological element clearly plays a role.

Environmental and Cultural Aspects of Pain

Consider a climb of Mount Everest. The highly conditioned and prepared Westerner is attempting a feat that few members of his society can do. He has trained, jogged, climbed smaller mountains, eaten completely uninteresting food; he is as physically fit as he can be. His body is ready for high-altitude exertion. And he has conditioned himself psychologically to endure more discomfort than his friends back home.

Walking beside the Westerner is a Nepalese porter. He has lived in the mountains most of his life. A Sherpa can carry a seventy-seven-pound pack at high altitude, with little outerwear, even in freezing temperatures. He does this with no complaint and with such assuredness that some have speculated that people of his culture have a special capacity to endure such hardships, or that they munch on some local plant that gives them special power, or perhaps that their brain is wired differently. Until recently, every conceivable idea has been put forward to explain the Sherpas' extraordinary perseverance.

In 1982, two American psychologists investigated this contrast among six Nepalese and five Western trekkers. The Clarks administered painful stimuli under tightly controlled experimental conditions using a mathematical, statistical procedure. The method cleverly distinguished between the ability to sense a stimulus and the attitude of the subjects about the stimulus itself. The results were unequivocal. The Nepalese could endure much higher levels of stimulation than could Occidentals. In other words, the Nepalese had a much higher threshold of pain. Yet, and most important, the same tests showed that the Nepalese were as sensitive as the Occidentals in discriminating between two stimuli, being equally able to distinguish between a high- and low-intensity stimulus. In short, both groups' sensory systems were relaying information to the brain in the same way. But once the painful stimulus was inside the brain, the psychological nature of the individual took hold. The Nepalese had simply been inured, and responded stoically, to stimuli that Westerners would complain of as unbearable.

War and pain have an almost paradoxical relationship. It is commonly reported that soldiers who have sustained the most grotesque bodily injuries involving loss of limbs or open abdom-

inal wounds rarely complain about pain. If the same men were
wounded just as severely in a peacetime accident, they would
react with violent pain and signs of anguish. As Beecher observed
after his extensive experience with World War II battle casualties:

> The common belief that wounds are inevitably associated
> with pain, and that the more extensive the wound the worse
> the pain, was not supported by observations made as carefully
> as possible in the combat zone. . . . The data state in numeri-
> cal terms what is known to all thoughtful clinical observers:
> there is no simple direct relationship between the wound
> per se and the pain experienced. The pain is in very large
> part determined by other factors, and of great importance
> here is the significance of the wound. . . . In the wounded
> soldier [the response to injury] was relief, thankfulness at
> his escape alive from the battlefield, even euphoria; to the
> civilian, his major surgery was a depressing, calamitous
> event.

Ronald Melzack and Patrick Wall, two of the primary researchers in the field of pain, reviewed other studies on the
psychological aspects of pain in their book *The Challenge of
Pain*. Studies similar to the World War II observations were
recently carried out following the Yom Kippur War in 1973.
Like the World War II soldiers, Israeli soldiers reported feeling
no pain after severe injury and used neutral terms like "bang"
and "thump" to describe losing a limb. However, unlike the
World War II victims, they were not euphoric about leaving
the battlefield. That agreeable prospect was tempered by the
fear of deserting their comrades and facing an uncertain future.
In Israel, everything is related to everything else. It is a small
country, and everyone knows the state of war intimately. The
Israeli soldier is fighting on his own doorstep, as it were, while
American soldiers in World War II were fighting thousands of
miles from home. What is important for the present discussion
is that in both wars, the soldiers' response to physically painful

stimuli was minor and was affected by their psychological state.

In everyday practice, any dentist knows that his patients' tolerance for pain varies enormously. But we can also see a variation in tolerance from one culture to another. Today in Bavaria, it is not considered appropriate to ask for anaesthesia when having a tooth filled, yet two hundred miles to the north, the vast majority of Germans demand an anaesthetic.

Dozens of studies have been done on how cultural factors influence the pain perception threshold. Mediterraneans tolerate pain poorly. Radiant heat that northern Europeans feel as merely warm is considered intolerable by Israelis and Italians. Melzack and Wall also reviewed other experiments comparing attitudes about pain. In one study of Jewish and Protestant women, Jewish women increased their tolerance to a painful stimulus when told their religious group had a low tolerance to pain, but the Protestant women did not increase theirs when told the same thing. Finally, other researchers have found that Jews and Italians are big complainers about pain. They differ, however, in their responses. Jews tend to wonder what the meaning and implication of the pain are, while the Italians simply want relief.

Studies of animals also demonstrate the psychological dimensions of pain perception. One of the classic observations comes from one of Ivan Pavlov's animal-conditioning experiments. Dogs intensely dislike having a paw shocked with a brief electrical pulse. They withdraw the paw swiftly from such a stimulus. Pavlov observed, however, that if each electrical pulse is made in association with the presentation of food, the dog quickly adapts to the aversive shock. Once conditioned, the dog salivates, wags its tail, and looks eagerly for the food dish. Clearly, the dog had re-evaluated the significance of the shock, accepting it as a necessary condition for receiving the food and sublimating the physical pain.

All of these studies and observations suggest that how we respond to pain is largely the result of learned behavior. Ronald Melzack and his colleagues in Montreal dramatically demonstrated the connection between learning and pain in a study of Scottish terriers. The dogs were raised in isolation from infancy to maturity and therefore were protected from the normal scrapes and bruises encountered in early development. More important, the puppies could not observe their more experienced elders' reactions to painful situations. When these restricted animals were allowed to go free to explore a real environment, several dramatic events occurred. The terriers would sniff at burning matches and not jump back as would dogs reared normally. When exposed to hot heating pipes, the animals gleefully licked them, showing no indication of pain. Melzack and his colleagues observed the dogs for two years. Some remained totally fearless of painful situations. They never yelped or complained about conditions other dogs would find intolerable.

Such observations suggest that there is what biologists call a critical period in the development of pain perception. If during infancy there is no social model in the environment from which to learn, the animal acquires no particularly negative view of pain. In humans, if an infant always sees a parent scream at the slightest pain, he undoubtedly will learn similar responses for his own life. The Spartans and Athenians, for example, raised their children differently. From a very early age Spartans were trained to endure pain and were able to remain stoics throughout their lives.

The Chronic Pain Patient

An interesting example of mind-brain interactions in the perception of pain is the patient with chronic pain. Chronic pain sufferers often consult a doctor for the slightest reason, and their medical records are thick. For them a simple scratch becomes a calamity. Doctors tend to classify this condition as psychogenic—that is, not real pain. Yet to the patients the pain is real enough. Although they are not malingerers or fakes, they are the most abused patient group in medicine because they appear to be neurotic, and it is common for the physician to write them off as such. Usually the problem continues to grow worse.

What is so curious about these patients is their psychological profile. On a personality test such as the Minnesota Multiphasic Personality Inventory (MMPI), they score high on scales measuring hysteria, depression, and hypochondria. The question, then, is which came first, the chronic pain or the mental state that tends to interpret certain stimuli as painful? In recent studies, researchers have found that the pain is frequently the cause of the neurosis, not the other way around. After certain patients with chronic pain underwent a variety of medical procedures that successfully alleviated much of their pain, their subsequent testing on the MMPI showed a drop in scores on hysteria, depression, and hypochondria.

With the chronic pain victim, we can begin to see how our brain's interpreter becomes a powerful determinant of behavior. That patient usually starts out with a real pathology. The physicians solemnly report to the patient that there is apparently nothing wrong. After several such episodes, the interpreter goes to work on the self and concludes that it is the patient who is at fault. The patient's self-esteem drops sharply, as the MMPI tests show. But when patients are lucky enough to find a procedure or a drug that helps to alleviate the pain, the self-esteem measures go back up to the normal range. In these cases the rational interpreter of the brain has another set of data to consider, and it arrives at a different and more positive conclusion.

The patients who are not successfully treated for their pain, however, have nothing but heartache ahead. In addition to having to adapt to their mysterious pain, they now have to adapt to the social rejection that befalls such people. No one wants to be around chronic complainers. Faced with this, patients who begin with only a heightened sensitivity to discomfort can quickly develop a serious illness with psychiatric dimensions. They look on their pain as something unique, and the border between physical and psychological pain blurs. One becomes as real to them as the other. At present, no one has a treatment for this mind-state form of pain.

If the psychological factor in pain perception is real, so too are the physical mechanisms. Over the past hundred years, much has been learned about the physical basis of pain. There have even been certain discoveries within the last ten years that appear to have finally established how pain is generated in the brain and how it can be effectively treated. One of the most interesting was the revelation that the body produces its own opiates for pain. This optimism has, however, given way to more realistic views. Still, the understanding of pain mechanisms has come a long way, and these advances have been made in the face of some very puzzling phenomena.

Physiology of Pain

We know a great deal about the brain mechanisms of everyday, real, felt pain. Long ago, when scientists started to consider the problem, they immediately proposed the simple idea that there was a special set of nerves for the management of pain information. First advanced by Johannes Müller in 1842, this postulate is known as the theory of specific nerve energies. It proposed that all information about the environment came to the brain through one of five types of sensory nerves. Vision, smell, taste, hearing, and touch each had its own neural input system.

It wasn't until years later, in 1894, that the German physician Max von Frey expanded Müller's doctrine and argued that the nerve system for touch included four other, more specialized subsystems. He believed that temperature, pain, joint sense, and touch all had specific receptors in the body, and that each receptor relayed information only of a specific nature into the brain: pain neurons went to pain centers in the brain, temperature neurons went to temperature centers, and so on. Taken together, this was a clean set of ideas about how the brain and the peripheral nervous system were organized, and it has dominated neurological thought for the last eighty years.

There is now ample evidence that the way the brain receives pain information is much more complex. But the absolutists' position that all pain is transmitted by specific nerves has had the bad effect of inhibiting the development of ideas about pain mechanisms that take the psychological process into account. The old ideas have persisted, in no small part because of our knowledge of how aspirin, the most common and effective analgesic, works.

Aspirin As a Pain Reliever

In 1763, the Englishman Edward Stone wrote to the Royal Society and informed them that an extract of a willow tree proved effective against the pain of rheumatism and fever. It was not until 1827 that a French chemist by the name of Leroux isolated the compound and named it salicin. It was heavily used throughout the nineteenth century and finally was commercially marketed by Bayer. To this day, aspirin is the most effective analgesic for common pain. It is also a billion-dollar-a-year industry.

Aspirin does not work on the brain. Instead, it appears to modify the inflammatory response to the damaged or bruised body area. You can understand the simple, common, constant sequence of events that occurs when tissue has been damaged by running a fingernail up the surface of one forearm from the hand to the elbow. If you scratched hard enough, you will experience the four processes that always take place with inflamed tissue: redness, heat, swelling, and pain. The redness is the result of the vasodilation (dilation of the veins) at the site of injury. Heat is produced by the sudden delivery of large amounts of blood to the skin's surface because of vasodilation. The swelling is due to the release of other fluids into the surrounding tissues, and the pain is generated by what are called free nerve endings that are embedded throughout the skin. These nerve endings cover our body surface and are an important factor in sending pain information to the brain. Aspirin intervenes in this sequence of events by influencing another chemical system, the prostaglandins.

Cells in the injured region produce prostaglandins, body chemicals that sensitize the free nerve endings in the skin and make them send the pain cues to the spinal cord and from there up to the brain. Aspirin blocks the synthesis of prostaglandins, thereby reducing the sensitivity of the free nerve endings. Thus, aspirin does not directly influence the brain but has effects on nerves going into the brain. Also, aspirin can be injected locally into damaged tissues and result in pain relief.

Not surprisingly, it is not an analgesic for pain caused by electrical shock, an injury that does not produce inflammation.

An Alternative to Specific Nerve Energies

While the spectacular success of aspirin was welcomed with open arms, the difficult problem of understanding bodily and mental pain remained. The pieces began to fit together in 1964 when clever experimenters in Sweden showed that the old idea of specific nerve energies was far too simple. The Swedish scientists invented a method of logging the activity of a single sensory nerve. They were able to record the number of times the neuron discharged, according to the type of stimulus applied to the skin. At the same time they could ask the subject to tell them what the stimulus felt like and how painful it was. First the scientists isolated one nerve and applied heat to the skin surface at that point. As soon as the subject said the stimulus was painful, the scientists noted the frequency of discharge from the nerve. Then they applied pressure instead of heat to the same place on the skin.

If there were indeed nerves specific to pain, they reasoned, then the degree of perceived pain ought to depend on the rate at which the "pain nerve" fired, no matter what the stimulus. However, the subject felt pain from a pressure stimulus only when the nerve was forced to fire at five times the rate caused by painful heat. Thus, the type of stimulus did make a big difference. Clearly, the nerve fiber was not sending a simple pain message from the skin. Instead, it was sending a more complicated code to the brain; there, the information became integrated with other signals from the skin area and elsewhere. In the brain there must be some central system deciding when to judge a volley of incoming stimuli as painful.

Histologists, who study the body's tissues at the microscopic level, have been gathering additional evidence that disputes the theory of a specific pain-receptor system. They have observed that each neuron has dendritic, or branched, connections to numerous points on the skin, and that many points are served by more than one neuron. The complex network of connections is contrary to von Frey's suggestion that each sensitive spot on the skin is served by one and only one specific nerve ending. The new picture is that a network of cells innervates, or supplies nerves to, most tissue, and the entire network reports to the brain about the status of the unwanted stimuli. The brain, using its central processors for pain, evaluates those incoming signals and decides what to label as pain.

The Interpretative Role of the Brain

Consider the problem of trigeminal neuralgia. Known as tic douloureux, it is considered to be one of the most painful human conditions. It is a disorder of the trigeminal nerve, the huge nerve responsible for much of our facial sensation. Trigeminal neuralgia is usually of sudden onset and occurs in older people living in colder climates. The pain is described as, well, indescribable. Attempts to characterize this feeling include statements about darting pain and deep, gnawing sensations that can spread to the entire face and upper torso. It can be powerfully disabling. In a small percentage of cases the symptom is triggered by a tumor on the trigeminal nerve, but most of the time autopsy finds no abnormalities in the neuron.

This disease exemplifies the active role of the brain in determining what is and what is not painful. A painful episode with trigeminal neuralgia usually lasts a few seconds and cannot be retriggered for several minutes thereafter, even though a very light stimulus applied to the facial area can usually set off an initial attack. A neurophysiologist would predict that the sensory nerve is almost instantly ready to respond again after the first attack because the nerve surely continues to send messages to the brain. Nevertheless, the brain's *central* processes seem to call a halt for the time being and do not recognize the new information as pain. When pain messages from the periphery come into the higher, central brain centers, other factors become involved in the perception of pain.

When a surgeon severs the sensory branch of the trigeminal nerve, thereby supposedly abolishing all sensation in half the face and tongue, the original pain may disappear. It is replaced, however, by new tingling, crawling sensations in the supposedly anaesthetized zone. This condition, called anaesthesia dolorosa, can persist for life. How can this happen? The central brain system must be interpreting phantom signals from the facial area in a manner that generates psychological pain.

Even the common slipped disk, which generates very tangible low back pain, offers evidence of the importance of central processes in pain perception. The ruptured disk touches a sensory nerve and sends an abnormal electrical volley that is interpreted as pain by the brain. The compression of a sensory nerve at the spinal cord sometimes increases the rate of firing from the nerve and sometimes decreases it. Both changes from the normal rate create the perception of low back pain. Surgical removal of the irritating stimulus, the disk, is usually completely effective, providing long-lasting relief. Yet occasionally patients do not lose their pain even after removal of the disk. In these cases, central brain processes must still be interpreting some peripheral message as painful.

Gate-Control Theory of Pain

In 1965, when Melzack and Wall considered all the evidence and peculiarities of pain research, the challenge as they saw it was to postulate a mechanism that takes into account a set of irrefutable and hard-won facts about pain. First, there is a high degree of physiological but not psychological specialization of the nerve cells that transmit pain information into the central nervous system. This means that while there is little doubt that certain types of receptor cells have special functions, it does not mean that the cells and the neural circuits that feed off them register only one kind of sensation. That crucial distinction is a major clue to how the brain manages pain. It forces the scientist to consider a more complex neural model and leads to possible explanations for why psychological approaches, as we have already seen, can be so effective in pain control.

The second crucial fact is the role of temporal and spatial patterning of nerve impulses. As we saw from the Swedish experiments, pain perception is determined not just by the pattern of firing from the nerve cells but also by how the brain interprets the firing. Finally, the theory must have an explanation for clearly psychological phenomena such as the spread of pain and the persistence of pain after healing.

Melzack and Wall's gate-control theory takes account of these facts by suggesting that the brain can simply turn off incoming information from any part of the body where nerves end—the periphery—by commands emanating from deep within the brain itself. This area is in the spinal cord and is called the substantia gelatinosa. It serves as the gate and receives information from the periphery and also from the brain. There, incoming messages from the periphery can be altered by information coming down from the brain, so that the subsequent message from the substantia gelatinosa back up to the central brain processes may not dictate a pain response. In short, the substantia gelatinosa is a place where information gets mixed and returned in its new form to the central brain system by means of certain cells. These so-called T-cells (transmission cells) are projected to the central brain regions and trigger the ultimate psychological response of pain. While the gate-control theory is a little weak on tracing the pathway of the T-cells and the ways complex psychological processes can modify the message it delivers to the brain, the theory is elegant in explaining how messages from the periphery can be modified in a way that is consistent with all of the bizarre pain phenomena previously discussed— such as the evidence that some people can endure more physical pain than can others.

The substantia gelatinosa is crucial for other reasons. It is obviously a complex network of neurons that normally function in a delicate balance to produce meaningful information about the state of the body. One can see how any disturbance to its input might result in the T-cells' sending out erroneous messages. With chronic low back pain, for example, the death of some sensory nerves in the area of the pain could throw off the balance of information coming into the substantia gelatinosa from the periphery and trick it into sending a pain message up to the brain. It is easy to imagine that people with such pain may have some nerve cell death that is very subtle and not observable by modern methods of detection.

An important aspect of the gate-control theory is that the physical mechanism it proposes is completely consistent with one of the major findings of the last decade concerning the control of pain. Starting in the seventies, the world was introduced to the concept of self-produced opiates. It had been known for years that opiates like morphine were the best pain relievers. Modern neurobiologists assumed there are some cells in the brain that are sensitive to the drugs, and that these cells are part of a network that could either transmit or block pain messages. The hunt was on for a chemical produced by the human body that had a morphine-like effect on the brain.

Investigators have long known that morphine blocks contractions of smooth muscle in the intestine. Several scientists made brain extracts and were able to isolate a substance that exactly mimicked this effect of morphine. The substance, called enkephalin, is a compound that occurs naturally but in small amounts. Shortly thereafter, the endorphins (from "endogenous morphine-like compounds") were discovered. The first to be named, beta-endorphin, is produced in the pituitary gland. In the years to follow, scientists found special receptors for the endorphins and enkephalins all over the brain, the spinal cord, and other tissues as well.

The researchers discovered the greatest concentration of receptors in an area of the brain called periaqueductal grey, and this is particularly important for pain theory. Periaqueductal grey sends fibers down into the brainstem and from there to the spinal cord, where they can influence the pattern of messages about possible painful stimuli coming from the periphery. These appear to be the messages to open or close the gate in the substantia gelatinosa, as posited by Melzack and Wall's theory. It appears that the self-produced opiates are a type of neurotransmitter that starts a sequence of signals that eventually order the gate closed to possible painful stimuli.

In the late seventies and early eighties there was an explosive amount of research on endorphins. Scientists hoped that they had found the magic bullet for pain. Under conditions of severe pain, the body's natural ability to make its own endorphins was not sufficient to produce the level of analgesia needed. Why not supplement the body's endorphins with artificially produced endorphins? Once again scientists discovered that the brain is not as simple as they would like it to be. While some studies on endorphins indicated they would be effective drugs

for pain, other studies showed no promising results. At this
writing, the view is that endorphins are effective in treating immediate, intense pain. Afterward, however, comes the chronic
phase of pain, and for that other analgesics are needed.

Morphine is still the medication of choice for chronic pain
associated with cancer. Contrary to common medical and public
beliefs, morphine remains an effective painkiller for these patients, with little indication of tolerance being formed. Tolerance
for morphine is clearly observed when it is used to try to relieve
other kinds of brief but intense pain. In recent years, techniques
have been developed for the cancer patient where the administration of morphine is completely under the patient's control. There
was no evidence that patients indulged in more morphine than
was needed. Instead, they were found actually to reduce their
dose to a level that relieves the pain but also leaves them mentally
alert.

Lately the endorphin story has been tempered by further research, which has shown that there are other descending neural
systems in the brain that modify incoming signals from the
spinal cord. These other pain control systems use other neurotransmitters, and at present there is a complex array of systems
that appear active in the control of systemic pain. It will be a
long time before all of the mechanisms for the management
of pain are comprehended.

Pain, while essential to our well-being, is psychologically awful
and unwanted. The heartbreak of pain problems is, however,
that all too frequently they are not helped and remain persistent.
At the same time, from a scientific point of view, chronic pain
reveals certain secrets about brain organization and the mind.
Among other things, it shows us how psychological states of
mind can influence the interpretation of nerve signals heralding
pain. Pain messages sent to key brain structures can be modified
when other information, from more central brain processes,
arrives. These more central brain processes are responding to

a lifetime of attitudes and beliefs about pain, about how to endure or not to endure such things. What finally arrives in the brain is a mix of all of this information, where it gets a final judgment as to whether it is painful or not. In short, the psychological state of mind and views about pain endurance play an important role in the moderation and interpretation of painful stimuli.

Pain states can also exist as an interpretation of a former pain. In this case what the patient feels, most likely, is not pain from damaged tissue. He is, in fact, reliving a past pain experience—which can be very real. Pain and the mind are hopelessly linked.

Memory and Thinking
after Forty

When Ronald Reagan was re-elected President of the United States at the age of seventy-four, a question often asked was: Will his aging brain support the complex tasks faced by the leader of 230 million people? It is the kind of question that should be asked of any public official of that age. The doctors examine the colon, why not the brain?

Formal tests of brain function are not commonly administered to our highest elected official. This aspect of health is left for the casual judgment of all those around the President, and unless something is radically wrong, no signal is sent and the issue is dropped. Yet all of us past the age of forty begin to recognize certain changes in our mental life. We find it more difficult to remember the name of something new. A little later we can't recall the name of something familiar. And after that we struggle to penetrate new concepts. Memory, just like pain, is a product of brain and mind. Listen to W. Somerset Maugham at the age of ninety:

> My memory leaves much to be desired these days and I find that, as I walk the meagre tightrope which separates me from death, such memories as I have of my 90 years are so dim as to fill me with regret for the past.

Perhaps the most vivid memory left to me is the one which has tortured me for more than 80 years—that of the death of my mother. I was eight when she died and even today the pain of her passing is as keen as when it happened in our home in Paris.

Other memories there are but most are so dim that I find it easier to forget than to remember. Neither do I think of the future, for at 90 there is only emptiness before me. . . . I have no wish to write further. My head is empty now of the thoughts, plots, and the makings of a story. I have long since written the words that were inside me and put aside my pen. . . . And so, when my obituary notice at last appears in the *Times* and they say, "What! I thought he died years ago," my ghost will gently chuckle.

What happens in the brain and body that makes this a "normal" state in the advanced years of a human being? What are the known brain changes that occur with normal aging that may be involved in this key process? Are there substances or psychological strategies that can ward off brain and memory decline? The first issue to grasp when dealing with memory degeneration is the inevitable brain changes that begin with variable force after forty.

Physiological Changes of the Aging Brain

The most noticeable changes are found in the cerebral cortex, the structure in the brain that supports our ability to think and serves as the repository for memories. Several differences emerge between the brain of forty- to sixty-year-olds and that of twenty-year-olds. First, there appears to be a decrease of some 15 to 20 percent in the number of cells throughout the cortex, and this number drops even further by the age of seventy-five to over 40 percent of our cortical cells. Interestingly, the most dense loss is seen in regions of the brain that are thought to be exceptionally important in the storage of memory, the temporal lobes.

What remains a total mystery, however, is what happens to the missing nerve cells. When a disease process hits the brain, the loss of nerve cells is easy to detect, but in the normal aging process there are no signs of pathogenesis, the process by which cells usually die. There is no inflammation, no telltale sign of virus attack, no phagic cells are apparent—that is, cells that eat up the remains of dead cells. Our normal neurons, up to 40 percent of all of our cortical cells, appear to vanish. This prevalent view is now being challenged by some who claim the cells don't actually disappear; they simply change their size and function, as we will see.

There may be a change in the big neurons in the brain. These neurons may take on a new configuration, becoming smaller and responding differently. Although counting cell alteration and loss is a difficult enterprise for the brain anatomist, all scientists agree that there are substantial changes in the individual neurons themselves. These changes range from downright atrophy of cell parts to loss of the cell's capacity to respond to neurotransmitters. As I described in the Introduction, most neurons have large input components called dendrites, which are frequently splayed out and look like trees. The dendrites receive incoming signals from hundreds of other neurons. In the normally aging cortex, many of the dendritic elements are lost. This loss should affect how and when cells normally discharge and, in turn, how the whole nervous system functions. As already noted, the observed losses mostly affect layers of the cortex that are thought to be active in memory storage.

Other changes prevent the neuron from transferring chemicals from the cell body down the axon to the tip of the nerve cell. So-called plaques also appear and further disrupt neural activity. When they emerge in large numbers and are particularly placed, they can lead to diseases such as Alzheimer's. To some extent, though, all aging brains possess these new and unwanted elements. Where plaques come from and what they are caused by is not known.

There are also changes in one of the key factors of normal nervous function, the neurotransmitters. Although obtaining measurements of these chemicals is difficult in dead brains, certain important observations have been made. Specific neurotransmitters are thought to be most active for particular purposes. Thus, dopamine is important in movement control, and with its loss, severe Parkinsonian motor problems are seen. With aging, the number of cells in parts of the brain normally rich in dopamine-producing neurons drops by about 40 percent. When it falls more than that, it can lead to disease. Similar reports are made for other transmitters, such as acetylcholine and gamma-aminobutyric acid, which seems to influence psychological functions. All is not bad, however. Oddly, there are claims that other chemicals, such as monoamine oxidase, thought to be active in the management of depression, increase with age. Perhaps the added supply of monoamines keeps the aging population more cheerful than it ought to be, given the other reports.

The brain site rich in noradrenaline, the neurotransmitter that supposedly affects arousal and attention span, is called the locus ceruleus. This structure, deep in the brain, sends out fibers to absolutely everywhere. Before the age of fifty there are approximately seventeen thousand neurons in a specific cross-section of the locus ceruleus. By the time the brain is seventy years old, there are only eleven thousand neurons in the same area, a drop of approximately 35 percent. This observation would lead some to suggest that a brain mechanism is in hand that explains lower attention span in the elderly. Is this why President Reagan nods off at cabinet meetings? Or is it because they are boring? Or both? It is too soon to tell.

Finally, with such a huge decline in the number of brain cells as we age, it should not be surprising to learn there is a marked and easily observable change in the brain's size. In mod-

ern neurology, this is easily detected with the CT scan, a computer-based technology that provides exact pictures of the brain.
The brain volume of seventy-year-olds is nearly 11 percent
smaller than that of the brain of forty-year-olds. Correlated
with this change is a loss in overall brain weight as well as an
increase in the size of the brain ventricles, the sacs within the
brain tissue that are filled with cerebrospinal fluid.

Implications of Brain Changes

These basic facts of brain change raise many questions for
theoreticians of brain science and bemuse those who believe
there is less to most people than meets the eye. First, what
does the loss of brain cells mean?

As we will see, although there are real problems with memory,
language, and general motility in later life, these debilities in
our mental domain do not seem to reflect to the same degree
the huge changes occurring in the brain. Put differently, if memories are supposed to be stored in neural networks in some
way, why doesn't loss or drastic change in nearly half of our
neurons find us almost totally amnesic? The answer to that
question is completely unknown. The code by which the brain
stores and retrieves information gained over a lifetime still eludes
researchers. Indeed, scientists argue over the accuracy of memories. Some feel they are poor record keepers and that what
passes for a vivid memory is a reconstruction of what ought
to have been, given a couple of recalled facts. These issues are
brought up here to illustrate how difficult it is to achieve true
insights into how the brain supports our mental lives.

With all the tangible changes in brain structure, there ought
to be effects in functioning brains that are easily detectable using
standard equipment found in most well-equipped hospitals. Results of routine tests such as the electroencephalogram (EEG),
which is a measure from the scalp of the brain's electrical activity,
ought to change, since there are far fewer neurons functioning

in the older brain. With fewer neurons, less electrical energy would be generated in response to stimulation, which would reduce the size, or amplitude, of the EEG. Changes are reported, but they are unremarkable until the eighth decade of life. Likewise, there are now ways to measure the rate of blood flow and the rate at which cells metabolize in the brain. Such data are thought to reflect the rate at which cells discharge and also the number of cells present. There are several reports that blood flow and metabolism are reduced in the aging brain. Yet these methods are costly and elaborate. It still remains true that the best place to look for effects of a normally deteriorating brain is in the standard neurological and psychological exam.

On his eightieth birthday Malcolm Cowley observed that "age is no different from earlier life as long as you are sitting down." He is not far from the truth when considering speed of actions. It is motility that gradually goes in the aging adult. This can be seen in the athlete. In 1980, the New York City marathon was won by a twenty-one-year-old with a time of two hours and ten minutes. In the same race, a seventy-six-year-old rather remarkably finished in three hours and fifty minutes. By the age of forty there can be a 20 percent decrease in an athlete's speed. In simple tasks like copying words or tracing figures, there is a 30 percent increase in the time a sixty-year-old needs to do the task as compared to a twenty-year-old.

Reduction in our overall ability to move quickly is thought to be related to the loss in cells in the brain areas rich in the neurotransmitter dopamine. Such claims are also made for the walking problems usually seen in the elderly. It should be pointed out, however, that there are many other factors playing a role, including arthritic changes, possible damage to other brain areas, as well as side effects to the enlarged ventricles described earlier. The elderly also are virtually unable to stand on one leg with eyes closed. This example of loss of their sense of balance is poorly understood but is thought to relate to the loss of a neuron that sends information about the body's position from the legs up through the spinal cord into the base of the brain. This is one cell, the longest in the human body, and it is thought that keeping such a huge entity alive over a long lifetime may be difficult.

All of these basic changes in body mechanics are real and common as we grow older. A brain that slows down in the management of such simple acts as moving the body must also be affected for the other activities we hold dear, such as thinking. Most of us would gladly accept slowness in our tennis game so long as our mind remained at full speed.

The most frequent complaint for the normally aging person after forty is the sense that the memory is not what it used to be. Recalling names is harder, with proper names being more difficult than simple facts. Complaints are also heard about decreased capacity to remember new vocabulary and proper names. "Let me write that down or I'll forget it" is the cry of the middle-aged. Memory starts to malfunction just when visual acuity changes, both just after forty. All the jogging in the world can't change these facts of life.

In order to grasp what may be happening, it is necessary first to consider how memory works. Much of what is known about the process seems almost intuitively obvious. Generally, there are three stages to memory. There is the very short-term phase that amounts to a photographic image that fades quickly. Then there is short-term memory, which lasts a few minutes and can be read out directly or maintained with rehearsal. Last is long-term memory, which we retain for years and must be retrieved effortfully. Sometimes those efforts are unsuccessful.

In the early 1950s, a famous case in the neurological literature was reported that dramatically illustrated this straightforward view of the stages of memory. As the result of a surgical procedure (which is no longer carried out), the patient, case H.M., could remember information for the short term but could not transfer new experiences into long-term memory. He was unable to retain any new experiences, but at the same time, he had access to all of his old memories. In addition to not being able to recall any new events, he was also very bad at recognizing whether or not a recent event had occurred. Psychologists have known for years how much easier it is to recognize previously experienced events than to try to recall them. Because of his failure on both kinds of tests of memory, case H.M. was viewed as a person who was unable to record new information of any kind. This finding welded into the minds of all psychological investigators the value of thinking of memory as having three stages. While information could be retained for the short term, none of it could be transferred to the long term.

Over the years, case H.M.'s extreme amnesia has been the fodder of dozens of clever and resourceful experiments. The unfortunate aspect of the studies is that they have emphasized a simplistic model of how new information is stored in the brain. In contrast to this case, the vast majority of people with memory problems can store new experiences of some kind and at some identifiable rate. They tend to be more impaired in their capacity to recall the information. It is studies of these patients and also of the normally aging adult with recall problems that have led to a deeper understanding of the human memory process. The experiments all show that most memory problems are problems of recall. Somehow, the brain is usually capable of recording information. What it loses is its capacity to access the recorded information through recall. Why this is so has to do with several factors such as the "automatic" processes of memory. Consider the following.

Recent research has shown that there is a host of automatic processes that occur during the acquisition of new information, which takes place in a particular space, at a particular time, in a particular mood, and in a particular mental context. We do not consciously take note of all of these parameters that are crucial for the proper recall of the information being learned; they happen automatically. It is now known that these automatic processes can be impaired in the neurological patient, giving rise to a behavior that mimics the behavior that begins to occur in the normally aging brain. Patients with this kind of amnesia are usually very poor at freely recalling whether or not specific events had occurred in their recent past. However, when forced to choose between two alternatives, they are quite good at determining whether or not an event had occurred. In short, as we just described, they have good recognition memory but have a poor ability to recall. It is that impairment that begins to creep into the aging brain. It hits different people at different rates, but it hits us all.

Once psychologists began to study long-term memory per se, they realized it may be divided into two main categories. Endel Tulving of the University of Toronto has for years been working on the kinds of memory in our long-term stores. He distinguishes between semantic and episodic memory. Semantic memories have to do with our general knowledge about the working of the world. We know what cars do, what stoves do, what the laws of gravity are, and so on. Episodic memories are largely events that took place at a time and place in our personal history. Remembering specific events about our own actions, about our family, and about our individual past falls into this category. With amnesia or in aging, what dims, as Maugham reminded us, is our personal episodic memories, save for those that are especially dear or painful to us. Our knowledge of how the world works remains pretty much intact.

Tulving recently studied a brain-injured young man who suffered a head injury. Case N.N. revealed a remarkable pattern of memory behavior after the injury that fits nicely into his theory. The patient was alert, intelligent, and fully capable of explaining anything one cared to hear about how the real world functioned. Yet, save for one or two personal memories, he had no capacity to recall any of his past life; it was a blank for him. Because of that, he was also unable to plan for the future. What he just did was not remembered, and so on. Clearly, the brain injury had selectively hit those brain regions that were responsible for the maintenance and storage of his episodic memories while sparing those areas storing past knowledge about the real world.

This distinction between the kinds of long-term memory we have fits with the facts about learning and memory in the aging. Knowledge, or semantic memory, stays relatively intact. It is episodic memories that fade, with important notable exceptions worth mentioning. First, established memories remain very real and relatively easy to access. In one study, a group of people were asked questions about their catechism, which they had not used or rehearsed for thirty-six years. They were able to recall about 80 percent of their lessons. This is not to say we have excellent recall for all preceding events of our lives. When one tries to recall childhood, there tend to be some very vivid and wonderful memories (as a rule) while the rest of the enormous amount of time spent with one's family remains beyond recall. As a result, it is generally believed that long-term episodic memories are more vulnerable than semantic ones. Earlier episodic memories are more insulated from the generally deleterious effects of brain aging than are more recently acquired episodic memories.

A more interesting and positive aspect of memory in the aging is that if enough extra time is given to an elderly subject to learn a new task at the same level of competence displayed by someone in his early twenties, the older person will retain the task at the same level as the young adult. That is to say, the mechanism for learning and remembering, while not performing normally in the aged, can function. Why this is so requires the introduction of another useful concept, that of general resources.

The human mental system has a finite amount of resources for working on a problem. What are these resources? The concept is very similar to the monetary realities of personal income. You make so much a month (those are your resources), and you desire to do so many things a month, all of which require money. You obviously have limited resources (unless you are Imelda Marcos), so you have to decide which activities you will take part in and which you won't. In psychological parlance, resources are thought of as energy—psychological energy, which at some level translates into brain energy. The brain has limited energy, and it must allocate the amount that is going to be consumed or applied to any problem or task the brain is working on.

Scientists believe that in the aging brain, the overall amount of resources available is gradually being reduced. The decreasing amount of energy is distributed, but it no longer can cover the entire job. As a consequence, certain activities are not carried out, which means that when an older person attempts to recall new information, the system can come up short.

Such a model for our brain activity does not suggest, however, that even with diligent effort the system will not work. With additional practice the resources become increasingly distributed over all of the automatic processes that need to be active in learning something new, and gradually the information is properly recorded. Such information is then available in the same way it is for the young. It is a reassuring view, and one that is probably correct.

Another major fact that emerges when considering the learning and memory skills of the aging is that all people are more receptive to meaningful information. That is, if new facts build on an existing knowledge base, they can be retained far more easily and at a rate comparable with that of young adults. If, however, the task is to learn information that is totally new, severe problems arise. For example, for an adult who speaks French and English, learning Turkish is most difficult, whereas learning new words in a familiar language is much easier. Needless to say, this single fact about the aging brain may well be the reason that maturing adults tend to become more and more fixed in their ways. They simply find it very difficult to retain something that is not already part of their view of the world. The scientist, of course, wants to know why all of this is true.

When these observations about decline in memory are pulled together, a picture emerges suggesting that a bottleneck appears in the short-term phase of the learning sequence. It is clear that long-term memory in older people works, and that with more time applied to learning, new information can be inserted into long-term memory. We also know that in the immediate short term ("photographic" phase), memory is fine, since the aged can easily repeat back strings of numbers read to them. Thus, something happens to new information in the second short-term phase before it goes into the long-term phase. The fact that meaningful material is dealt with and learned more easily than the nonmeaningful suggests that the short-term system is aided during this critical phase by long-term memory, allowing it to work somewhat more normally. What is wrong with the aging process that finds things abnormal at this point in the memory system?

Current research suggests the psychological difficulties relate to the well-documented neural cell alterations that occur throughout the brain, which have the overall effect of slowing down brain function. Physiologically, one can detect that information no longer moves around the brain as fast when serious aging starts after forty. At a psychological level, this is easily measurable. One simple technique to illustrate how timing is disrupted is to use what is called backward masking. In this test, a picture is presented very briefly and is quickly followed by another. Depending on how long the picture is presented and/or how long the interpicture interval is, the first image may or may not be seen. If it is not perceived, the second image is said to (backwardly) mask the first. In sixty-year-olds, the times that will produce the masking effect can be extended by as much as 20 to 70 percent. This suggests that the original stimulus is not getting out of a particular part of the brain and moving on in the overall processing sequence. While it dilly-dallies, along comes another image, which has the effect of erasing the ultimate perception of the first. It is easy to imagine the disastrous effect such an eventuality would have on trying to learn new information.

Other psychological experiments are also revealing. It is well known that the speed at which one can identify a particular item as part of a list is directly related to the number of words on the list. If the list to be remembered has only one word— "apple," for instance—subjects can judge very quickly whether or not it or another word was presented to them. However, the longer the to-be-remembered list, the longer it takes to decide. Each time an item is added, the subject has to spend more time searching the list to discern whether or not a new item is present or absent from it. Subjects up to the age of forty take about 400 milliseconds to respond to one item, and an additional 30 milliseconds for each item on the list. Thus, for a four-item list the subject takes about 490 milliseconds to respond.

After age fifty the story is different. The initial capacity to respond is slowed down to 500 milliseconds for only one item. More interesting, the search time is increased for additional items. It takes approximately 45 milliseconds to search for each new item, which means for four items a fifty-year-old takes about 635 milliseconds. So the fifty-year-old is approximately 30 percent slower in both finding the information in the brain and then responding to it than someone under forty. Such a huge difference in quickness of response must have serious effects on the capacity to remember a series of items.

It is important to note that all these processes proceed differently in each of us. For people whose vocation does not require extensive use of memory, the deterioration is less noticeable and less trying to them. For those continually called upon to remember new names, new dates, and new relationships, the naturally deteriorating system is not only noticeable to them; it is annoying. We all try to compensate by covering our holes in name finding by using circumlocutions, since we can't be constantly saying "what's the name of whatyoumaycallit." Whether or not any of this is fixable or avoidable will be discussed at the end of this chapter.

Thinking after Forty

"But wait a minute," says the CEO. "I may have a small problem with memory, but I'm still running this company with an iron fist. Profits are up. I feel great. That I can't remember the names of all my new salesmen doesn't mean I can't see what's good for this company and grasp all the issues at hand. My aging brain seems to do that kind of thing very well. I can still think!" This claim is both right and wrong. The good news is that verbal IQ remains largely unchanged with age. In a wide range of studies that measure verbal IQ, no significant changes are seen until the seventh decade of life. The capacity to define words, to note similarities between words, and to abstract ideas from reading are all intact until an advanced age. Even in the eighth decade there appear to be two groups. While some begin to falter on such tests, others continue as though they were twenty.

What this seemingly remarkable capacity reflects is that adults have learned to recognize patterns of behavior and thought. Over the years they have absorbed these patterns, and they are very neatly catalogued and filed for easy accessibility. In that real sense they are prepared for the societal posture of conferring wisdom on the elderly. The aging adults who have led observant lives have learned hundreds of scenarios, hundreds of lessons about how people behave and think given a certain set of circumstances. In this light, they are advanced and offer a fabulous capacity to assay what may strike a younger person as a new dimension in human knowledge. And, as they drag out one of their insights, it is frequently so illustrative and subtle that the notion of intact intelligence is immediately assumed in the aged adult. The question is whether or not the seemingly intact intelligence is more apparent than real.

The aged brain is not unlike a highly efficient special-purpose computer. That is, if asked the right question, a question for which it knows the answer, the system appears wonderfully smart. If asked, however, to think about wholly new information requiring the application of a set of concepts not exposed to the brain before, quite a different picture emerges. Under such circumstances the aging brain cannot compete with the young brain. Fortunately for all of us, this situation rarely occurs in the normal life of human beings. Most of us deal with a limited set of concepts that we are well rehearsed in using. We are quickly able to recognize and apply them throughout our lives. We therefore appear intelligent at a time when our brains are, in fact, markedly impaired at deducing from scratch the new concept that is being applied.

Aging: Individual Differences and Cures

So the problems for the aging brain are real, tangible, and inevitable for most humans. This reality led one psychologist to ask, "Why do people save themselves for the worst years of their lives? Live intensely while you are mobile and can enjoy." It is a profound point, especially when considered in light of research suggesting that much of what happens to our aging brains is under genetic control. In all the preceding discussions, we have been talking about group norms, what happens to the average person. There are always exceptions at both ends of the scale. There are worst cases—those with disease— and there are best cases where the performance of an aged adult can compete with that of a twenty-year-old. These extremes are thought to be the clearest instances of genetic influence. As longevity runs in a family, so does brain health.

Even more disconcerting is the fact that at present there is no clear way to prevent the onset of these brain changes. Jogging doesn't help. Jane Fonda's exercise program doesn't help. Eating lettuce and bananas doesn't help. The disappearance of some brain cells and the change in size and functional capacity of others appear to progress regardless of our attempts to prevent them.

This leaves the question of what can be done to help those with the major mental difficulty of those past forty—the problem of impaired memory. There are two levels at which to attack the problem: the psychological and the biological. The first is the area where there is the most help, using straightforward management tricks. The simplest support strategy is to take notes of important needed information. If your internal memory system is faltering, try to develop efficient external memory aids. In patients with intact intelligence but severe amnesia, this method has proven helpful in assisting them to a normal way of life.

The second strategy for improving memory is to utilize imagery aids. It is well known that the ability to remember new information is enhanced by tying it to a mental picture. In the laboratory this is easily demonstrated by giving subjects a long list of word pairs to remember. First the list is read out loud by the tester, and the subject is instructed to remember the words by saying them over and over to himself. Then he is asked to recall the second word after the examiner has read the first word of each pair. Another version of this experiment is to give the list of word pairs to the subject and instruct him to make mental images of them. Thus, instead of rehearsing a word pair such as "apple/car" over and over again, the subject is told to create a picture: a car made of an apple, perhaps, or an apple sitting on top of a car. The effects on memory of this simple trick are truly astounding. The overall scores in recall can go up as high as 100 percent using such a mnemonic.

This strategy can be easily applied in everyday life. You have just seen a new species of dog and are told it is a Bichon Frise. How are you going to remember that? Easy. Think of a hot day in Paris, and you are standing outside Fouchons, where they are serving a wonderfully cold drink. It will be practically impossible to forget the name.

But the civilized world has become accustomed to the quick fix. Why can't we pop a pill that will make remembering as easy when we are ninety as it was in our youth? Modern medicine has reinforced this view with its seemingly endless series of cures for common maladies. Where is the pill for helping memory? It is being worked on, but not too successfully.

The approach is largely motivated by the grand success psychopharmacologists had with finding a drug to control the symptoms of Parkinson's disease, which, you recall, causes loss of movement control because of a marked decrease in the brain's capacity to produce the neurotransmitter dopamine. In addition, the number of cells that respond to this neurotransmitter is abnormally low. It was discovered that administering L-dopa, a chemical agent appearing early in the biochemical chain that leads to the synthesis of the neurotransmitter, causes patients to be markedly better by improving their motor control. Huge doses of L-dopa did the trick.

The same simplistic logic is being used for memory loss. For this brain system, researchers currently believe that the neurotransmitter acetylcholine may be important. The brain areas suffering the cellular loss described at the beginning of this chapter are rich in this transmitter, and acetylcholine metabolism decreases in the aging brain. This has been discovered by observing that choline acetyltransferase, a marker for neurons that synthesize acetylcholine, is dramatically reduced in patients with real dementia. At the same time, these patients have in place the neurons that respond to this neurotransmitter. Additionally, it has been shown in normal people that administration of a drug called scopalamine, which prevents acetylcholine from working properly, causes disorders in the normal brain. Implication? Try to increase the synthesis of acetylcholine in the aging brain.

Although there have been attempts to do this, and some report that moderate success is possible, the current view is that the administration of a variety of drugs that manipulate the brain metabolism of acetylcholine has not been helpful. When you stop to think about it, it is no wonder. Brain scientists still have only the sketchiest idea of how the brain stores memories and how they are initially established. While at one level the local synapse has to be important in understanding the physical basis of memory, it must be only a small part of the picture. Memories surely involve vast networks of neurons that use several neurotransmitters in widely different parts of the brain. Timing of impulses among the millions of neurons active in memory storage must also be important. To unilaterally increase the metabolic rate of one transmitter is to take a shot in the dark. The shot hasn't worked, and probably won't until brain scientists have a better idea about the normal mechanism by which the brain learns and remembers.

Modern medicine can fix backs, control hypertension, cure many forms of cancer. It cannot for now fix the memory system, which begins losing its efficiency after the age of forty. It is clear that there are enormous changes going on during normal aging, affecting virtually every aspect of the nervous system. It is also clear that the psychological system managing how we store new information is undergoing tremendous changes. In the heyday years of youth it is a complex system with many components interacting to produce normal memory. With age, the shrewd intellect, which remains markedly preserved in a deteriorating brain, finds new ways, new tricks to store information. It creates images and lifts the storage process from using traditional brain systems into new systems that are not understood in the least. Yet, at a level of personal consciousness, with age we tend to avoid information-rich experiences. It is as if our left-brain interpreter quickly constructs theories why we shouldn't travel or attend social functions or consider new ideas. The cocoon of later life begins to be woven around us, and the interpreter gives us a clear reason why. But underneath all of this is the greatly decreased capacity caused by a markedly changed brain, and the interpreter, observing this, constructs theories that explain why we are changing our social behavior.

Memory, like pain, is an essential feature of a normally working brain and mind. At this point in human history there are no quick fixes for memory loss. If there were, all kinds of uses would be found for the drugs. Not only would they be used for the aging; they would be called upon to help those who do not appear as "bright" as others. This brings us to another "hard" feature of the brain—intelligence. What is it and how does such a property of brain and mind influence our lives?

3

Intelligence

George is a schoolboy of twelve. George is retarded. Everyone agrees. His IQ is below 70. He goes to a special school paid for by the taxpayer. Pete, his friend, is dyslexic. He has a learning disability that is real and tangible. Almost everyone agrees that his disability reflects a brain deficit of some kind, but no one knows its exact nature. He goes to a special teacher, also paid for by the taxpayer.

Susan is smart and Jane is not. Their parents know, their teachers know, their friends know, and most of all, they know. Almost everyone would agree that George and Pete were born with handicaps that care and training can ameliorate but will never overcome fully. Yet when someone observes that Susan has a higher IQ than Jane and that the higher IQ is largely driven by genetic factors, it spurs everyone to become agitated, heated, and abusive. That intelligence is largely inherited is an idea most people accept privately but won't acknowledge publicly. The reason for this double standard is that no one wants to believe that, once established, a perfect environment might still nourish imperfect human beings. The very existence and purpose of social systems seem to mandate the opposite idea. Where did the idea come from? Most important, what are the brain factors responsible for the wide range of individual differences obviously apparent among humans?

What is meant by human intelligence? Although our capacity to adapt, to come in out of the cold, to easily see cause and effect, certainly reflects some kind of baseline competence for our species, it does not capture the notion of intelligence. Cockroaches, after all, are quite adaptive; some might say more so than people. Human intelligence refers to the computational capacity of a particular individual. It has to do with the ability to solve problems and to think about relations between variables. Most intelligence tests assess this computational aspect of the mind. If you are good at these tests, it means you will tend to do well in school, because the generally accepted goal of good education is to enhance one's general knowledge and ability to solve problems. It should not be particularly surprising that this is so. But when it comes to the topic of intelligence and schooling, feelings run very deep.

Nature Versus Nurture

It all started with Francis Galton and John Stuart Mill. Galton was a cousin of Charles Darwin and was born into a privileged English family who urged him to be a university scholar. For most of his early life he was passionately consumed with this goal. He quickly came to the view that intelligence, like rich land and money, was inherited, and it followed that there was a privileged intellectual class. At Cambridge University he excelled until the final exams, where, in the course of seeking honors, he received a test score that proved to be only good rather than excellent. He was flabbergasted by this and withdrew from further competition.

Galton went into a serious depression. He was aimless until his father persuaded him to attend medical school. But he disliked medicine, and after his father died, he withdrew from medical school. He received a substantial inheritance and quickly began to live the aristocratic life. Then Galton, too curious for idleness and frustrated with his own lack of purpose, went to see a phrenologist. The session proved most helpful. The phrenologist claimed to have detected that while Galton was highly intelligent, his skull shape—and therefore his brain capacity—suggested that his skills were not scholastic but rather for roughing it on difficult challenges. This analysis must have relieved Galton of his sense of failure in academia, and shortly thereafter he commenced his long and distinguished scientific career.

Galton coined the term "nature versus nurture" and carried out a series of new statistical studies that argued for the importance of heredity in intelligence. He introduced the study of how twins brought up in different environments compared as adults in terms of intelligence. He also devised the adopted child method of study. Here children with biological histories different from those of their parents were compared with the biological children of those parents. Finally, he developed statistics for the mathematical method of correlation coefficients. This measurement, which is used throughout all of science, helps determine how related two different variables are to each other. It is essential to the study of intelligence.

Having convinced himself of the role of genetics, Galton suggested that IQ tests should be developed and eugenics programs should be started at once. Like most of the scientists who followed him, Galton believed so strongly in the importance of heredity as the basis of intelligence that he advocated absurd social reforms in the name of eugenics. Yet the notion of breeding a higher intelligence into our species persists and sometimes interferes with the dispassionate analysis of why people have different competencies.

Mill saw it differently. The son of the famous cleric James Mill, John Mill was educated at home by a father who believed that environment was all important. The father taught all of his children at his desk, and even though it was John only who excelled, the family held tightly to the view that "mental potential" was built up from simple associative learning. Although John significantly advanced his father's sophisticated philosophy of associative learning, he produced some fairly wild concepts. For example, he felt that differences in talent between artists and scientists could be explained by differences in associative learning in early periods of their lives. His reasoning was that children who have intense experiences will develop strong connections between them and ideas synchronously. Children with milder experiences will develop associations with events that occur successively over time. The synchronous children will become artists, since their connections will favor objects and things existing in a moment of time. The children with mild experiences will become scientists, since their experience, according to Mill, favors knowledge about successive events. This predisposes them to think about phenomena and processes. This rather ingenious account of how the environment can lead to the development of various mental skills is one of the best post-hoc explanations I have come across in a long time.

Unlike Galton, Mill believed that the mind was delivered to this world as a blank slate upon which experience was written. His political views were consistent with his psychological ideas, and he was the consummate egalitarian. Mill and Galton fought continually, and it is no wonder, with a history like this, that the nature–nurture question in intelligence remains as heated today as it was over a century ago.

Measuring Intelligence

The entire history of intelligence testing spells out a story of how the personal beliefs of each investigator correlate with the side of the nature–nurture question each defends, from Galton and Mill right on through the development of IQ tests and their current use. Following up on Galton's notion that various sensory and motor abilities could be measured and correlated with overall intelligence, the American psychologist James Cattell of Columbia University developed a series of tests in 1890 that he felt would reflect the large individual differences seen in the normal population. He was the first to dub them "mental tests" and is credited with initiating the concept. They were focused on the physical aspect of the mind, however, examining such factors as muscle strength, amount of pressure necessary to cause pain, reaction time for sound, and so on.

The idea of having physical tests that supposedly measured intelligence was enthusiastically received, but it soon became apparent that they revealed no useful characterizations. One of Cattell's own students, Clark Wissler, showed that the measures in no way correlated with student performance at Columbia University. Cattell was devastated by this result and dropped the enterprise. It wasn't until 1900, when French psychologist Alfred Binet appeared on the scene, that the idea of "mental tests" was revived.

Binet was actually trying to measure individual differences in the way children solved problems. He had observed how his own children, whom he presumed to be of equal intelligence, approached and dealt with novel situations. He also was fascinated to note that children who are at the developmental stage where they are equal to adults on neurological tests only gradually learn to handle intellectual abstractions. Binet's tests centered more on reasoning capacity. He felt that if he could capture how children moved from one level of understanding to another, he would gain insights into what intelligence was all about. In a way, he saw children as adults in slow motion, and by studying them, he could figure out the components of adult intelligence.

Over the years the approach has made many advances. Binet's test, with much additional work by others, has become the dominant one for children. Lewis Terman at Stanford University picked up on one of Binet's versions and standardized it to take population norms into account. This test became known as the Stanford-Binet. Soon after its development, Terman adopted psychologist William Stern's notion of an intelligence quotient. Stern recognized that children have different capabilities at different ages, so he developed a ratio to express in one term what a child's intelligence might be. He divided the mental age, as determined by intelligence tests, by the chronological age and multiplied the ratio by one hundred to get what is now universally called IQ. It is that measurement of human competence that drives people to passionate debate.

There is little doubt that IQ tests are fairly good at assessing competence in school and at predicting scholarly achievement within the culture where the test is given. At one level, this predictability is surprising, since the items and problems in the tests are picked largely at random. But since intelligence is defined operationally as that which intelligence tests test, the test makers are chasing their own tail. They are not guided by any independent theory of what intelligence is in terms of how the brain or mind processes information. As a result, the test makers develop different problems that require reasoning of one kind or another and see if people sort out in their ability to solve the problem. If there is a variance that does not seem to depend on some natural advantage, the problem qualifies as a test item. In one of the initial efforts, for instance, the test kept showing that women consistently scored fifteen points higher than men. The test makers noticed which questions were being consistently missed by men and threw them out, thereby evening the norms for the two sexes!

Still, the tests do identify people who are better or worse at solving the kinds of problems that schools employ in teaching. The central question, however, is why do people score so differently? The modern-day argument still revolves around the issues that Galton and Mill established. Are the differences in intelligence due to heredity or different environmental circumstances?

Hereditary Influences on Intelligence

In an effort to determine how intelligence may be influenced or controlled by genes, researchers in the thirties followed Galton's suggestion and took to studying twins and adopted children. The twins method allows one to measure the influence of hereditary factors, since identical twins have the exact same genetic history. In studying how they perform on tests of all kinds, one expects to see less variation in their performance than, say, that of nontwin brothers and sisters. In normal sibling pairs there is some genetic similarity but the differences are large. Observations of their performance in psychological tests indicate that they behave far more differently from each other than do the identical twins. As for adopted children, who are unrelated to and therefore genetically distinct from their parents, the role of an enriched or impoverished environment, as the case may be, can be observed.

The first studies of twins at the turn of the century suggesting that heredity played an important role in intelligence were roundly criticized. However, Sir Cyril Burt, a respected British psychologist and a professor at University College in London, in 1943 began to publish a lengthy series of studies that initially silenced many of the critics. He demonstrated that most of the variance seen in human intelligence could be explained by heredity. The work stood out as a landmark. Then came the big surprise: Burt had made serious errors. Stated more strongly, he had completely fabricated his data! It was a major scandal.

Nonetheless, there were many other studies supporting the role heredity played in intelligence. Some of the research reported new data on twins that refueled the notion of a strong genetic component. Modern neurobiology, too, offered some researchers hints as to how the brain might support individual differences in intelligence. But first the research on twins and adoptees.

We go to Europe for new insights into these questions. The first study capitalizes on the tremendous effort made by the Norwegian government to offer equal education to all after World War II. Before that time, the affluent had access to excellent schools while the poor got a more rudimentary education.

In support of the effort, the Norwegians established a "twin panel" that keeps relevant data on twins and their families. A recent study of Norwegian twins, conducted by American scientists led by A. C. Heath from the Medical College of Virginia, has received much attention. He sent out questionnaires to 8,389 twins and received almost 5,000 responses.

The American researchers were trying to determine whether the new, more liberal educational policies of the postwar years in Norway had had a beneficial effect on educational attainment. At the same time, they could assess the relative role of hereditary versus environmental factors in gaining a higher education. Correlations were made between identical twins and their educational achievement under the old system and under the new reforms. The same was done for the less genetically similar fraternal twins. Comparisons of educational attainment were also made between twins and their parents.

The results were striking. First, there was no difference in educational attainment for identical twins who were educated under either the old or the new system, suggesting that, overall, genetic and familial contributions to educational attainment had not changed in the Norwegian culture. There was an extremely small change between the educational achievement of prewar and postwar parents, thereby indicating that the parental "stock" had not significantly changed. In other words, parents of children educated under either system had themselves achieved roughly the same educational level and, therefore, were creating similar "educational environments" for their children.

The surprise came in the correlations for the fraternal twins. Prior to the war, there was a high correlation of educational achievement between fraternal twins of both sexes. After the war, the fraternal males, enjoying the improved school system, began to show marked differences in accomplishment. One fraternal twin would far outdo the other. Thus, when two twins given nearly equal academic chances vary so widely, the reason would seem to lie in their slightly different genetic heritages.

While this finding had been predicted by several investigators, including Sandra Scarr at the University of Virginia and Richard Herrnstein at Harvard, Heath's study provides new evidence in support. The researchers went on to show that in the male dizygotic twins, the hereditary factor accounted for a whopping 74 percent of the variation seen in educational attainment.

The effect of the postwar educational equality did not have a large influence on females. For them, only approximately 40 percent of the variation in educational attainment was accounted for by genetic factors. No explanation is given by the authors for this difference between the sexes. The implication that sex differences may exist in the genetic influence on intelligence is largely unexamined territory.

The other major study to come out of Europe, shortly after Heath's, was based on a careful examination of the Danish adoption register. T. W. Teasdale and David R. Owen unearthed several comparison groups. They looked at both intelligence and educational attainment of biologically related adopted children reared apart as well as biologically unrelated ones living together. The related adoptees brought up in separate households that differed a great deal in income and social class tell us much about the role of nature—the genetic factor. The unrelated adoptees reared in the same surroundings give us insights into the nurturing role—the environment. After a thorough and complex analysis of the adoptees' intelligence scores and educational levels, the authors came to conclusions similar to those found in the Norwegian study: genetic factors played an important role in determining intelligence scores, but both genetic and environmental factors were involved in predicting educational level.

These kinds of studies will always be criticized, redone, and argued about, since there are so many variables involved and so much political contention about the implications of the results. It will be a long time before all agree. Indeed, when these new studies came out in the prestigious British journal *Nature,* there was a long editorial by the editor, John Maddox. Anticipating the reaction to the new studies showing that intelligence may have a genetic component, he voted for continuing to support scientific inquiry on the topic, saying a fuller answer to the question would not be socially divisive and would only lead to more questions of scientific interest. Certainly that is true.

For years this controversy has centered on whether or not the as yet undefinable cognitive entity—called intelligence—is largely under the control of hereditary factors. While the argument has been raging, precious little attention has been given to what actually may differentiate one brain from another. Is it known that brain lesions affect intelligence? Is the neural circuitry different from one brain to another? Does one brain work more efficiently than another? Do brains have different metabolisms? These questions are now being investigated, and, from what is now known, it seems apparent that there are dozens of ways for brains to be different.

Early and Late Brain Injury and Intelligence

Direct evidence for the brain's role in the development of intelligence comes from the examination of children with injuries sustained at a very early age. It is important to keep in mind the adult pattern of brain injury. In approximately 97 percent of all humans, damage to certain regions of the left hemisphere of the brain has serious effects on language and thought processes. Damage to the corresponding areas of the right causes other problems that are commonly associated with spatial orientation. Injury to the young child's brain produces a wholly different picture. Damage to the right hemisphere during the first year of life produces grave consequences for both verbal and spatial functions later on. Remarkably, damage to the left affects spatial processes only, with verbal processes being almost completely spared. In other words, the specific brain functions active during the development of language and thought mechanisms are located in brain areas distant from their final location. Apparently, there are distinct brain processes active during early life that are crucial for establishing normal language and thought mechanisms. Most important, because they exist as specific, localized systems, they become evidence for the key role brain processes play in mental functions such as intelligence.

Individual Variation in Brain Circuitry

The first fact of human brain anatomy is that even at the gross level, brains are different. Their pattern of convolutions is different. The amount of tissue in each of the major areas of the brain varies from one person to another. Even the major fiber pathway that connects the two halves of the brain, the corpus callosum, has a different shape in virtually everybody. With such easily noted distinctions, we might expect that vast differences would exist in cell-to-cell interactions.

In animal experiments, researchers have looked for possible differences in cellular organization between male and female rats. Variations were clearly observed in several brain structures. In humans, with the billions and billions of nerve interconnections that are possible, the truly phenomenal result would be to discover that the interconnections are the same for all of us. There is, of course, no suggestion that this is the case.

How do these brain differences come about? If we take the simple and extreme view of genetic influence, the DNA, or genetic chemicals, ought to spell out in detail all aspects of development. Strict hereditarians hold this view with some reason. In the early forties, the work of Roger Sperry put the brakes on runaway environmentalism and brain mechanics as argued for by his mentor, Paul Weiss, and dozens of others. The biological view at that time was that the brain developed nonspecifically: it was only after a neuron was used that it took on a specification. The notion was, for example, that a nerve that grew out to the arms could just as easily have grown out to the feet. The nerve was initially capable of doing any function. It was only as the arm began to be used in the way arms are used that the nerve became specially adapted and dedicated to arm functions. Sperry showed, in a brilliant series of experiments, the incorrectness of this view. In brief, he found that nerves grew to their destination points with their function already specified. If the sensory nerve of the right hind paw of a rat, for example, was sectioned and neatly transposed so that in effect it served the left hind paw when regenerated, a most remarkable and consistent thing happened. When the left hind paw was shocked, the animal thought it was his right paw that was being shocked, and as a result, he quickly retracted the wrong—that is, the right—paw. The left paw, the one actually receiving the shocking stimulus, stayed put. Clearly, the nervous system had developed in predetermined fashion. The right sensory nerve from the start was created for the right paw, and even surgically directing it to the left paw could not change that fact. Any stimulation of it, no matter where it was placed in the body, would find the brain treating the messages as if they were coming from the right paw.

These studies were extended to other animals, with the result always showing how specific and genetically determined neurons seemed to be. Yet most of the observations were on peripheral nerves. Could it be that the same kind of specificity held for the billions of cells in the brain? It wasn't until the work of David Hubel and Torsten Wiesel, at Harvard in the early sixties, that insights into this aspect of brain cells became known. Their work also supported the idea of predetermined neural capacity.

Hubel and Wiesel made some fundamental discoveries about the visual system of the cat. Using microelectrodes, they determined the way cortical cells, receiving information from the retina, responded under strict experimental conditions when visual stimuli were presented to one or the other eye. They showed that a preponderance of cells in the normally developed visual cortex responded to stimuli presented to either eye. These cells were called binocular cells. They also noted that far fewer cells responded to stimuli presented to only one eye. These were called monocular cells. Knowing this about how the settled, adult brain of the cat was constructed, they studied newborn kittens. Would their brain look the same as the adults'? They quickly discovered that the kittens had the same distribution of cells—that is, most of the visual cells in the kitten also responded to stimuli presented to both eyes. This strongly suggested that the basic organization of neural inputs was under genetic control.

Hubel and Wiesel also discovered that manipulation of the cat's visual world could change the proportion of binocular and monocular cells. Here was an effect of the environment on the cellular organization of the brain. While genetic mechanisms gave the broad structure, the fine detail could be influenced by different surroundings if the manipulations came early in the animal's life. The major pathways and general features of brain organization are under tight genetic control, but deviations can exist at the cell-to-cell level. These local changes in cell-to-cell connection are not so bound by heredity.

The work of Hubel and Wiesel demonstrated that the tension that exists between the genetic program and the effects of environment can be examined and measured physiologically. Other researchers have further demonstrated that brain changes due to environment can be directly observed.

First, when a cell under genetic control has to grow from point A to point B, it does not do so by simply sending out the exact number of neurons to the destination point. Instead, it is now known that so-called exuberant growth occurs. The number of projections to point B is several times greater than what it ultimately will be. This pattern of overinnervation followed by a retreat and death of the unwanted neurons works in some as yet unspecified way. Scientists, in trying to understand what factors determine which cells stay and which ones die, alter the environmental experience of the developing animal and look for systematic differences in the brain zone being studied. One such study of young chicks showed that a brain area retained more neural innervation when exposed to a simple single tone as opposed to the clucking sound of a normal hen. It was as if the rich clucking sound, with its varied harmonics and complex tones, required more specific neural apparatus for support than did a simple tone.

There are dozens of problems yet to be worked out with such studies. For example, perhaps the variations in the chicks' brain zone was due to a different level of arousal stimulated by the more "ecologically relevant" cluck. The arousal level, with the concomitant change in hormonal response, might be responsible for the nerve growth difference. Hormone levels are known to affect such growth, yet it seems as if the genetic program leads to an exuberant growth that is then trimmed by experience.

Other, more interventive studies also show how brain circuits can change their largely predetermined course of connection. When young monkeys are subjected to minor cortical injury, the nerves that would normally innervate the injured zone are sent off to hook up elsewhere. One can imagine that subtle changes in the chemical or metabolic rate of a brain zone could thus affect whether an incoming nerve makes connections or not. Some pediatricians think that caesarean babies are brighter than their siblings, suggesting that the trauma of the birth canal delivery might have a negative effect on ultimate brain capacity.

Finally in the brain circuit story are the new findings of Michael Merzenich and Jon Kaas, who have studied the somatosensory—the body nerve—system of the monkey. These investigators have shown that the "maps" for the body that exist in the brain differ enormously in location, size, and extent from one animal to another. They also vary in how much of any given map is devoted to a particular body area. These maps were discovered by monitoring the nerve cells on the surface of the brain's cortex. The cells discharge when specific body areas or zones have been stimulated. By carefully noting how each cell in the brain responds to what body stimulus, researchers can identify the maps. They have been studied for years and are one of the clearest results from classic neurophysiology. The recent research, using new methods of measurement that define with greater accuracy the boundaries of the maps, shows that while monkeys may look alike, their brains are all subtly different. Each map varies, and Merzenich and Kaas have done further work in an effort to understand why and how these differences come about.

They examined whether the maps could change as the result of experience. They amputated one finger of a monkey's hand, expecting to find a silent zone in the brain map of the hand area that they had already determined was usually active to stimulation only from the now missing finger. Instead, to their amazement, the brain area was almost immediately responsive to stimulation of the other fingers. This suggested to the investigators that the adult brain can be incredibly adaptive to change, and that either the underlying circuits changed quickly in response to the injury or the existing circuits were quickly reprogrammed to respond differently.

In a follow-up experiment Merzenich and Kaas examined whether less severe manipulations could also produce changes in cortical organization. They trained monkeys to use their middle finger in carrying out a particular task. They reported that the brain map for that finger became larger! This suggested to them that experience changed the neural network, although it remains unknown whether the change was due to cell-to-cell changes in position and connections or to reprogramming of the existing cells. In short, their new view was that the brain is in a constantly changing state, and information is represented in a dynamic rather than static pattern. The idea is revolutionary and is more supportive of the notion that the environment is constantly influencing the structure of the nervous system.

But there are problems with this interpretation, and they show the difficulties in research, even when it is as clever and elegant as this work appears to be. For example, it is known that the capillaries that feed blood to the cortex expand and contract, depending on how active are the nerve cells they nourish. Their expansion and contraction could cause the cortex to expand and contract slightly as well, simply as the result of physical displacement of tissue as the blood rushes into and swells the capillaries. It is possible that the changes the neurophysiologists see might reflect this mechanical aspect of brain physiology. It may be that the actual map size in terms of neural connections is not changing at all. Evidence to prove which of the two interpretations is correct is not yet in hand.

Still, there is overwhelming evidence that within a species, brain circuitry is different from one animal to another. These same researchers who found evidence of dynamic changes within a brain region also found the overall brain maps different in each animal they tested. This kind of data could serve as a basis for explaining individual variation in intelligence.

Efficiency of Cell-to-Cell Transmission

The genetic hold on the development of intelligence could act in other ways as well. Instead of circuit differences, the amount or efficiency of neurotransmitters crucial for the actual communication between cells might vary from one person to another. Specific suggestions on this aspect of the problem have been put forward by T. Edward Reed of the University of Toronto. He points out that the loci for genes controlling enzymes that are important in the manufacture and metabolism of neurotransmitters are polymorphic. That means there are at least two genes at each site, thereby assuring a wide variability of expression. If the amount of an enzyme available differs from one person to another, then the efficiency of a nerve circuit will also vary. In rats it has been shown that both conduction velocity—that is, how fast an electrical impulse travels down a nerve—and synaptic transmission time vary with specific genetic manipulations.

Brain Metabolism and Intelligence

If brain efficiency is heightened in some people who have more efficient synaptic activity because of more robust neurotransmitters, it would suggest that their brain cells are more active. The more active the brain cells are, the more they need food to carry out their activities. Food comes to them in the form of glucose, which is pumped into the brain via the blood. One way to measure how active the brain is is to measure the rate at which glucose is utilized. This can now be done, thanks to radiochemistry and positron emission tomography (PET), in which the chemist cleverly makes radioactive a molecule that can track glucose metabolism. The PET process is a way to take pictures of where in the brain the molecule travels and also to trace how much of it travels to one place as opposed to another. If the PET technique discloses that one part of the brain is more active than another, we can assume there is more neural activity going on there than in other parts. Using PET, one can begin to ask whether people with higher IQs have different rates of brain activity than people with lower IQs. There have been some new experiments that support the idea.

A group of researchers at the National Institutes of Health report that verbal IQ is related to activity in particular areas in the left half brain, and performance IQ—that is, the ability to solve problems requiring manual dexterity—is linked to part of the posterior right half brain. These results are consistent with earlier ones obtained from studying patients with localized lesions. However, the implication of the work goes further. The analysis of brain activity suggests that people whose IQ varies have different metabolic rates in the zones responsible for verbal as opposed to performance IQ. If these findings are confirmed, tying intelligence to brain activity will be one step closer.

Modern research on brain mechanisms now points the way to how we might explain individual variation at a neural level. People's brains are different, and the spookiness of that idea is behind us. We are not stamped out of a mold. We are all wonderfully varied, and the variation in brain mechanics is measurable and verifiable. Yet, having said that, we are left doubling back to the psychological level of evaluation. O.K., O.K., yell the psychologists, brains are different, but what, operationally, is the smarter person doing that the less smart person is not doing? There must be some qualitative difference. After all, sheer efficiency cannot be the answer. Faster and more efficient memories may help, but they are far from a complete explanation. To use the computer metaphor, faster computers do not mean smarter computers. What is the something else?

The quick answer is that no one knows for sure. The more interesting answer, however, is that for the first time new work is beginning to identify human thought processes in a way that allows for the understanding of individual variation. It all has to do with a new concept that is not unrelated to the notion of the brain's interpreter outlined earlier. It is called the psychology of explanatory systems.

Many tests of intelligence are directed at assessing skills of deductive logic, such as the ability to decide that *If P,* and *If P, then Q,* it follows that Q. But these rules do not apply to many real life situations—for instance, those involving beliefs. If Mary believes *If I look in the cupboard, I will see a box of Cheerios,* and *I am looking in the cupboard,* then by the rule of deductive logic just stated, Mary should also believe *I see a box of Cheerios.* But if, unbeknownst to Mary, someone ate the Cheerios yesterday and discarded the box, Mary should not believe *I am seeing a box of Cheerios that is not there.* That would be absurd, but strict application of the rule of deductive logic would force Mary to such a conclusion. What Mary would do in the real world is forget the rule of logic and proceed to revise her beliefs, changing her initial premise in an attempt to *explain* why she is not seeing the box of Cheerios.

The human ability to explain unexpected situations is overwhelming. It is the heart of categorization and reasoning. I will argue in the following chapters that the attempts the mind makes to explain essentially unexplainable and aberrant brain activity can often lead to serious psychological problems. But the same tendency to interpret and explain guides everyday thinking about cause and effect and, at its most sophisticated, is the stuff of good science. If intelligence is anything, it is this capacity to offer reasonable explanations. Intelligence tests, if they are to measure anything, should assess these explanatory skills. And theories of intelligence, if they are to explain anything, must articulate the way knowledge and actions are represented in the mind so that explanations are as easy and natural to man as they appear to be.

Questions about intelligence—how to manage it, administer it, account for it, ignore it, yield to it—are more often avoided than discussed, even though it is a commodity of mental life called upon daily. An example of the perplexing questions raised is: should people of low intelligence be considered handicapped, say, the way people in wheelchairs are? Certainly they are shut off from a wide range of human activities that require higher computational skills. Because of that, they are often denied higher incomes. Issues of this kind point up once again how a brain state affects the mind and how we adapt to our own levels of biological capacity.

Intelligence is a brain state that is dictated by innate capacities. Because we possess it, we respond to various aspects of our environment in different ways. Memory and pain are qualities of mind that also rely heavily on the state of basic brain structure, and how we deal with our particular capacity becomes important in what we choose to do and how we choose to live. There are still other, more aberrant disturbances in brain tissue that feed an individual into more bizarre response strategies. These are the brain changes that lead us to the problem of crazy thoughts, a state of mind that proves most instructive for students of mind and health.

Crazy Thoughts

Schizophrenia can be called a "hard" disorder of brain and mind. During an attack, its victims cannot think in a logical way from A to B. When in full bloom, it appears dense and unapproachable through purely psychological methods. Although physicians immediately call upon drugs to control the symptoms, all too frequently the disease itself remains in place. To a large extent it is held out as an example of how little we know about mind and brain. Yet that kind of thinking seems an oversimplification. Schizophrenia can be very instructive about mind-brain mechanisms and may well hold lessons about how normal people organize their environment.

This disease can sneak up and grab hold and never let go. Or it can grab hold for only a short while and then disappear into the night, never to return. It comes in many shapes, many intensities, and many styles. Determining the nosology—that is, the specifics of each possible manifestation—has occupied psychiatrists for years and continues to demand further investigation. It is as if each category represents a new subspecies of the human condition, with each needing its own behavioral description and having its own biochemical reality.

Curiously, there is some argument over the origins of the disease. While most people assume it has always existed, and even though it is now known to occur in every culture, including very primitive ones, there is evidence that it is a modern disease, first detected in the early nineteenth century. Historians note that before then there is essentially no reference in literature to anything that resembles our modern descriptions of the disease. There is, however, no argument over who described and coined the word "schizophrenia."

The two pioneers in the field were the German Emil Kraepelin and Eugen Bleuler of Switzerland. Kraepelin called it dementia praecox, while it fell to Bleuler to name it schizophrenia. He was after a term that would describe the apparent split between affect and thought, a shrewd characterization. Both investigators felt the disease was brain-based, even though they had no idea of the specifics. Yet this notion was more or less furloughed for dozens of years and did not become the dominant view until relatively recently.

Although there are new and intriguing reports on the particular biochemical abnormalities that exist in schizophrenia, this recently acquired knowledge alone does not help explain why a schizophrenic may think he is the King of Siam. Nor can terrible experiences be an explanation. The most onerous and stressful psychological ordeals rarely lead to schizophrenia. It hits 1 percent of the world population, no matter where they live, what their culture, what they believe, or whether or not they have money in the bank. Consequently, the purely psychological view—the idea that the disease can be traced to antecedent psychological events in the life history of the schizophrenic—must be considered only in the context of the biological state the person was in during the period of his affliction.

An Interpretative Theory of Schizophrenia

My view is that schizophrenia is a disease that finds the brain's interpreter going wild in its attempts to bring order out of what is most likely endogenous, or inner-generated, brain chaos.

Examining the extreme example of schizophrenia reveals how powerful the interpreter may be and how much it wants to succeed in generating reasonable ideas about unreasonable experiences and thoughts that most likely arise out of spurious neural actions precipitated by faulty biochemical brain states. It may well be the brain's interpreter, the system that has been discussed before, that produces our everyday beliefs and, surprisingly, the severe delusions of the schizophrenic as well. Appreciating the presence of the brain's interpreter and the range of biochemical conditions that can exist in altered brain states gives us powerful tools to better understand this awful disease.

There is a veritable constellation of symptoms associated with schizophrenia. A common progression for the disease can be seen in the case of Georgia. Hers was a drug-induced psychosis that mimicked the chronic schizophrenic state. Georgia suffered from narcolepsy (sudden lapses into deep sleep), and in coping with that disorder she took too much amphetamine.

> Georgia experienced hypnogogic hallucinations, the perceptions of visual or auditory stimuli that are not really present. These sometimes occurred at the beginning of the period of her sleep paralysis. Georgia, however, was reporting that the hallucinations had become more frequent and were occurring throughout her waking hours. Hearing voices several times a day led to inevitable and obvious personality changes. These became profound. She slowly withdrew into the world of her auditory hallucinations and constructed a complicated paranoid delusional system around them. She believed that these voices were intruding into her head and controlling her will. In fact, she began believing that all her thoughts were public knowledge and that anyone could read exactly what she was thinking. Before long her friends noted her extreme withdrawal, and when they interacted she seemed strange and emotionally inappropriate. They brought her to the hospital emergency room.

> It was clear that Georgia was in the throes of a serious

thought disorder most like schizophrenia. The reasons for this break became clear only when the nurses emptied her purse. They found enough amphetamine to supply an ordinary narcoleptic for several months. Unknown to her doctors, Georgia's need for amphetamine—Dexedrine—had increased beyond all reasonable limits. While Dexedrine was appropriate pharmacologic regimentation considering Georgia's narcolepsy, she had begun taking more than her doctor prescribed. Taking upwards of 200 mg a day, though, was unquestionably dangerous and the chronic ingestion of such a dose of amphetamine commonly causes paranoid behavior and auditory hallucinations; then thought disorder, personal withdrawal, and inappropriate affect all characterize the spontaneous disorder called schizophrenia. Here the disorder was drug-induced with chronic amphetamine overdose.

In this example, we see the almost cascade-like progression of one form of the disease. There is some brain state change that produces the hallucinations, clearly a very disturbing state of mind. As one copes with these unwanted intrusions into thought, thought itself becomes very disordered and interrupted—full of static, as it were. A first response can be a wild embarrassment, and the victim withdraws from social contact as much as possible. That isolation compounds the problem, as the interpreter, first having had to deal with imagined sounds and voices, now has to comprehend them without the steadying influence provided by contact with friends and family.

The phenomenon of delusions can provide insights into the mind-brain interaction. We are all paranoid at times. The sense of momentarily overwhelming vulnerability that can arise in the absence of a threatening stimulus is most likely due to some transitory biochemical imbalance in certain brain structures. But when the condition moves beyond the episodic moment to the more chronic condition, severe paranoia can result. The famous case of Dr. Daniel Schreber illustrates the sequence of events. (This account is from the *DSM-III Case Book,* which is a fascinating supplement of case histories of most kinds of mental disorders, published by the American Psychiatric Association. *"DSM-III"* stands for *The Diagnostic and Statistical Manual of Mental Disorders, Third Edition.*)

Dr. Schreber was a highly intelligent judge who lived at the turn of the century. He served as a case example for Freud and also wrote insightfully about his own condition. In 1884 he had an attack of hypochondria that completely cleared. Then in 1893 he got the idea that he was going to be transformed into a woman. His attending physician, Dr. Weber, reported that

> he was chiefly troubled by hypochondriacal ideas, complained that he had softening of the brain, that he would soon be dead, etc. But ideas of persecution were already finding their way into the clinical picture, based upon sensorial illusions which, however, seemed only to appear sporadically at first, while simultaneously a high degree of hyperaesthesia was observable—great sensitiveness to light and noise. Later, the visual and auditory illusions became much more frequent. . . . He believed that he was dead and decomposing, that he was suffering from the plague; he asserted that his body was being handled in all kinds of revolting ways; and as he himself declares, to this day, he went through worse horrors than any one could have imagined, and all on behalf of a sacred cause. The patient was so much occupied with these pathological phenomena that he was inaccessible to any other impression and would sit perfectly rigid and motionless for hours. . . . On the other hand, they tortured him to such a degree that he longed for death. He made repeated attempts at drowning himself in his bath, and asked to be given the cyanide of potassium that was intended for him. His delusional ideas gradually assumed a mystical and religious character; he was in direct communication with God, he was the plaything of devils, he saw "miraculous apparitions," he heard "holy music," and in the end he came to believe that he was "living in another world."

Clearly, a brain state produced the sense of vulnerability, and in this case there were also hallucinations. The hypersensitivity to visual and auditory stimuli also suggests a change in Schreber's brain chemistry, as does the illusion of femininity. In assessing all of these felt states, the interpreter constructs hypotheses that seem delusional and bizarre to others but apparently fit the data as it (he) perceives them. In short, this suggests that the delusion represents an effective coping strategy; it is the interpreter weaving together a story that fits *his* facts. The judge wrote in his own memoirs: "Now, however, I became clearly aware that the order of things imperatively demanded my emasculation, whether I personally liked it or not, and that no reasonable course lay open to me but to reconcile myself to the thought of being transformed into a woman." And that insight of the judge's led to another conclusion. "The further consequence of my emasculation could, of course, only be my impregnation . . . by divine rays, to the end that a new race of men might be created." For the judge, it all appeared to fit and make sense. This was the interpreter trying to come to grips with all the altered brain states shifting at random, it would seem, beneath the mind.

As with so many schizophrenics, the judge passed through his intense phase and took on another profile. But the delusional ideas, once established, had their own life. There was learning and new memories associated with the discovery process, and these new memories now existed in their own right to support the experience. At the same time it appeared that the judge's biochemical imbalance had disappeared, leaving only his delusional ideas, isolated, as it were, from his newly healed brain. Dr. Weber wrote seven years later, in 1900:

> For the last nine months Herr President Schreber has taken his meals daily at my family board, I have had the most ample opportunities of conversing with him on every imaginable topic. Whatever the subject for discussion (apart, of

course, from his delusional ideas), whether it concerned events in the field of administration and law, or politics, or of art, or of literature, or of social life—in short, whatever the topic, Dr. Schreber gave evidence of a lively interest, a well-informed mind, a good memory and sound judgement; his ethical outlook, moreover, was one which it was impossible not to endorse. So, too, in his lighter talk with the ladies of the party, he was both courteous and affable, and if he touched upon matters in a more humorous vein he invariably displayed tact and decorum. Never once, during these innocent talks round the dining-table, did he introduce subjects which should more properly have been raised at a medical consultation.

The flow of symptoms outlined in the judge's case has been formalized in recent years. There is a sequence and duration of events that must be met in order for someone to be diagnosed as schizophrenic. In general, patients must be chronically ill for at least six months and must have either auditory or visual hallucinations, or bizarre delusions, or disordered thinking. The disease usually initiates with a psychotic episode followed by less bizarre manifestations. The patients have a flat affect, show little emotion, isolate themselves, and sometimes display eccentric behavior. All in all, the description sounds like the scenario of a brain event triggering a mind event, which in turn causes the brain's interpreter to respond with theories, bizarre to the outsider but perhaps meaningful to the victim.

The Dopamine Theory of Schizophrenia

Speculation on the meshing and interaction of brain states with mental processes is credible only when we can identify physical brain abnormalities present during schizophrenia. It is only recently that this has happened. Prior to these discoveries, students of mental disease were confined to purely psychological models in their search for an explanation of what goes wrong when people suffer from major thought disorders.

The birth and early vigor of psychoanalysis were motivated by some basic truths. There was a patient, like the judge, who was mentally ill. No question about that. There was also an ingenious intellectual framework, largely constructed by Freud, for attempting to identify what was wrong. This framework rested heavily on the importance of the psychological history of the patient. Given his present diseased state, the reasoning went, there had to be something in the patient's history and psychological background to explain his current disorder. For dozens of years, psychiatrists analyzed, catalogued, and described each case, then formed a hypothesis as to why the patient had developed a mental illness. And that process still goes on, even though the objective observer has long ago begun to note that the psychological histories of most schizophrenics are identical to those of others who are completely normal. There must, it seemed, be something else—a biological trigger of some sort. Such a link has recently been discovered quite by accident.

At the turn of the century, the German dye industry developed a number of new chemicals in an effort to obtain better substances for coloring clothes. Medics had already used several of the by-products to treat malaria, with some success. A new product, phenothiazine, was formulated and used experimentally against malaria but completely failed. Undaunted, other researchers tried the drug on a variety of diseases. In 1949, a French surgeon asserted that phenothiazine helped to calm surgical patients. As various derivatives were made, each was tried and finally one called chlorpromazine was found to be effective in treating schizophrenia. There was no theory behind any of this. The patient was viewed as a black box. Put something in and see if it works. If it does, use it. And use it they did. Chlorpromazine emptied out the psychiatric hospitals in the 1950s and 1960s, putting the better part of two million seriously ill people back into American society. It didn't cure their schizophrenia, but it did make them manageable. They stopped having hallucinations and hearing voices. They were able to function somewhat rationally most of the time. As we shall see, however, the chronic administration of these types of antipsychotic drugs can start another clock ticking in the brain, with the end result that other troublesome disease processes develop.

The immediate hope was that understanding how the phenothiazines affected brain cells would give clues to the nature of the brain disorder present in schizophrenia. Shortly thereafter, however, it became apparent that other drugs with totally different chemical compositions were also effective in controlling the behavior of schizophrenics. For example, haloperidol, a highly effective drug, and one that is most used today, has the same effect. What was the action of these two substances and how could both work?

The discovery that these drugs had an impact on the disease unleashed a torrent of research. Scientists took to the test tubes to study the effects the drugs had on brain cells from animals, looking for some event that was influenced by both chlorpromazine and haloperidol, and they found one. Both drugs bound to (that is, formed a molecular union with) dopamine receptors, thereby blocking the action of the neurotransmitter dopamine. And they discovered that the more potent a drug was in controlling the clinical symptoms of schizophrenia, the more completely it bound to dopamine receptors. As a result, current thinking is that dopamine is somehow involved in schizophrenia. Some mechanism must cause too much of it to be produced in the brain, and that overabundance leads to the first psychotic episode that triggers the entire sequence of psychological events.

This dopamine hypothesis is also consistent with the observed effects of drug-induced psychosis, as seen in the clinical case of Georgia described earlier. Amphetamine, the drug that induced her psychosis, stimulates the production of dopamine and also prevents its reuptake, or recycling. This means there is an excess of dopamine at the synapses, or junctures, of critical brain structures, which could lead to an induced psychosis.

In addition to the effects of amphetamine, the overabundance of dopamine could also be brought about by a number of brain events. It could be that the schizophrenic brain (a) secretes too much dopamine, or (b) has more dopamine receptors than normal, or (c) that the dopamine receptors are hypersensitive to a normal amount of secretion, or (d) that normally antagonistic mechanisms are not working, or (e) it could be something else! In an effort to identify which possibility is most likely, postmortem schizophrenic brains were studied using special cellular identification methods. In patients who had been chronically treated with antipsychotic drugs as well as in patients who never received drugs, increased numbers of dopamine receptors were noted. This newly discovered evidence ties the biological aspects of the disease to the genetic processes that are clearly involved in the formation and distribution of such cellular variations and thereby link schizophrenia to genetic causes. The case is made even stronger by the fact that the concordance rate for the disease among identical twins is extremely high. Finally, recent radiochemical studies using PET, carried out on schizophrenics who have not been previously treated with drugs, show they have an abnormally high number of receptors in a part of the brain called the basal ganglia.

Taking the dopamine hypothesis to the next step—identifying where in the brain these dopamine processes are malfunctioning—presents the neurobiologist with a great many conceptual problems. It is one matter to find the place where the changes are occurring and quite another to suggest why those changes produce the bizarre behaviors that result from those biochemical abnormalities. An overproduction of dopamine does not make someone think he is the King of Siam. It is how the dopamine abnormality makes nerve circuits misfire that is critical, and how that in turn creates a state of mind that finds being the King of Siam a way to cope with the world. In short, it is neural circuitry, just like the electrical circuitry in one's television set, that makes systems work to produce the picture. And yet, when applied to neural circuitry, the hypotheses about what goes wrong remain hypotheses. The facts are sparse but the opportunity for speculation is rich.

Let us reflect for a moment on the overwhelming feeling of vulnerability that invades the mind of the person entering a state of schizophrenia. Most of us maintain our personal sense of worth by the relatively careful management of interpersonal rewards that come from social contacts, interactions, personal relationships, and the like. We seek out friends who have a positive effect on our moods. Friends reinforce one another. We get an automatic support from association with our children, our parents, our spouse. We seek recognition for our work and our contributions to the community. When we have these rewards daily, we behave with self-esteem and usually with confidence. While we may have doubts about the future and unknown situations, we deal with such feelings successfully because of our psychohistory. We have survived in the past and life has worked out—witness the overall sense of satisfaction we feel each day. But what would happen if we started to lose our perception of these automatic rewards? After all, they reflect a brain circuit system that is working. We see a friend and associated good feeling is automatically triggered. What if seeing the friend did not trigger that response? What would we come to think?

I am suggesting that this new, negative experience would evolve into a state much like schizophrenia. With our personal reference system at loose ends because it has trouble producing those automatic rewards, we feel suddenly vulnerable. In this disorienting state, we begin to see the world through a haze of paranoia. If indeed the dopamine change does alter brain circuits and those circuits are no longer able to make pleasant associations produce rewards in the mind, it is easy to imagine how bizarre feelings and thoughts might fill the void. (Without occupying thoughts from the normal rewards system, the schizophrenic is in a chronic informational vacuum.) He casts about for information from his current environment, but because of the new isolation, there really isn't much there. What makes this theory plausible is the particular location in the brain where the dopamine deficits are found.

The part of the brain that is heavily involved in the management of reward processes is the limbic system. There are several structures associated with this neural system, and many of them are located in or near the temporal lobes. The limbic system, one of the oldest parts of the brain, has been called "the emotional brain." The interesting aspect for this discussion is its rich input from dopamine-producing cells. Disruption of normal processes here is known to have disastrous effects on the reward-generating system in the brain. When lesions are made in particular parts of a monkey's temporal lobes, they will result in a condition called the Kluver-Bucy syndrome. In this state, postoperative monkeys are unable to learn new visual problems because of their failure to make a link between rewards and visual information. These animals have a nerve circuit disconnection between their visual system and their reward system.

Another aspect of schizophrenia that may be related to temporal lobe dysfunction is the hallucinations schizophrenics invariably experience. Hallucinations can occur in patients when temporal lobe tissue is electrically stimulated, as happens during the course of brain surgery for epilepsy. The surgeon frequently must determine where in the brain he is operating before excising diseased tissue. Because the patient is operated on under a local anaesthetic, he is free to respond to the surgeon's probe. Temporal lobe stimulation will often elicit old memories. Sometimes the patient will describe hallucinations or nonsensical memories that may be the stuff of hallucinations. The limbic system and temporal lobe disturbances could account for triggering the emotional aspects of schizophrenia and be responsible for the hallucinations of schizophrenics. Since this part of the brain is so rich in dopamine receptors, the hypothesis of some dopamine malfunction there is made even stronger by the preceding observations.

A Role for Endorphins?

The dopamine hypothesis dominates the latest scientific interpretations of schizophrenia; however, research continues on other substances that may also be involved. The ongoing hunt for alternatives is motivated in part by problems with the dopamine story. From a clinical point of view, there seems to be a disparity between the time it takes for the antipsychotic drugs to affect cellular events and the time it takes them to affect behavior. The cellular events occur almost instantaneously, whereas the clinical changes evolve over a few weeks. The commonly asserted explanation for this phenomenon is that secondary changes are occurring through other neural systems as the result of altering the dopamine system.

This is a highly reasonable notion. But more interesting, in terms of our present hypothesis, is the recognized clinical fact that the antipsychotic drugs have little or no effect on the residual aspects of the disease. These are sometimes called the negative symptoms: the lack of motivation, the desire for social isolation, the flattening of affect. The antipsychotic drugs hit the so-called positive dimensions of the disease that are commonly the triggering symptoms: the hallucinations, the paranoia that leads to delusions. Taken together, these facts fit well with the idea that the brain's interpreter responds to the endogenous, or inner-generated, events of brain activity. All the delusional theories a patient develops have their own referents in the brain. They have their own memories. They become established as part of the patient's experiential history and as such influence his future perceptions. It would be bizarre to find a biochemical manipulation that would alter both the endogenous events and the new memories that are stored as a result of the interpreter's coping with the endogenous turmoil.

Nonetheless, the new avenues of inquiry are fascinating. Most of the current ideas are based on the belief that the endorphins, the self-produced opiates, are not working normally in the schizophrenic. Once again, the possibly disastrous effects of dysfunctioning brain processes that mediate our sense of pain or reward become apparent. The new interest in endorphins is based not only on their current popularity among brain scientists but on over 130 years of observation that externally administered opiates have effects on schizophrenics. Shortly after endogenous opiates were discovered, a study indicated that schizophrenics' symptoms could be dramatically relieved by beta-endorphin. Several other variants followed, and soon scientists began to suggest that the schizophrenic suffered from a lack of endogenous opiates.

Yet those who accepted this new view were soon faced with further puzzles. Other researchers reported that the activity of endorphins in the schizophrenic follows an enigmatic pattern. In the cerebrospinal fluid of acute schizophrenics they found levels of endorphins ten times higher than normal. At the same time, they discovered that chronic schizophrenics had reduced levels, about half the normal concentration.

The picture of increased endorphin level in acute schizophrenics was supported by other research. One theory advanced the idea that schizophrenics had a flattened evoked brain potential to painful stimuli, which is consistent with a high endorphin level. To observe this, researchers administered an electric shock to the skin, and the electrophysiological reaction to it was recorded from the scalp. Normally, there is a hefty response over the part of the brain receiving impulses from the peripheral area where the shock is applied. The flattened response of the schizophrenics suggested that they had high levels of endogenous endorphins clipping the incoming message by means of mechanisms already described in our discussion of pain. Even more telling was the discovery that if schizophrenics were given naloxone, the antagonist of endorphins, their evoked response looked far more normal. Finally, to cite an animal model, injections of beta-endorphins produce a catatonic-like response in rats, which, it has been suggested, resembles the schizophrenic state.

At this writing, several major studies have been carried out in efforts to confirm or reject these ideas, because not all previous human experiments had been done with appropriate controls. The new research investigated, for the most part, the hypothesis that schizophrenics lack the proper amount of endorphins. These experiments were correctly controlled, and they paint a different and somewhat equivocal picture. The majority of the studies found no effects of endorphin level on behavior. One out of five reported some changes on a psychometric measure, but the difference had no clinical impact. Still, the results were not conclusive. Beta-endorphin has been difficult to make and is very expensive. Future investigations that vary the dose and time of administration with impunity may well unearth critical relationships. The importance of this freedom cannot be underestimated. In the widely heralded success of L-dopa in treating Parkinson's disease, it took years and bravado on the part of one investigator to hit upon the dose that effected the grand and medically helpful result.

The attempts to verify the opposite notion, that the schizophrenic has too many endorphins, have led to more provocative but still tentative results. In these studies, naloxone was given to patients to counter endorphins. In the original study of six patients given the drug, four reported a reduction in auditory hallucinations. Several follow-up investigations that kept the dose of naloxone high confirmed these observations. In addition, some of the researchers also reported improvement of orderly thought and a reduction of paranoia. Such results are intriguing and frustrating. They are intriguing because any systematic change in the complex of behaviors and brain chemistry leads to new possibilities and new questions. Could it be that the overabundance of endorphins brings about what might be called hyper-reward? The human system is indiscriminate as to what it rewards, including faulty associations of thought. But as I say, those results are also frustrating in that there is no apparent common denominator for the various bad symptoms that naloxone seems to mitigate. In the long run, however, the results point the way to more basic truth about brain and cognitive links.

It is no longer possible to believe that a specific behavioral abnormality results from one specific biological abnormality. Neurons—billions of them and their billions of interconnections—all interact. If we manipulate the level of one chemical, that affects innumerable nerve networks that are predominantly active in producing other chemicals. The entire dynamic neural net that comprises our mind and our emotions is vulnerable and can be influenced by any adjustment to the net. Some manipulations will have greater effects than others. In that light, it is no wonder that several different brain chemicals influence the symptoms of schizophrenia.

Yet the overall pattern in this most distressing of all mental disorders remains fairly clear. Endogenous brain changes create new circumstances, to which the brain's interpreter must react. That reaction, in turn, produces memories that can become powerful guides for the mental outlook of the patient. Any endogenous state that is quickly induced (as in the case of Georgia) by a fast, artificial manipulation of brain chemistry can be fairly easily dismissed as an aberration after the biochemical system returns to a more normal state. If the brain changes last longer, then the interpretations given the altered state of mind become more embellished and the memories associated with it take on their own life and become powerful influences on the personal life history of the disorder. Crazy thoughts are manageable for the normal person because they occur quickly and they can be considered as part of some unusual context and rejected. Continually crazy thoughts, evoked by a more chronic abnormal chemistry, become more acceptable. They do so because they succeed in building up a context of aberrant thought—that is, a crazy memory that welcomes crazy ideas.

Most neuroscientists write off the schizophrenic patient's problems as teaching us nothing concrete about the mind. In fact, they may be teaching us quite a lot. It is just possible that this disease could be viewed as the fate of the human mind when exposed to long-term distortions of reality. In the biological case, as with schizophrenia, the distortions are dirty tricks of Mother Nature. The brain's interpreter tries to bring order to the chaos brought about by biochemical abnormalities. In this sped-up version of reality upheaval, the consequences are disastrous. Yet perhaps the lesson here is that when the normal mind is allowed to entertain, for long periods of time, erroneous data about people, about power, about sex, about social relations, it too begins to construct strange theories about reality. The strange thoughts of some otherwise normal, mature brains and minds serve as a constant source of amazement to the even-handed student of human behavior. When we choose not to correct other adults' false assumptions about the nature of the social and psychological environment they live in, we are contributing to their ever-deepening set of delusions about how the world works.

As the brain greatly influences the fundamental matters of life—memory, pain, and thinking—it also plays a powerful role in our emotions. For years, scientists have been dancing around the complex structures of mind that we call feelings and emotions. Poets and artists have been putting up No Trespassing signs, but for a scientist, a person totally seduced by the appeal of logic and data, no part of life is off limits. The thorny problems of mood have recently come under their scrutiny, and insights into abnormalities and normalities of these states are beginning to accumulate. To those who are curious about ephemeral states such as love or destructive states such as depression, to those who are fascinated with how mind and brain interact to produce our whole lives—read on.

5

Anxiety

Modern man's brain has been essentially unchanged for approximately forty thousand years. Given what is now known about the biological nature of the mental state called anxiety, one must assume it has been experienced by humans for all of those years. Yet it wasn't until 1844, when Søren Kierkegaard wrote *The Concept of Dread,* that anxiety was truly defined. We tend to think such everyday mental states as anxiety are part of the dynamics that have always driven human behavior. In the English language, however, the word did not appear until 1525, and it was first used to describe a pathological state in 1661. It was only after Kierkegaard, in 1880, that the word was medically defined.

What is anxiety? It was best described by Rollo May as that "nameless and formless uneasiness" that besets all of us in varying intensities at various times. It is a complex mental state because it can be triggered by endogenous biological events that are seemingly outside any direct mental control as well as by exogenous, or external, stimuli. The interpretation of this state, which is in effect a state of arousal, takes many forms. For some, anxiety leads to action. For others, complications occur that can lead to neuroses, phobias, and other crackpot theories of reality.

In the past twenty years, a huge industry has been built up in response to the mental state of anxiety. Biologists, largely through luck, have uncovered several drugs that seem to block the brain state that produces anxiety, making even the extreme version of the state tractable through good medical care. The antianxiety drug industry started with Librium, which belongs to the class of drugs called benzodiazepines, and moved ahead in 1969 to the more effective Valium. Continuing pharmacological advances have been so promising—even though there is still no agreed-upon theory about what brings on the anxious state—that psychoanalytic approaches to the problem have been largely abandoned. In this chapter we will examine both the psychological and biological aspects of anxiety, its medication, and what it teaches us about the brain and mind. First, however, it is worth considering why this mental state seems so ubiquitous. Donald W. Goodwin, a psychiatrist at the University of Kansas, has written compellingly, in his book *Anxiety,* on why the twentieth century appears to be plagued with the problem of anxiety. Once Kierkegaard coined the description, anxiety seemed not only to be everywhere but also to have intense reality for modern man.

A Historical Account of Anxiety

According to Goodwin, the rise of anxiety may be the inevitable consequence of the existential view that man is free to choose from the plethora of options available to him. In existentialism, which did not take hold until after World War II, you are only what you choose. Prior to the existential view, most people made choices on moral or ethical grounds—grounds defined by religion and philosophy. In the new view, all truths were determined by the individual, and each had to be weighed and analyzed. Kierkegaard's most famous book, *Either/Or,* argued that you can pick either Christianity or atheism, although it makes little difference which you choose. The important thing is to make the choice, to deal frankly with reality.

While Kierkegaard was a Christian existentialist, Jean Paul Sartre was an atheist existentialist. Unlike Kierkegaard, who despaired at the choice the Christian must make between good and evil, Sartre simply concluded that there was no point to life, no meaning. Like Pascal before him, he felt that man had been dumped on what amounted to an island in some small corner of the universe, and that there was no way to know why or how, or to find out what might be his fate. In short, there was no way to know anything substantial about the conditions of life. This human-centered view of the world is powerful, especially if one had been beholden to a religious outlook. Sartre went on to argue that the only way to put meaning into life was for modern man to make decisions that "affirm" himself as an individual. He felt that the first choice was whether to remain alive or to commit suicide. If the choice was in favor of life, the chore was to make personal decisions *as if* life had meaning.

There is a complex theoretical history for the rise of existentialism, which according to Goodwin is the source of the rampant modern-day anxiety syndrome. Goodwin traces the possible antecedents, starting with the emergence of the Age of Reason in the seventeenth century. The Age of Faith had passed, and with people like Spinoza leading the way, rational men—who embraced logic and science—were going to better the human condition. This transition would lead only to greater anxiety. In the Age of Faith, the guidelines were laid down from above. There were no choices. With the Age of Reason, there was nothing but choices, and therein were the seeds for doubt, which is the father of anxiety. But philosophers like Spinoza felt that serenity could be achieved by reason alone, by simply "ordering our thoughts and images."

Existentialism came on the heels of the Age of Reason. During the French Revolution, the cathedral of Notre-Dame de Paris was converted into a Temple of Reason while thousands of people were being executed after mock trials. Such contradictions prepared the way for twentieth-century existentialism. Traditional religion had fallen first, and now reason proved so fitful that life seemed meaningless. In 1947 W. H. Auden, in his famous poetic work *The Age of Anxiety,* wrote that disillusionment was everywhere: in science, in religion, and in family life. Man was as "unattached as tumbleweed."

Goodwin's book is a fascinating account of this historic theory, which seems to fit the awful truth that people have become increasingly anxious. It is, as they say, simply a "just-so" story. It could be relevant to the causes of the current condition, but it might not be. There were many other major trends in twentieth-century Western culture that could have led to the same result. Freud, for example, dwelled on the problem of anxiety, no doubt because he himself suffered from it. While he first interpreted anxiety in a psychosexual context, he later described it (as did others) as the condition of anticipating danger. Freud's generally uncritical acceptance in the West, particularly in the United States, gave great currency to his concept of anxiety and its newly recognized dangers. The very vogue of this novel complaint probably helped to affect the mental states of many people. A society whose medical profession heralds the existence of a new disorder will also provide many subscribers.

The State of Anxiety

Anxiety may well be the mental condition that is most instructive in gaining an understanding about how a brain change can lead to rich psychological response. The human mind leaps to interpret everything, from overt behaviors to covert "moods." Anxiety is an identifiable state of brain arousal produced by real physical events in the brain. In some of us, through casual chains not yet understood, chemicals are unleashed that cause a change in brain dynamics that in turn leads to a "felt" state of mind. Our conscious system jumps in and generates a theory, an interpretation as to why this particular mood state exists. That theory can have extremely negative psychological effects, as we will see. But the point is that the psychological level, while very real and ultimately the only level at which we know things, could be far mistaken in identifying the origin of the anxiety. Either the genes or some spurious physiological event, in fact, triggered the release of a chemical or a set of chemicals that led to an aroused state. Yet the mind refuses to accept "I am aroused." It seems always to need "I am aroused because . . ."

There are two general kinds of anxiety: endogenous and exogenous, which is also called generalized anxiety. The latter type is considered far more prevalent. It is my view that the two are highly related. The mechanism that somehow triggers for the endogenous type may also trigger when identifiable external sources seemingly create the circumstance for anxiety. In short, the biological system that responds to internal and external stimuli may be very similar, if not identical.

Much of what is known about the brain mechanism of endogenous anxiety comes from studying patients with the extreme form of endogenously driven anxiety, the panic attack. The panic attack affects approximately 5 percent of the population, with women being more susceptible than men. The disorder has a strong genetic component and appears to be dominant; that is, if one parent has it, there is a 50-50 chance that each child will also. It does not start until the teens and can then occur as often as daily or as infrequently as once or twice per year. Unlike exogenous anxiety, a panic attack occurs spontaneously and has no obvious link to environmental stimuli. It gives rise to a devastating sensation, yet it is not life threatening.

The symptoms are telling. The victim usually suffers chest pain and has trouble breathing. There can be the sensation of choking or smothering, dizziness or vertigo. Frequent symptoms include tingling in the hands and feet as well as hot and cold flashes along with sweating. Trembling and shaking are also part of the picture, and sometimes a sense of dying or going crazy. Most eerie is the sudden sense of unreality. In his book *The Anxiety Disease,* Dr. David Sheehan, a psychiatrist at Harvard Medical School, writes about such an episode, experienced by one of his patients:

> I feel I'm in another world. It's like I know I'm there, but I'm really not. I feel removed from the situation I'm in. I feel like I'm in another dimension—like a hollow or vacuum—outside the situation I'm in. It's like watching the whole thing from a distance, like I was looking at everything through the wrong end of a telescope—it seemed to get more distant and smaller. Sometimes the opposite would happen and everything would feel closer and larger.
>
> Sometimes I feel disconnected from the ground under my feet like I'm walking on air or floating. Last week I was driving my car when I felt the wheels weren't connected to the road. The car seemed as if it were floating along about two feet off the ground. I felt I didn't have control, I couldn't reconnect with the ground properly.

Examples of what is called depersonalization or derealization are relatively common in the normal population and also in sufferers of brain disease, particularly of one area called the parietal lobe. Some transitory event is probably occurring in the nerve cells of the brain, but the episode can be triggered by any of a number of physiological changes. The search is still on for the specific physiological events that lead to the clinical syndrome of panic attacks.

Toward a Biological Explanation of Anxiety

One of the first major clues for the underlying biological cause of endogenous anxiety was discovered in the 1940s, when it was observed that patients with panic disorders tired easily when they exercised. Researchers determined that the level of

lactate in their blood was high. Lactate is produced by the muscles during exercise, and it was assumed that this high level
was due to the fact that either panic attack patients overproduced
the substance or they had an impaired ability to break it down.

Years later, this finding was picked up by Drs. Ferris Pitt
and James McClure at Washington University in St. Louis.
They injected lactate into patients with panic disorder and into
normal control subjects. They discovered that patients with
the disease immediately had an attack, while nothing happened
to the control subjects. Although such knowledge was helpful
for the diagnosis of the disease, it was not until the 1980s that
more light was thrown on the disorder. This advance took
advantage of that new technology in brain science, positron
emission tomography (PET). Conveniently, PET was largely
developed at Washington University, and it wasn't long before
the psychiatrists hooked up with the PET scientists.

As already noted in chapter 3, the PET scanner is a computer-
based radiation-sensitive machine that is used to measure things
like the metabolic rate of different brain areas. Because of the
nature of the radioactive chemicals injected into the patient,
and because of how these chemicals release their radioactivity,
a special "camera" surrounding the patient's head is able to
relay to a computer information that is used to generate an
image or map of the brain's metabolic rate in each region. This
technique is proving very helpful in determining possible brain
abnormalities for a variety of diseases. The range of normal
metabolic rates for the brain is compared to that of patients
with a disease, and a mismatch provides a clue that can lead
to a better understanding of the underlying physiological mechanism. In the case of patients with panic attack, an intriguing
discovery was made.

In the normal brain, when metabolic maps of the left and
right hemispheres were compared point for point, no major
differences were found except in one small area. Not surprisingly, panic attack patients showed a different picture. While

the rate of metabolism for a brain area called the parahippocampus gyrus was within normal limits, the parahippocampus gyrus on one side of the brain was metabolizing at a faster rate than was the other. This brain structure, which is known to be crucial for a number of psychological processes, was working out of synchronization. The different metabolic rates suggested that the neurons were not functioning under normal timing constraints, and this in turn could have had an apparently disruptive effect on psychological processes.

It is too soon to tell for sure what the actual mechanism is, but implicating the hippocampal regions ties the disease to another relevant network of the mind and body, the stress system. Bruce McEwen at Rockefeller University has discovered that the hippocampus is rich in receptors responsive to corticosteroids, the chemicals produced during stress. Perhaps in the panic patient the hippocampus has an abnormal amount or distribution of the receptors sensitive to such a crucial body chemical. Or there is another possibility. Perhaps the conditioned emotional responses we all have to hundreds of stimuli in the real world trigger a stress reaction. The stress causes the production of corticosteroids, which are then dealt with abnormally by the special hippocampus the panic patient appears to possess.

It is also intriguing to consider how the triggering of a stress response may actually be the result of some kind of conditioned response, which appears to be a spontaneous physiological event. In fact, however, a conditioned response may well relate to nonconscious but very active memories that function as a result of a person's psychological history. This is speculation, to be sure, but it illustrates how one biomedical finding can generate ideas for specific experiments that could lead to a final discovery of how panic attacks have their effect.

The basic insight that panic attacks are largely physiologically induced raises questions concerning the popularly held notion that anxiety in general is a response to the psychological demand to make decisions. "The more decisions, the more anxiety" has been the traditional interpretation. But when applied to a real life setting, that kind of analysis becomes problematic. Consider a surgeon, a person who makes more decisions in a day than most people make in a month. The surgeon is also a person of great physical stamina, sometimes having to stand in a small area for eighteen consecutive hours. If the surgeon could not tolerate exercise—which is effectively what he is doing during his day—he would have to change careers. Put differently, the surgical profession is selective for people with physical stamina and low levels of anxiety.

Our interpretative mind is always attributing a cause to felt states of mind, and we now know that these interpretations are frequently irrelevant to the true underlying causes of a felt state. Our mind's explanations become more relevant only as we come to believe our own theories about the cause of a state like anxiety. The fact appears to be that some people are genetically disposed to an anxious response while others are not. Those who are anxious search for a theory to explain their anxiety and commonly seize on the number of decisions they make a day as a likely source of their state of mind. As we see from the example of the surgeon, this explanation is most likely spurious. Yet as the anxious person comes to believe his own theory, he begins to change his life pattern in ways that can easily be imagined.

When it comes to treating the panic disorders, there is an odd twist to the story. While at a psychological level the panic attack is an exaggerated example of general anxiety, it is not treated effectively with antianxiety drugs, Librium, or Valium. Instead, it is the antidepressants that work well, including the monoamine oxidase inhibitors (Nardil) and the tricyclics (Elavil), which are discussed in the chapter on depression. This paradox suggests that the biological mechanism causing the panic attack is not the same as that causing general anxiety, even though, at the psychological level, one is seen only as a more severe form of the state of mind. Some have taken this

evidence to imply that anxiety is related to the depressive illnesses. Yet a variety of tests have shown that while patients
with depression can have panic attacks, panic attack patients
are not primarily depressed.

The Psychology of Anxiety

A successful medical diagnosis is only the very beginning
of treatment for panic attack. If the patient is well into the
disease, he has developed an independent psychological reality
for it, and that can make patients very tentative about trying
the "cure." In short, fears and anxiety over the possibility of
failure are one problem that prevents some from wanting to
find a cure. Or, alternatively, after starting a course of medication
that alleviates the symptoms, a patient can show a complete
reversal. A patient who was inhibited about living life to its
fullest might then attempt too much, frequently at the expense
of people who have tried to help him in the past. Such patients
become demanding and seek out unrestrained activity. These
kinds of difficulties reveal that there is the profoundly important
problem of psychodynamic management that accompanies any
drug therapy. When it comes to balancing the mind, there is
no quick cure, as there sometimes is with other systemic diseases.
When you stop to think about it, there can be no other way.
The theories that the interpretative brain has generated to fit
the felt state of mind are now stored as memories and as potential
behavior patterns. They exist in conscious reality even though
the stimulus that provoked their creation has now been successfully treated.

There is a natural tendency in all of us to think we have an
illness, particularly after it has been described to us. Medical
students routinely feel they must be dying from dozens of diseases. Given that caveat, consider the following test questions,
which are meant to assess the extent to which an individual
experiences anxiety. The questions were adapted by Sheehan

from an earlier test developed by I. M. Marks that has proved useful in objectively measuring anxiety. In the full test there are some forty-six queries, and each item has to be judged as to the severity of feeling it elicits. The subjects are instructed to think back to a problem and are asked, "How much were you bothered by . . .

1. lightheadedness, faintness or dizzy spells.
2. sensation of rubbery or 'jelly' legs.
3. feeling off balance or unsteady as if about to fall."

and so on. If you score in the mild to moderate zone on the set of questions, it indicates that you suffer from a generalized anxiety. It suggests that while you can function in life, you are nonetheless jumpy, sometimes irritable, you startle easily, have sweaty palms, ruminate excessively, and are generally on edge.

When such states start to appear with regularity, they can distract you to the point of being unable to concentrate and work. This is particularly true if you were raised in a household that tolerated such a mental state and didn't urge you to push on in the face of uncontrollable events. Both Emily Dickinson and E. B. White were afflicted with anxiety and wrote about their condition often. White felt he had a mouse in his mind and expressed this feeling in a poem called "Vermin."

> The mouse of Thought infests my head,
> He knows my cupboard and the crumb.
> Vermin! I despise vermin.
> I have no trap, no skill with traps.
> No bait, no hope, no cheese, no bread—
> I fumble with the task to no avail.
> I've seen him several times lately.
> He is too quick for me.
> I see only his tail.

No matter where you turn, the victims of anxiety experience a state of mind that seems to be arbitrarily inserted into their normal consciousness. Even mild anxieties seem endogenous in origin—that is, they are triggered by a brain mechanism that produces the felt state. How can the endogenously generated general anxiety be distinguished from the exogenously triggered anxiety? While both ultimately invoke similar bodily mechanisms and responses, such as cold feet and hands, exogenous anxieties are the result of real concerns of any conscious person. For example, a highly educated and responsible person is constantly monitoring his strengths and weaknesses. If he is called upon to lecture to an informed body of professionals, there is every reason in the world to expect the speaker to experience some anxiety. The understandable fear of an inferior performance would be enough to create such a state. Under the circumstances, it would be folly to suggest that he should seek medical help. The exogenously produced anxiety is identifiably clear, and the victim has no problem attributing the correct cause to his state of mind. Another important variable for many exogenously induced anxieties is that the act that produces the anxiety is freely chosen. The lecturer has willingly agreed to give the talk. Thus, the anxiety is willfully brought on. He knows that he will be nervous but also that the reward will justify the minor discomfort.

Phobias

Phobias can result from anxieties, and they surface in special situations or settings. They can be terribly debilitating and are likely formed as a result of the endogenously based anxiety system's being triggered in specific psychological contexts. In many people suffering from anxiety, the development of extensive phobias is the inevitable end product and the most psychologically disruptive of all the manifestations of the disease. A phobia is defined by Goodwin as "a persistent, excessive, unreasonable fear of a specific object, activity, or situation that results in a compelling desire to avoid the dreaded object, activity, or situation. The fear is recognized by the individual as excessive and unreasonable." According to the National Institute of Mental Health, phobias are common enough to be harbored by one out of every eight adults and, as in anxiety, are more prevalent in women than in men. They generally appear after the age of eighteen.

Phobias come in all sizes and shapes. A common one is agoraphobia, which is the dread of open and public places. It is reported to affect one in twenty persons and is a multifaceted disorder. Some people cannot tolerate crowded buses or trains or other gatherings, while others cannot bear to be alone and require constant companionship. When thrown into one of these situations, the phobic's usual reactions are high anxiety, dizziness, sweating, and all the other physiological responses that can go along with an anxiety attack.

Other simple phobias include a fear of some kinds of animals, fear of heights, and fear of illness. These are reported to have a good prognosis, since they are isolated and usually singular in nature. For social phobias, yet another class, the prognosis is not as good. They include such concerns as sexual performance, eating in public, public speaking, and so on. None is pleasant, and all are psychologically real to their victims.

Phobias are a fascinating aspect of the anxiety disease. As outlined in Chapter 1, trying to understand their formation and maintenance may help not only to understand anxiety but also a host of disorders that feed off an endogenous brain event. In an effort to explain how and why phobias form in the anxious patient, let us take a step back and look at research on animals.

One of the cleverest psychologists of the twentieth century, John Garcia at UCLA, has for years studied a fascinating phenomenon called "the bait-shy effect" in all kinds of animals. Garcia trained rats on a maze with many arms. At the end of each arm was a food well, and the rats were always pleased to find the food reward after learning which of the arms contained food. Garcia was interested in studying the psychological laws of learning and wanted to examine the effects of an aversive stimulus in the learning situation—that is, in the maze. He wanted to introduce it not at the time of learning but hours after the animals ran the maze. To learn that an animal would avoid a place in the maze after it was punished on the spot would be no surprise. But what if the food the rat consumed in one arm of the maze was spiked so that hours later in its home cage the rat became ill and vomited? After such an experience, would the rat remember the source of its problem? Indeed it would, and the rat actually developed a phobia about that part of the maze where it found the spiked food. In humans, this has been dubbed "the sauce béarnaise effect." If something you eat in a restaurant makes you ill, you will find it hard to return to that restaurant ever again.

Consider another effect discovered by psychobiologist James McGaugh of the University of California at Irvine. McGaugh has been studying animal memory for years and has come across a phenomenon corroborated in humans. If an animal is given a stimulant such as epinephrine just before exposure to new information, subsequent tests reveal that memory of the information is enhanced. For humans, the natural equivalent of this test would be to assess someone's memory of an event under conditions of arousal and to compare it to a memory registered when the subject was not aroused. Persons asked to recall a scene experienced in the context of arousal—for example, a narrow escape from being hit by a car—show an extraordinarily detailed memory of the scene. It is vivid in their minds, welded in, in a manner of speaking.

If the human brain can remember with impressive speed and accuracy the details of an event when aroused, could this phenomenal memory also account for the formation of the acquired phobias? Say a person is in a particular setting—a crowd, for instance. Suddenly, the brain goes into its anxious state for no apparent reason. Such a psychological vacuum exists for only moments, and the internal interpreter immediately attributes a cause for the anxious state. In this case, the crowded room gets the blame. The person concludes that crowds produce anxiety and therefore that they are to be avoided. That conditioned association, the link between the anxious state and crowds, most likely goes on automatically, both at the level of conscious awareness and at the level where a conditioned memory is formed. Thus, the next time the person is in a crowd, the automatic conditioned memory begins to respond, precipitating the associated anxious state, which in turn activates the conscious memory of the possible ill effects of crowds on anxiety. The processes feed off each other and are interrelated. Soon, however, this person can become a full-blown agoraphobic.

If our interpretation of how phobias are formed is correct, it makes certain predictions. The first is that phobias have a life of their own. They are psychological constructs placed in the human mental system by the process just described. The phobic stimulus becomes the trigger for anxiety, and as such, an external stimulus has gained control over the anxiety system that initially was governed by internal processes. The original brain abnormality has developed into a complex psychobiological problem.

Since phobias have their own construction in the brain, it would seem that the drugs effective in treating anxiety per se might not be helpful in treating them. This in fact has been the case. Antianxiety drugs such as Valium have little or no effect on neutralizing phobias. All they do is calm people down in the presence of the aversive stimulus, the phobic trigger. Once established, phobias are very conscious memories of places and things that are part of other brain systems. Their elimination has to come from psychological sources. In other words, the phobia is dissolved by the gradual understanding that it is irrational or harmless. This takes time and knowledge, and may be why, years after they are formed, or years after taking antianxiety drugs, phobias do tend to disappear. It is reported that few persist in people over the age of thirty-five.

Finally, perhaps the most common phobia, stage fright, is worth a special note. "Phobia" is probably a misnomer for what an experienced performer contracts on opening night. There is a lot riding on performing well on such an occasion. For the rank amateur to appear in front of a crowd or class and to have a phobic response is quite another matter. In some instances it could well be triggered by the kind of mechanism just described. But in both cases, the people involved are aroused and anxious. The heart is beating fast, the pulse is high, the lips are dry, the voice may be shaky. All these symptoms reflect well-known responses of the autonomic nervous system. Could a drug be developed that would stop only these peripheral systems from acting up? Would that have a calming effect? A drug exists that does seem to do this. It is called propanalol, invented for other reasons but effective in this case if used carefully.

To sum up, anxiety is clearly a complex mental state that is fed from several sources. Both the extreme and mild forms are triggered by an imbalance of brain processes that can be manipulated by a range of antianxiety drugs. When the imbalance occurs, a variety of psychological responses occur that interact with the brain condition. People develop theories about why they feel the way they do, and these theories become beliefs. The beliefs are usually erroneous and can be destructive as they evolve into phobias. It is a fascinating condition from a scientific point of view. From the sufferer's point of view, it is an unpleasant mental state but one that can be treated.

6

Depression

It is Saturday morning and you have just awakened. The previous night wasn't unusual; it was a perfectly pleasant evening with friends. Life is great, the new baby is a delight, the job is going well, the new house deal worked out. All in all, this year has been good to you, and you have stored only fond memories of life. Yet you awake depressed. You feel gloomy about everything. Your wife, up before you and excited about the day's outing to the Metropolitan Museum followed by a late lunch at Lutèce, bustles in with coffee. You make every attempt to hide your mood because you hate to dampen anyone else's feelings. You yourself can't stand to be in the presence of a depressed person. You say good morning and try to pretend you are still a little groggy from sleep. Your wife understands and doesn't remark on the unmistakable flatness in your voice or your lack of animation.

You get through the day, then the week, covering as you might to avoid giving pain to others, but things get worse. You can't sleep well; you wake up very early. You lose interest in food. Your wife gently suggests there has been no sex for weeks. Your job seems dull. You are reminded of Hamlet's observation, "How weary, stale, flat, and unprofitable seem to me all the uses of this world." You are at sea, almost unable to seek help because it all looks like tinsel, glitzy, silly; all those enjoying life do not appreciate how pedestrian it truly is.

You are suffering one of the many forms of depression, probably what is called a unipolar depression that is endogenously driven. That means you usually have a normal affect, when out of the blue comes this state of mind. It is not precipitated by the environment. Something in the brain triggers this feeling, this view of the world. You notice it is worse in the morning. You investigate the problem and discover that women have it twice as often as men. It usually begins at forty, although it can occur earlier, especially in adolescence. You try to think of a reason why you feel this way but you can't. You see a therapist, who confirms that you are depressed but is unable to help. You are told that about 10 percent of those with the disorder go through a manic phase that lasts about a week and is characterized by hyperactivity, grandiosity, and talkativeness. This form is called bipolar depression and recurs twice as often as unipolar depression. You couldn't care less about another form of depression. In fact, you don't care about anything.

You are one of eight million Americans suffering from this disorder. If you do nothing, you will come out of it within four to twelve months, although there may be no one left around you by then. Unless, of course, you commit suicide. Twenty-five thousand of you do, but it is interesting to note that you won't do it when you are the most severely depressed. You won't do anything at that stage, won't even wash. You wait until things begin to improve; then you kill yourself. Or, if you are lucky, you get by that phase and actually feel better. Sparkle comes back, you smile, you tell a joke. Food looks good. Your wife looks good, and because she is patient, she has stayed with you. Sexual interest returns, plans are made, all life's little rewards begin to mean something to you again. You are feeling normal, and wonder what on earth happened to you. Then your wife tells you that if depression strikes again, she will not allow it to go untreated. She has investigated the matter and has found that untreated depression is frequently unfixable and can become long lasting. The biochemical remedies that are known to work are not always effective for the hardened depressed patient. If you are wise, you firmly agree with her and continue with your life.

Depression comes in many packages and can be precipitated by sudden changes in brain chemistry or by surrounding personal conditions. At this writing, it is not known for sure whether or not the depression precipitated by circumstances can change the brain chemistry and thereby create the depressed state of mind. I assume it can. This form, called exogenous depression, is common and is usually dealt with through psychological therapies. What is also very common and more disturbing is the brain-triggered, or endogenous, depression we have just described. Fortunately, a lot is known about it and how to treat it.

What causes this awful disease? How can a chemical disturbance make you change your view of the world, your sense of pleasure? This affective disorder has been recognized since the advent of history. Hippocrates suggested it was due to an imbalance in the four bodily humors: blood, phlegm, yellow bile, and black bile. He blamed black bile in particular, and this thought gave rise to the description of melancholy. Modern medical knowledge suggests that the disorder involves a malfunction of the hypothalamus. Yet to say these things seems totally inadequate. While we will explore the biological dimension of this disease, we are faced with this recurrent problem in all mind–mood research: how can a chemical imbalance change our view of things, which we so compellingly feel is derived from our rational understanding of life? The answer to this question is nowhere in sight. What is beginning to be in hand, however, is knowledge about what constitutes the chemical imbalances that lead to depression, and why these imbalances can lead to disastrous long-term behavioral and mental consequences if they are not rectified.

Brain-based Depression

As we know, a traditional way to begin the check on whether or not there is a biological component to any disease is to examine how frequently identical twins suffer from a common disorder. This ratio is compared to the rate for fraternal twins and to that of non-twin siblings. Identical twins are very susceptible to the same afflictions, and if one suffers from depression, 50 to 70 percent of the time the other will too. This statistic compares with a 10 percent figure for fraternal twins and non-twin siblings. Similarly, if an adopted child had natural parents who suffered from depression, the child is two to three times more likely to develop depression than an adopted child whose natural parents were not depressed. And the depressed adopted child is six to ten times more likely to have suicide in the background of its real family than the adopted child who suffers no depression.

The genetic link for endogenous depression is clear. During the brain's development, at which time it is under direct genetic control, something like a time bomb is established in the brain's circuitry. At some later point, the error in brain formation will result in the onset of endogenously produced depression.

It is the fashion in modern medicine to develop, when at all possible, physical evidence for a psychological state. People want to be shown they are different, not merely told they are. In a court of law, it is physical evidence that sways a jury, not psychological testimony. Holding up a CT scan showing a hole is far more persuasive than describing the defendant's psychological history. So, too, in everyday medicine. As a consequence, various tests have been developed to assay for depression, some reasonably successful. None, however, is as reliable as the good clinical interview.

The most common test for depression is the dexamethasone suppression test (DST), although it is not a very good one. This is a blood test that measures whether or not cortisol, a hormone produced by the adrenal glands, is suppressed in response to dexamethasone. That is, following the administration of this drug, the normal body produces less cortisol, a chemical that is easily measured in the blood. In about 50 percent of depressed patients, cortisol continues to be made at the normal rate. The questionable aspect of this test, however, is that it sometimes shows a positive result when there is no depression. In these cases there is usually another illness present. All in all, the DST is not conclusive and is used only in conjunction with other diagnostic means.

Scientists have known that depressed patients have an abnormally high level of acetylcholine, a key neurotransmitter, in the brain. There is a new claim that in these patients certain skin cells called fibroblasts are rich in receptors to acetylcholine. Thus, researchers examined these skin cells, because they recently discovered that various body organs tracked levels of brain acetylcholine, and it is a lot easier to count the receptors in skin cells than it is to measure abnormal levels of acetylcholine in the brain. One hypothesis stated that fibroblasts might have more receptors than normal in the depressed patient, and early tests have shown this to be the case. In the original study by a team of scientists from the National Institute of Mental Health, seventeen of eighteen patients tested positive for greater receptor density for acetylcholine than did controls. This is a hopeful sign, and the test may prove useful.

There are still other tests that look for other metabolites, but for now they all have limited predictive power. A neurologist can tell within five minutes whether or not someone is demented. A trained psychiatrist can detect depression in about the same time. A surprisingly accurate method is a questionnaire called the Beck Inventory. In short order, one can obtain a pretty good idea of any patient's state of depression.

The pharmacological agents that best control endogenous depression are the so-called tricyclic compounds and monoamine oxidase inhibitors. Why they work is not fully known, but they are about 70 percent effective for all patients using the drug. Some psychiatrists maintain that if the dose is increased and blood levels of the drug are carefully monitored, they will work 85 percent of the time. When first treated, the patient does not leap off the couch cured. It usually takes three to four weeks for the pharmacological action to take hold. Then, however, the effects can be dramatic. The patient's glum demeanor reverses, and animation and interest in life return. The inconsequential rewards, such as a friend's smile, a cup of coffee with a colleague, or a meal at a restaurant, all again begin to play their sustaining role.

The current explanation for why the monoamine oxidase (MAO) inhibitors and the tricyclic compounds work is that they increase the concentrations of two of the brain's neurotransmitters, serotonin and norepinephrine; this is the so-called biogenic amine hypothesis. In the 1950s researchers discovered that when electrodes were placed in the brains of rats, in areas that produced these two chemicals, and the animals could activate the electrodes, they preferred to self-stimulate these brain areas than eat. It was immediately suggested that a depressed patient might lack a sufficient supply of these chemicals. Scientists think that MAO inhibitors increase brain levels of serotonin and norepinephrine by blocking the degrading influence of monoamine oxidase on these two neurotransmitters. The tricyclics, on the other hand, work by inhibiting reuptake of these transmitters out of their site of action, the synapse.

The work leading up to this view started in 1950 when scientists observed that reserpine, a drug extensively used for the control of high blood pressure, caused depression in about 15 percent of hypertensive patients. In addition, when reserpine was given to animals, they became lethargic and looked almost sedated. National Institutes of Health researchers discovered that reserpine deactivated the compartmentalization of storage granules in vesicles, the places where neurotransmitters are stored and readied for action at the synapse. The vesicles would empty their supply of nerve transmitter while still inside the nerve cell, and the neurotransmitters would be broken down by monoamine oxidase. As a consequence, there would be an overall depletion of the neurotransmitter, such as serotonin and norepinephrine, in some nerve cells. You can clearly see the corrective role of an MAO inhibitor. It would block the action of monoamine oxidase, which would keep the neurotransmitters dumped into the cytoplasm from being broken down, letting them remain available for use at the synapse.

Soon after these discoveries were made, it was noted that the tricyclics blocked the reuptake of serotonin and norepinephrine. If you remember the description of chemical dynamics at the synapse from the Introduction, this means that these two neurotransmitters were not being returned to the cell that emitted them into the synapse. Instead, they remained in the synapse and thus were effective in firing the postsynaptic cell once again. Thus, the tricyclics, in effect, increase brain levels of serotonin and norepinephrine and thereby relieve depression.

If you've come to the conclusion that any drug or chemical that increases levels of serotonin and norepinephrine in the brain might well lead to lessening of depression, you are, in fact, correct. In normal people, amphetamines, which are thought to release more norepinephrine and to help block reuptake, can cause a big change in mood and give rise to a sense of well-being. Surely, these neurotransmitters are active somehow in pleasure perception and in warding off depression.

The biochemical evidence of what is wrong in depression is persuasive. But there are problems. One of the issues that bothers some researchers is that some antidepressants, such as the tricyclics, work within minutes on their site of action, yet, as already noted, the clinical response can take three to four weeks. The pure brain scientist asks how this can be, because he fails to appreciate the extent to which a patient can reorder his views of the world in a state of depression. Then, the brain is busy generating new interpretations of previously neutral events. While a conversation with a friend was once reinforcing, it no longer is. The friend does not mean as much to you as you thought he did. That becomes a belief, which takes time to reverse itself once the biologically induced state of depression is treated with drugs. To think that depression could be reversed by a single switch, ignoring the preceding months of psychological re-evaluations and theory development, would be odd indeed. This view is supported by the well-known fact that patients, suffering depression are best helped early in their disease. When the mind creates a structure of thought, current ideas and experiences are made to fit that structure, even in normal, nondepressed humans. Put an old Catholic in a Jewish home and compare the response to the change of beliefs with that of a young Catholic in the same home.

More troublesome for the simple neurotransmitter hypothesis is some new experimental work. The original idea was that certain brain areas were not getting enough of either dopamine, serotonin, or noradrenaline. The new data suggest, however, that many confounding events go on at the critical synapses. There is now evidence that the noradrenaline receptors become less sensitive to noradrenaline, which ought to decrease the effectiveness of noradrenaline. There are also reports that the secreting presynaptic cell begins to falter in its reuptake role. This means that there is more noradrenaline at the synapse for greater synaptic efficiency. In short, seemingly contradictory events are taking place, and this has led to the new idea that either too much or too little of a neurotransmitter will cause abnormal function, leading to the state of depression.

There are also other chemical candidates for how depression is produced in the brain. The failure to have an airtight explanation stimulates continuing research, even though the theories just stated are still the dominant ones. Further study is also motivated by psychologists, who, as a rule, have a more complex and accurate view of the world than those who deal with molecules alone. It is from the psychologists that we have learned much about the concept of reward, which is potentially applicable to the problem of depression. In order to understand rewards, one has to take a step back and understand an overall psychological context for action.

If a chemical has proved rewarding, we are likely to want to experience its effects again. Seeking the sensation of reward would keep us functioning members of a social group. According to the biogenic amine hypothesis, the brain of the depressed person is not delivering a sufficient amount of reward, and so he asks, "Why should I do X if I'm not rewarded for doing X?" As a consequence, he withdraws into inactivity.

We can see the relation between reward and depression at the behavioral level. For instance, it is well known that moving from a familiar place to an unknown place can cause depression. This has proved to be a great problem for families of executives that are always being transferred. While the husband, whose new job is consuming all his energies, tends to be quite happy, the wife and children are usually less well off. Back in the old home town, the wife and kids knew how to play the life game. They could make dozens of responses that resulted in reward. They had contact with friends, they knew the restaurants, playmates were abundant, and so on. In the new town, all of these things must be re-established. During the course of this adjustment, depression usually ensues because the daily rewards are fewer.

But there is another, more complex side to rewards. As we have just seen, the desire for reward can induce us to action, but some chemicals have the opposite effect. They are called satisfiers and are thought to be part of another brain chemistry system. These drugs, which resemble morphine, satisfy and simultaneously alleviate the drive to do anything while they are working. Could it be that the reward process involves several steps in a complex release of biochemical events? Perhaps the biogenic amines are active in guiding behaviors to an appropriate end, but once that is achieved, another class of chemicals is triggered to produce the sensation of gratification. Such a scenario has been proposed by several researchers, and in order to test it, they first had to determine that the satisfier chemicals actually had a rewarding effect.

Larry Stein, for years a leader in the field of the chemistry of reward, was the first to demonstrate that the body's own opiates—the enkephalins, which were described in our previous discussion of pain—can serve as chemicals for rewards. Dr. Stein placed catheters into the brain ventricles of rats, and when the rats pressed a lever, a small dose of enkephalins was injected into their brain. The result was that they worked hard to gain more enkephalins compared to their rates for normal saline solution. The next step in the study was to draw back and see if the release of the animals' own enkephalins through self-stimulation would accomplish the same thing. Stimulating electrodes were placed in the brain areas rich in enkephalin-producing neurons. If the rats pushed a lever, a small electric current would be delivered to the enkephalin neurons in the brain. Sure enough, Stein showed that the animals would work hard for this sensation.

It is easy to imagine how any of these chemical systems, if impaired, could lead to severe behavioral disorders. A brain that did not deliver the sensation of gratification after a long guided journey to the reward box would be a depressed brain indeed. ("What's the point?" screams the brain.) And so, the obvious but ill-conceived experiment of injecting opiates into depressed patients occurred. The results were confused, to say the least. And why shouldn't they be? The experimenters were delivering gratification apropos of nothing. They had removed all worldly contingencies and then dumped endorphins into the brain without any psychological context. Rewards are perceived as rewards only in a psychological context. A contingency is always necessary. Something is done to obtain something else. Consider the work of David Premack.

Premack discovered the reversible relationship between rewards and responses. What served as a reward in one setting would serve as the thing to do to get a reward under other conditions. The key concept in Premack's theory of motivation was the notion of a probability of response. In order to increase response A, a more probable response had to be made contingent to it. Thus, let's say an animal had equal access to water and running. Let's also say that prior to being exposed to these two, a rat had had ample opportunity to run but not to drink. It would come as no surprise to observe that such an animal would spend more time drinking than running during our equal access test. When the opportunities were reversed, so were the results. Premack then went on to show that the thirsty animal would run in order to have the opportunity to drink, and that the confined animal would drink in order to have the chance to run! In short, what served as a reward was not absolute. It depended on the context, the psychological state of the animal. Such a powerful concept as this leaves simplistic pharmacological experiments doomed to failure. It will remain for future work to get the psychological as well as the pharmacological elements coordinated so that we can get a deeper understanding of depression chemistry.

Finally, treating endogenous depression is possible not only with drugs but also through a controversial procedure called electroconvulsive therapy (ECT). ECT sounds like a holdover from the dark ages of scientific experiments. Between 70 and 100 volts of electricity are passed through the brain in an effort to bring on electrical seizures. If seizures are not induced, the therapeutic effect does not occur. Typically, prior to a treatment, the patient is given an anaesthetic so that he will sleep through the entire procedure. Another drug prevents the induced seizures from causing severe muscle contractions and possible injury. On the average, six to eight treatments are given two days apart over a two-week period. After the therapy, the patient has no memory of it and for about one hour has confused memories about very recent events. This confusion clears, and frequently the patient's overall memory improves because of the cessation of the depressed mood. However, repeated and frequent ECT treatments can lead to a more severe disruption of memory. There are, in contrast, some recent reports stating that delivery of shock therapy to only the right half brain allows for the therapeutic effects without causing any disruption of memory.

ECT produces remission or improvement in about 90 percent of patients. In modern clinical practice it is used only when drugs seem to fail, usually in severe cases such as psychotic depression, where the depression is accompanied by serious delusional states. Practicing psychiatrists say it is a most effective technique. The outsider finds it disturbing that no one has any idea why the treatment works. This fact has led to all kinds of theories, ranging from the psychologically sinister to more cellular ideas. Some critics argue that it works because of the terror the patient associates with shock therapy: "Don't take me there again! I'll do anything—even stop acting depressed." The more biologically oriented critics feel the seizures produce a whole new biochemical milieu in the brain that somehow benefits the patients. The fact is that no one knows why it works; we only know that it does, and that afterward people who were so depressed that they contemplated suicide now find themselves back at work, leading functional lives.

The Manic-Depressive Syndrome

Bipolar disease, the manic-depressive cycle that afflicts about 10 percent of those suffering from endogenous depression, has its own medication. It is a simple salt called lithium, which can almost miraculously dampen each half of the cycle. Patients describe the effect with a curious detachment. They say that they begin to feel themselves slip into a depressive state only to have it clipped by the lithium treatment. The same is true for the manic mood, which is clipped just as quickly. People who have suffered this disease for years are cured with a daily dose of a five-cent salt!

The breakthrough came in 1949 as an Australian physician worked alone in a small hospital. J. F. J. Cade had cared for manic-depressives for years. Even though he had had no formal research training, he decided to embark on a project that later proved seminal. His first idea was that perhaps the bodily fluids of a manic contained some chemical that triggered the mood state. To test this, he took urine samples from manic-depressive patients and from normal subjects and injected them into guinea pigs. The guinea pigs receiving the manic-depressive patients' urine became lethargic. He quickly reasoned that he had to control for the mixed bag of chemicals present in urine. He injected some animals with uric acid alone, but since uric acid is not very soluble in water, he gave them lithium urate. To control for any effects that might be due to the urate, he gave lithium carbonate to another group of guinea pigs. The results were unexpected but clear. The guinea pigs with the lithium carbonate only also became lethargic. Their usual startle response was absent. When turned over on their back, they did not make their normally frantic attempts to right themselves. Instead, they looked up rather complacently.

Cade immediately began oral administration of lithium salts to human manic-depressives in Australia. The results were startling, and the new treatment was off and running. It was picked up in the 1960s by the Europeans, who refined dosages by monitoring blood levels. It was highly successful but remained isolated there. The United States was slow to pick up on the advance for several reasons. First, drug manufacturers saw no profit in it and were therefore reluctant to initiate the process of approval by the Food and Drug Administration. Second, lithium therapy had been tried on patients with congestive heart disease in the 1940s. The proper dosages had not been worked out, and several patients died as a result.

Why lithium salts help ward off this awful disease of the brain seems to be unfathomable for now. Most biological models of how lithium works involve understanding the salt's action on blood cells. Certain abnormalities in the way ions are transported across the membranes of blood cells have been detected in manic-depressive patients. Relating blood mechanisms to mood mechanisms is difficult, however, unless one hypothesizes a genetic influence that affects brain membranes as well as blood membranes. Such a two-tier effect is currently thought to explain the role of lithium in controlling manic-depressive disease. Lithium has been shown to interact with the normal sodium-calcium system of neurons so important in regulating the amount of neurotransmitters released in a synapse. Still other new evidence suggests that lithium acts on the receptors of these neurotransmitters—receptors that may be overactive—and normalizes their action. But a direct link among the lithium treatment, the sodium-calcium system, and manic-depression is a total leap of the imagination at this point.

Environment and Depression

It is estimated that most depressions are psychologically induced. There are undoubtedly many kinds of psychological depressions, and trying to define them objectively can be a nightmare. There are environmental situations that in fact are able to induce depression in a certain percentage of the population. The problem with seeking a completely environmental explanation for a depression is that in the same environment there are more people who do not suffer depression than do. These individual differences in case histories of depression have always found the psychiatric community looking for some underlying biological disposition for the disease. How else is one to explain the fact that most people do not get depressed?

But situational depression is real. People thrown into an environment that they do not like can take on all the aspects of being seriously depressed. They lose interest, they stop eating, they sleep poorly, and they show all the other symptoms. Yet are they depressed in the same way as the severely endogenously depressed patient? It is not clear, but there are hints that they are not. First, the antidepressant drugs are not as effective in their treatment. Second, if asked whether they would like to move from their current environment, they will respond with enthusiasm, while to the endogenously depressed a move does not matter. In short, it appears that the endogenously depressed are up against a real biochemical abnormality that then feeds into a psychological state, whereas the situationally depressed have constructed a rational framework and theory to explain why they are depressed. However, show them the way out, and they are quickly on the way to recovery.

This notion fails to explain why both groups appear depressed in the same way to the outside observer. The disturbances in body rhythms are real. What remains as a great challenge to brain science is how an idea, constructed by the mind, gains control of cellular processes in such a way that it directs certain cells to secrete more or less of something that in turn eventually causes symptomatic behaviors. That view implies that the mind, with the right defenses, could well ward off the incoming environmental information that triggers a depression in some people. This belief provides the basis for psychological treatment and might explain the success some therapies have for certain depressed patients. The trick is to connect the right therapy with the proper depression.

Let us imagine first the tried and true case of the endogenously depressed person, the one who for no apparent reason falls prey to the disease. The working assumption is that critical chemical events triggered by the person's normal psychological state are not occurring. The system of previously perceived rewards that activated certain brain pathways—releasing chemi-

cals that activated other pathways and circuits—is not functioning normally. In such a case, psychological manipulation of
the disease appears useless, since there has been a disconnection
between the psychological message and the physical response.
If the physical mishap can be remedied and the connection between the psychological level and the chemical level readjusted,
then the psychological world can again work to mend the disease.
That is precisely what happens for the endogenously depressed.
The physical error is corrected—for example, by supplying the
system with lithium—and with an appropriate amount of time
the patient responds psychologically and is on the road to recovery.

Just as intriguing a scenario is the result of exogenous depression, also named reactive depression or situational depression.
No matter what it is called, it is the class of depressive disorders
that is thought to be precipitated by psychological stress. What
seems to be awry in people who suffer from it is the ability of
the psychological system to instruct the physical system to send
out the reward messages. Again, antidepressant drugs frequently
do not work on these patients. Strictly speaking, their physical
system is not impaired, but the process by which the message
gets sent to the physical system is. Further, it is not that the
psychological system cannot send the critical message to trigger
the physical events; it is that it does not. Enter the role of
psychological counseling.

One of the current treatments receiving wide attention is
cognitive therapy. The therapy builds on a set of observations
psychotherapists have made about depressed people. Among
other traits, the depressed person tends to overgeneralize the
meaning of events. Instead of dealing with adversities as isolated
incidents, the depressed person sees them as part of a larger
pattern. She also tends to see things as black or white. A normal
mother trying to solve family problems, for example, realizes
that solutions to some will work well while others work less
well. But the depressive sees herself as either a good or bad

parent. Finally, the depressive tends to feel she is helpless to affect the future. The aim of cognitive therapy is to educate the patient concerning these patterns and then to begin to work on specific problems the patient perceives as applying to her. Several reports suggest this technique can be very helpful for the situationally depressed patient.

One of the intriguing aspects of both endogenously and exogenously depressed patients is the sense of helplessness. Over the past ten years, a rich literature has developed on what has been called "learned helplessness." In animal studies, situations were constructed in which an animal could do nothing to avoid shock. The animals quickly learned they were helpless and fell into a totally inactive posture. Even when escapes were made available, the animals did not respond, in large part because they were too helpless to learn about the new possibility. The interesting thing to consider is how human demographic data on depression correspond to the learned helplessness model.

In 1975, a large study by the University of Indiana revealed a number of insights into who suffers from depression in the United States. The survey suggested one major factor in the creation of depression: inferior education, which in turn leads to low income, which in turn leads to an inability to secure financial improvement. In short, when it appears there is no exit from a low economic level in a culture that prizes material wealth, depression is a very common end product. The solution, the authors somewhat whimsically observe, is money. With money, choices can be made because goods can be purchased. If choices can be made, there is a reason to be active, to take part.

Depression affects eight million Americans at any one time. Clearly, it can be a very serious disorder, and when it appears, it should be dealt with swiftly and aggressively.

7

Obsessions and Compulsions

All of us obsess, but few of us obsess to the point of illness. An obsessive-compulsive disorder is an extremely serious disease. Although these patients represent only 1 percent of the population undergoing treatment in psychiatric centers, in a door-to-door survey nearly 2 percent of the population was identified as obsessive-compulsive. They are a disturbing group of people to be around, especially in the early phases of the disease when they admit to the irrationality of their obsession but seem helpless to do anything about it. In a one-on-one situation, it is like having a silent third party in the conversation who can seize control of the obsessive person at any moment and drive him or her to behave without any of the commonly observed social constraints. Examining these extreme cases gives insight into some of our own impulses.

There is a clear, apparent, and mercurial brain side to the story of obsessions. Head injuries, drugs, or brain surgery can bring on the behavior. Yet, as we will see, for all of the knowledge about the possible neurological involvement, no specific mechanism is known to be the culprit. A slight chemical imbalance can trigger the obsessive thought, the kind we all have from time to time. In the normal human, this thought passes as other competing thoughts take over, because the chemical imbalance is most likely quickly met and neutralized. What remains intriguing in the obsessive individual is why an otherwise rational person cannot state to himself, "Look, I must have a biochemical disorder that finds me obsessing about this one little aspect of life. I am going to set it apart from the rest of my life and proceed as if all were normal." Such willing away of the disease is not possible. The reason will become apparent as we examine this state of mind.

The disease has two different aspects, inasmuch as one can be obsessive without being compulsive. Here's a typical current definition of obsession, from *DSM-III:* ". . . recurrent, persistent ideas, thoughts, images of impulses . . . that are not experienced as voluntarily produced, but rather as thoughts that invade consciousness and are experienced as senseless and repugnant. Attempts are made to suppress them. . . ." As one tries to cram that definition into one's everyday knowledge of people who seem to act obsessively, it is important to keep in mind that the psychiatric sense of the term may not strictly apply to everyday usage. Some authorities maintain that obsessions span a continuum, with the severe cases showing up in the clinic. Others suggest that the clinical case is distinct from the more common experience of seeing obsessive tendencies in an otherwise functional person. To deal with this more commonplace variety of obsessive behavior, another diagnostic category has been established: the compulsive personality disorder. Typically, this kind of person has a preoccupation with rules, trivial details, perfectionism, and excessive devotion to work. The compulsive person is unduly formal or conventional, and stubborn and insistent.

Compulsions are defined in *DSM-III* as "repetitive and seemingly purposeful behaviors that are performed according to certain rules or in a stereotyped fashion. The behavior is not an end in itself, but is designed to produce or to prevent some future event or situation. However, the activity is not connected in a realistic way with what it is designed to produce or to prevent, or may be clearly excessive . . . , the individual generally recognizes the senselessness of the behavior and does not derive pleasure from carrying out the activity, although it provides a release of tension." For reasons no one understands, the compulsions are expressed in behaviors such as hand washing, which correlates with the obsession of contamination, and counting and checking, which is associated with being obsessed with doubt.

Consider the case of George P.:

> He was a 38-year-old engineer who was married and had two children. He came for treatment at the urging of his wife, who could no longer tolerate his bizarre behavior. George reported that he was deathly afraid of being "contaminated" by germs. The germs were carried around on the soles of people's shoes, and he felt that he could be contaminated by touching the soles of shoes, or by touching anything that was touched by someone who had touched the soles of their shoes.
>
> George performed an elaborate series of rituals to avoid contamination, or to uncontaminate himself if he did come in contact with germs. When he got dressed in the morning, he put on his shoes by holding them with tissues, so as to avoid touching them. If he did actually touch them, he was compelled to wash his hands. Washing could only remove the germs if performed in a specific manner. Each finger was individually washed by seven strokes of the washcloth, and then rinsed seven times. The same routine was then followed with the other hand. Drying then also involved a series of seven rubs of each finger. If George were interrupted during this sequence or otherwise lost count, he was forced to begin the entire sequence over again. The routine was performed slowly and carefully, and often took one hour to complete. George reported that on one occasion, it took him three and one half hours to finish washing.

Once he left the house for work, George was constantly on guard to avoid touching other people, or anything touched by others. He used tissues to open doors, pick up the telephone at his office, and handle mail or papers. He avoided shaking hands with other people whenever possible, and refused to eat in restaurants. He kept his office locked, and carefully examined it each time he entered to see if anything had been touched. The examination involved visual checking of the office contents. He would stand in the doorway and look at everything seven times. If he "sensed" that anything had been touched, he used tissues to systematically clean the item using seven strokes to clean each section. Consequently, it took George anywhere from ten minutes to two hours to get into his office and get to work in the morning, as well as every time he left the office during the day. Of course, any time he touched something contaminated he had to wash his hands. George reported that he had spent up to six hours checking, cleaning, and washing while at work.

In addition to his behavior in relation to contamination, George was compelled to complete many other activities in sequences of seven repetitions, including: combing his hair, brushing his teeth, shaving, and completing such household chores as washing dishes and mowing the grass. These activities all took a great deal of time, and were repeated whenever the sequence was broken. Before retiring each night, George thoroughly checked the entire house to make sure everything was locked, the stove was off, and no water was dripping. The entire house was checked seven times, and each door and window was tested seven times during each of the checks. On some nights, he experienced doubts that everything was satisfactory even after checking, and so he was forced to repeat the entire sequence. This routine took anywhere from forty-five minutes to four hours to complete each night.

George could offer no explanation for his behavior. He recognized that it was irrational and wished that he could stop, but could not control the urge once it was aroused.

He reported that as a child he was always neat and orderly, and felt highly uncomfortable when he got dirty, or if his possessions were left in disarray. He began to perform his current rituals several years ago, when the firm he worked for merged with another company. He was afraid he would lose his job, and became very depressed. He now continues to become depressed every few months, and his compulsions intensify at those times. (From Kazdin, Bellack, and Hersen, 1980)

Relatively new knowledge about possible brain mechanisms involved in obsessive-compulsive disorders have changed our views, but all past attempts at explaining patients like George were psychological in nature. The psychoanalytic explanations have been largely abandoned, since the hypothesized causes are found to exist in many people who do not develop the disease. The notion, for example, that the disease is the result of being raised by a domineering mother does not explain why all other people raised by domineering mothers do not obsess. As with most psychoanalytic theories of the origins of mental disease, they are found to be "just-so" stories. All antecedent events become fodder for the theory. Sometimes these events may be important but often they are not.

Behavioral Analysis of Obsessions and Compulsions

The behavioral descriptions get closer to the mark. At a minimum, they accurately describe the characteristics of the behaviors seen in the disorder. Working at this level of analysis, we can see why the obsessive's thoughts persist even though they are counterproductive. We can also begin to consider why the thoughts have the same themes and why the associated compulsions are so ritualistic.

Obsessive-compulsives are often afraid of making an error.

They exert Herculean effort not to do anything wrong. An error is perceived as an indication that they are not worthy and is to be avoided.

Why, however, is their obsession expressed mostly in terms of contamination? In the cases that come to clinic, approximately 50 percent are obsessed with cleanliness, as opposed to other behaviors such as checking or shoe shining or whatever. One reason may be that germs and health are themes of the entire detergent industry, of mother, of science, of just about everything: "Cleanliness is next to godliness." The person about to succumb to this behavioral pattern may only be seizing on one of the more prevalent concerns of our culture.

Another possibility is that the statistic may simply mean that a hand-washing obsession is more readily detectable; other obsessions may be easier to hide. For example, a scientist is called upon to present a paper at a meeting. Instead of taking the event in stride, he views it with great alarm, alarm beyond simple nervousness about public speaking. "What if I can't answer a question about the data? What if I do something stupid? Or what if the point is dull?" A not uncommon response to this set of questions finds the scientist writing out the to-be-presented paper, checking every detail, rewriting it, editing it, correcting a word here and there, and, thanks to word processors, reprinting the entire draft. Such behavior can go on for days or weeks before the talk. It is clearly obsessive-compulsive behavior that is unsettling to the scientist and to his colleagues. Yet it is acceptable and is hidden from the statistics. Compulsive behavior is more prevalent than commonly thought and takes forms different from what clinical data suggest.

With a mind-brain disorder of the obsessive-compulsive type, it is of great interest to try to determine which part of the couplet process comes first. Do people adopt compulsions to relieve obsessive states, or do self-generated theories of why someone is obsessing come from the compulsive behavior? In other words, what is driving what? With current knowledge, it can be said only that the two are very closely linked.

Consider the following. If there was an internal brain state triggered by some set of independent or even psychologically identified circumstances, then an act like cleaning is simply the most likely behavior, given our cultural context, to begin the process of reducing the internally triggered state of arousal. It is known that if a compulsive behavior is prohibited, the level of initial arousal persists for hours and is perceived as being very uncomfortable. It is also known that by allowing a compulsion to run its course, the level of arousal associated with the obsession is measurably reduced. With that being the case, it is easy to see how the activities related to decreasing the unwanted arousal become reinforcing to the person. The patients learn that the compulsive activities, which soon become ritualistic, make them feel better. They do not wish to lose the transient feeling of well-being associated with the reduced arousal, so they continue the aberrant behavior.

Ritualistic behaviors that are a large part of the disease have been studied in animals. In one type of experiment, an animal is forced to respond to a stimulus but very infrequently receives an electric shock at random intervals. This unpredictable environment creates bizarre patterns of behavior. Animals adopt stereotypical movements between their responses, as if what they are doing would somehow decrease the chance they would get a shock. In short, they enact a ritualistic behavior that must have hugely reinforcing effects. Human obsessions and compulsions have a similar quality. After all, there are facts to support the obsessive person's theories about the world, even if they depend on events that are highly unlikely. It is possible that one might make an error or contaminate a friend. Such an unpredictable event would be highly detrimental, and fear of its happening sets the stage for the compulsive, ritualistic behavior.

Unlike many behavioral states that are difficult to analyze both psychologically and biologically, obsessions and compulsions most likely have a tangible physical basis. In the normal course of everyday life, one may wake in the middle of the night thinking obsessively about something. The world looks bleak, even though the factual circumstances of one's life are unchanged from the day before. During the night there are large differences in brain and body chemistry. Such diurnal-based changes in our view of the world and our own position in it suggest that brain chemicals may be playing an important role in exaggerated behavioral states such as the obsessive-compulsive disorder. Consistent with the view of there being a strong biological component is the fact that the disorder is not tractable to psychotherapy.

Establishing Obsessive-Compulsive Behavior in a Biological Framework

One source of evidence that obsessive-compulsive behavior is related to a physical mechanism was collected when von Economo's encephalitis swept through Europe at the turn of the century. C. von Economo, a neurologist, identified and described the rampant disease that killed thousands. Among other things he discovered that dozens of obsessives appeared in neurological clinics. In some patients, the behavioral disorder remained even after the encephalitis cleared up. The disease was thought to be related to a brain disorder, and it was proposed that in as many as two thirds of the cases the brain was involved, with measurable neurological abnormalities such as tremors, rigid facial muscles, and other mild neurological signs. By 1960 brain disease was accepted as a likely part of the obsessive disorder. One of the more interesting observations to emerge was that patients who had suffered head injuries and recovered were more likely to become obsessive than other patients. Traumas to other body areas resulting in similarly long illnesses do not produce the disorder.

Genetic research on obsessiveness is equally revealing. Scientists have been slow to examine this line of inquiry because of the low incidence of the disease. Nonetheless, studies that show a genetic predisposition to the disease have gradually accumulated.

Identical twins reared either together or apart reveal a high concordance rate of obsessive–compulsive symptoms. Although this fact underlines the genetic factor, the inheritance pattern is complex and suggests neither the simple Mendelian nor sex-linked model. Plainly stated, the level of concordance rate— which is to say, the rate of expression between the twins— suggests that an obsessive–compulsive parent may or may not transmit the trait to the children. Whether the trait is transmitted is a function of what is called the penetrance of the gene. This concept takes into account environmental factors such as stress when determining whether a genetic element is expressed.

Genetic analyses are crucial to understanding the biological aspect of a disease. One can postulate the actual location of a gene on a chromosome by using the gene linkage technique. Each gene locus is composed of two alleles, with one contributed by the father and one by the mother. Linkage refers to whether an allele related to a particular trait, such as eye color, systematically varies with another allele that is supposedly related to another phenotypic expression, such as depression. If, on a particular chromosome, we know the genetic trait of one allele, and that trait covaries closely with another trait, the second allele should reside on the same chromosome. This linkage has been found for depression and eye color. It is a clever way to gain evidence about the actual genetic source of a trait.

Researchers have determined that there is a high rate of association between the obsessive–compulsive disorder and blood type A. Obsessive-compulsive patients have a significantly higher proportion of type A blood and a significantly lower proportion of type O blood when compared to the general population. Other patient groups, such as schizophrenics and depressives with obsessive symptoms, do not have blood types proportionately different from the general population. A continuum of symptoms may exist: obsessives with blood type A predominating at one end, depressives with obsessive symptoms in the middle, and true depressives without obsessions linked more to type O blood groups. This is speculation, but it is fascinating to consider how molecular one can get in the analysis of mind-brain diseases.

The genetic biasing of brain structures, which makes them function abnormally, is another central focus in the history of research on obsessives. A vast amount of work carried out on the neurophysiological, anatomical, and biochemical levels of analysis points to one overall picture of the essential nature of obsessives. They are overaroused by events that nonobsessive people find easily manageable. Moreover, and most intriguing, they do not adapt or become habituated to repeated occurrences of an event that has excited them. Research in brain physiology has done much to explain why they overrespond to threatening events and why they produce so much anxiety, anxiety that must be released through some kind of compulsive, real, and immediate motor behavior. How might this sequence occur?

Neurosurgical Cures or Calamities

In the late 1930s, the Portuguese neurosurgeon Egas Moniz suggested that cutting out parts of the frontal lobe might help chronic and severe obsessive-compulsives, basing his ideas on the results of experiments on chimpanzees. Experimentally induced anxiety in the animals was markedly lessened by frontal lobe ablation—or surgical removal of tissue. Moniz theorized that the same procedure might work in anxiety-driven obsessive patients. In the operation actually performed, leucotomies were carried out in preference to whole frontal lobe ablations. In a leucotomy, the neural connections that travel from the limbic system—that part of the brain intimately involved with emotion and arousal—to the frontal lobes are severed. At least that is what the more refined operations tried to do. Earlier attempts had far cruder results.

The importance of disconnecting the frontal lobes from the limbic system was purely speculative in the early days. More recently, it has been shown that lesions in an animal's hippocampus, a part of the limbic system, caused actions resembling obsessive-compulsive behaviors. The animals became intense, rigid, and abnormally persistent in learning a new task, and they adopted various ritualistic movements. Although these descriptions fit the human case, it is still not known why disconnecting the hippocampus from the frontal lobes resulted in the reduction of obsessive-compulsive behaviors. Coming up with a theory is difficult indeed.

Nonetheless, hundreds of people have undergone the leucotomy operation, and most reports agree that 75 percent of the patients were vastly improved. On a variety of psychological tests, amelioration was noted, suggesting that anxiety lessened, obsessions retreated, and depression diminished. Physiologically, there was a measurable reduction in such indicators of arousal as heart rate, blood pressure, and forearm blood flow. Five years later, researchers conducted a follow-up study in which leucotomy patients were compared to other groups treated by pharmacological intervention, electroconvulsive therapy, hypnosis, behavioral therapy, and psychotherapy. The leucotomy patients had the fastest recovery response; their symptoms lessened within three months. However, at the five-year mark there was no difference between any of the groups! Add to this the immediate side effects that the surgical patients experienced, and it is no wonder the operation has been abandoned in the United States. These side effects included transient confusion, headaches, urinary incontinence, memory difficulties, apathy, and a host of other problems.

Another argument has been made that a brain structure called the cingulum, which is associated with emotional behavior, is crucially involved in the disease. In one study, during surgery for epilepsy, electrodes were placed in the cingulum in an attempt to detect the initial focus of seizure activity. Once they identified the area, surgeons would then remove it. Frequently, surgeons use the same electrodes to stimulate the same brain structures that they are trying to record from. Such stimulation of the cingulum impelled patients to perform stereotypical, repetitive movements much like those seen in the obsessive-compulsive. The patients maintained that they felt it virtually impossible to resist the urge to carry out the motions. Armed with this, surgeons began making small holes in the cingulum of patients with obsessions and reported great success in relieving many of their symptoms. One study reported that 87 percent of the patients included were helped. More than fifty thousand such surgeries have been carried out in North America alone.

There are a number of opinions as to why operations became popular. First, no one likes to contemplate dragged-out solutions to anything, and operations appeal to the doctors' preference for a quick fix. Psychiatry, in contrast, appears to flounder on with its long-term therapies. Second, the disease state is, as we pointed out, nerve-racking for the patient and those around him. When it seemed imperative that something be done, in the days before the advent of powerful drugs, surgery seemed an acceptable option. Nonetheless, most of the surgical approaches are no longer used, and, to some extent, it is almost unbelievable that such measures were undertaken to cure a mental disorder. Yet, in other cases, it is difficult to identify the true reason why the surgeries stopped, especially the cingulotomy. Starting about five years ago, it passed out of favor, and the reasons were more sociological than scientific.

Pharmacological Interventions

With the surgical solutions largely discontinued, pharmacology has come to play a major role in the control of obsessive-compulsive behavior. In starting the process by which helpful drugs are identified, researchers like to be as objective as possible in singling out patients with the disorder. Currently, there are two main clinical tests. Since the compulsive patient is frequently, although not necessarily, depressed, scientists suspect that biochemical systems regulating mood are involved. As already noted in the chapter on depression, the dexamethasone suppression test has been useful in the diagnosis of depression. In this test, dexamethasone is administered at 11 P.M., and the following morning blood levels of cortisol are measured. In normal subjects, the cortisol levels remained suppressed for twenty-four hours. In about 50 percent of the depressed patients, the cortisol was not suppressed, and a recent study of obsessive-compulsive patients showed that approximately 40 percent did not suppress, suggesting that the disorders of depression and obsession have a common biological cause.

The other test frequently used to identify a clinically relevant obsessive-compulsive disorder is the sleep study. A patient's EEG is carefully monitored during nighttime sleep, and the pattern of electrical activity is compared to normal levels. Obsessive-compulsive patients differ on eight of seventeen variables that are identified in the sleep brain waves. They sleep lightly, wake up frequently, and have briefer periods of sleep. They have shortened rapid-eye-movement phases of sleep as well, and in general show overall features reminiscent of the sleep pattern of depressed patients. Thus, both the dexamethasone test and the sleep studies suggest a relation between obsessive-compulsive disorder and depression.

These clinical tests suggest that pharmacological interventions similar to those used in depression might also work for obsessive-compulsive disorders. This early hope has to some extent been justified, though a key to the ultimate biochemical mechanism active in obsessives is not at hand. The most prevalent theory to account for the obsessive-compulsive disorder at a biological level centers on serotonin. This chemical has been implicated

in a number of psychiatric disorders, most prominently depression. If you recall from the previous chapter, it is believed
that substances classified as biogenic amines, which include the
neurotransmitters serotonin and norepinephrine, are depleted
at the synapse in patients with depression. The antidepressant
drug clomipramine, which works in the serotonin system, has
been found effective for the obsessive-compulsive as well as
for depressed patients. Not only does the depression clear when
the drug is administered, but many patients also have fewer
obsessive feelings. When taken regularly, the drug is able to
maintain its antiobsessive effect for years, but when it is withdrawn the symptoms reappear. On the surface it seems like a
tight story. Animal studies support this view by showing that
symptoms similar to obsessive behavior are associated with a
depletion of serotonin in animals. Lowered serotonin levels cause
sleep disorders like those seen in human patients. In a rat study,
low levels of serotonin caused excessive grooming activity, a
behavior possibly related to cleaning behavior in humans. Recent
work, however, complicates the picture (as usual).

Clomipramine works by blocking the reuptake of serotonin
at the synapse. But it also has a metabolite (a product of its
chemical action) that affects the action of norepinephrine. In a
recent study, researchers discovered that a drug called zimelidine,
which *specifically* blocks serotonin reuptake, has no antiobsessive
effects. This finding brings into question the claim that the
biological error in obsessive behavior is solely due to too much
serotonin at the synapse. To make matters worse, desipramine,
a drug that blocks the reuptake of norepinephrine, also has no
beneficial effects on obsessives. Thus, the known second action
of clomipramine, the effect it has on norepinephrine, also does
not seem to hold the explanation for clomipramine's effectiveness
in helping the obsessive patient. Yet, when the patients that
were used in these drug studies were put on clomipramine,
they immediately showed improvement! Clearly, the nature
of the drug's action is quite complex and remains unknown.

Although many drug studies create the impression that the psychological dimensions of a disease are less important than the biological aspects, one has to be careful. For instance, while research shows that clomipramine helps to control obsessive behaviors, these reports usually come from self-assessment by the patient. In contrast, family members frequently attest that there has been no change in the frequency of attacks. When considering the known side effects of the drug, it is no wonder such discrepancies are reported. Patients on clomipramine frequently become lethargic and constipated, gain weight, and suffer major sexual dysfunction. With such changes in behavior induced by the drug, it is easy to imagine the patient worrying and trying to interpret them. This becomes his preoccupation, instead of his previously few, set, stereotypical behaviors.

In addition to the quick-fix strategy of the psychopharmacological approach, there have been other attempts at alleviating the symptoms of the obsessive. For example, some obsessives' EEG's are markedly abnormal over the temporal lobes, parts of the brain implicated in schizophrenia and amnesia. It has been suggested that the obsessive patient may experience seizure activity in the temporal lobes, which sets off the behaviors we have described. To test this, obsessives have been placed on anticonvulsants instead of on drugs like clomipramine. The reports of symptomatic relief are equivocal, however, and when the results are positive, they are almost impossible to assess. Simply saying that a patient "gets better" means very little.

Research has continued to consider other possible brain mechanisms that may be awry in the obsession disorder. For example, the possible role for antianxiety drugs has also been examined. If the obsessive is simply trying to reduce a general level of arousal, commonly referred to as anxiety, then such agents ought to work. They don't. Many compulsive patients placed on these drugs discover that although arousal is decreased, their motivation to carry out a compulsive act is not. How could that be? Researchers know that blocking access to the compulsive behavior heightens the obsessive state, which they consider to be a form of anxiety. The fact that it is not that simple once again finds us confronting mind-brain interactions.

Distinctions between anxiety and arousal, and also general anxiety and specific anxieties, must be made. The distinctions were originally proposed to account for the fact that different anxieties are manifested in identical twins reared apart. What is inherited may be a general disposition for arousal. Each twin interprets this arousal differently, as a function of his own set of complex psychological views that have gradually accumulated from living in a different environment. The specific anxieties, then, are individual responses to the arousal. The failure of the antianxiety drugs on obsessive patients may reflect that the learned behaviors—which is to say, the compulsions—acquired to deal with the arousal came to be viewed as reinforcing in their own right. As such, even though the trigger to start the obsessive-compulsive sequence has been neutralized by an anti-anxiety drug, the pleasures of the compulsive behavior motivate their continued recurrence. Additionally, and more dishearten-ing, it may well be that the compulsion, with its positive rein-forcing value, conjures up the obsessional thought in a reflexive way that results in the patient's feeling no relief from the compul-sive action.

This hypothesis once again shows the delicate balance that exists in mind-brain interactions. It illustrates the powerful role of the interpreter in spreading the initial disease. The result of any such interpretation is not foreseeable. Yet the disorder is even more complex and ever reminiscent of behaviors we all manifest from time to time. You're off to Europe, and you keep checking your pockets for tickets and passport. You do this a dozen times while waiting at the airport. In everyday life you never check anything. But here, if you make a mistake, you miss your APEX ticket rate, the connection on the other end, and so on. The realities are there, but the behavior is silly when carried to the extreme.

The obsessive-compulsive disorder is fascinating for a variety of reasons. From a psychological point of view, it is frequently manifested by the feeling that something outside yourself takes control of your motor behavior and does things you do not wish to do. That is, it does not seem initially driven by your own thought processes. Later, compulsives become so linked to what has become the theory behind the compulsion that the two go hand in hand. (There are reports that it goes the other way around too.) The obsession, the inappropriate anxiety about something that has at least a statistical chance to occur, takes on major proportions, leading to endless worry about the consequences. These thoughts lead to anxiety great enough to require a release mechanism, which becomes compulsive and reinforcing, in turn encouraging the representation of the obsession. With a possible circle of action and reaction like that, it is not surprising that the brain side of the story is hopelessly linked with the psychological aspects. Neither the mind nor the brain is an island unto itself.

Addiction

To put it boldly, addiction is a human phenomenon. While it is possible to create in animals a physical dependency for narcotics and alcohol, it is virtually impossible to addict animals to substances that humans will sometimes commit crimes to obtain. If given the choice, animals will walk away from a drug that has been foisted upon them. This is true even though the physiological effect of the drug is the same for animals and humans. As we try to untangle the problem of addiction from a host of popular confusions about its origin and nature, we come to the inescapable conclusion that human addiction is largely a product of the mind, not the body. And, more pointedly, only a small percentage of our society become addicted to drugs. Most people use one or another pleasure-producing drug at some time, but only a few become addicted.

Addiction was originally defined in Roman law as a surrender or dedication of anyone to a master. In modern culture, it refers to the uncontrollable seeking of an experience, usually through use of a substance that either gratifies or relieves pain. We tend to think of alcohol, tobacco, caffeine, and other drugs with either a sedative or stimulating effect as the stuff of addiction. Although the addictions these substances produce are powerful, consider all the things around which people organize their lives.

One can be addicted to sports, trips to Italy, Chinese restaurants, power, passionate sex, and many other sources of gratification.

Of course, these latter "addictions" are entirely acceptable behaviors. They give life a sense of well-being and focused interest, making the humdrum aspects of everyday life bearable. Six months in Kansas is acceptable if there is going to be a week in Ravello. Money is saved, plans are made, duties are assigned so that one rapturous week can be spent at the Hotel Palumbo, feasting every night upon gnocchi and calamari with the scents of the Amalfi coast wafting up. The week is addicting. When it is over, plans are once again made for that special experience. It is a peak experience and it must be relived.

These acceptable, normal "addictions" are psychological in nature and can be contrasted with the physiological addiction of many drugs. The vacation habit is a "soft" addiction, in that it represents a desire for simple rewards that do not establish physical dependence and that can be delayed in their delivery. But realizing all the ways we humans become ritualized in certain habitual behaviors is to begin to understand what is called "hard" addiction.

The Concept of Addiction

The concept of addiction is obviously riddled with problems. American society, which seems consumed with the notion of helping the deviant, whether it be the drug abuser or the criminal, has become obsessed with addiction. We have sanitized the problem by suggesting that "hard" addictions can happen to anybody exposed to powerful drugs. Save our children from the devil's grasp, we proclaim, and say no to drugs. Yet most of what we hear is hyperbole, and it is encouraged by those who profit from a continuance of the drug hysteria. It is hyped by medical researchers who get paid to study drugs. It is hyped by the social service industry that gets paid to help rehabilitate the addict. It is hyped by politicians who get elected by showing they have a social conscience.

This urgency to solve the problem loses some of its force once we realize that addiction, in the sense of physiological need, is very limited and relatively easy to fix. Most so-called addicts are not suffering from physiological needs; their cravings are psychological, and one has to wonder whether all the helping agencies that concentrate on the physiological dependencies are not in fact serving the function of reinforcing various forms of dependent or fatalistic psychologically driven behavior. Consider a study by Professor Stanley Schachter of Columbia University.

Schachter spent years studying why it was so difficult to wean smokers from their cigarettes. He examined all the data from rehab services and observed that no matter what the treatment had been, 60 to 70 percent of the participants returned to smoking. As he puzzled this fact and unearthed relations between nicotine levels and cigarette use, he also wondered why he no longer knew anyone who smoked. Years before, a seminar room would be so filled with smoke that the blackboard was barely visible. Now, not only was the air clear, but a maverick smoker incurred the wrath of all those around him when he lit up. What was going on?

Schachter formally surveyed his highly educated colleagues at Columbia. He also polled residents of Amagansett, a middle- to upper-middle-class community on Long Island where he summered. He first determined who were smokers and who had been smokers. He took into account how long they had smoked, what they had smoked, and all other variables he could think of for such a study. It wasn't long before the truth began to emerge. Inform a normally intelligent group of people about the tangible hazards of using a particular substance, and the vast majority of them simply stop. That's all, they stop. They don't need treatment programs, support groups, therapeutic drugs—nothing. People who had been smoking for years on a daily basis abruptly quit. This suggested that the rehab centers were attracting only those people who were unable to stop.

As a consequence, the rehab patients are not a random sampling of the population with an addiction. They are a subculture that cannot easily give up their addictions. Yet it is the patients from these centers who make up most of the studies about addiction and about how hard it is to kick the drug habit. Clearly, the Schachter study strongly suggests that the world is getting a distorted report about the addictive process.

About 10 percent of the population fall into addictive patterns with drugs. They frequently switch drugs, as is happening with crack. Heroin users are switching to it, so crack sales are going up, heroin sales are going down. What is *not* happening is any significant rise in the number of addicts. Similar conclusions can be made from a large drug study on returning Vietnam vets ordered by Richard Nixon.

Nixon, who rarely relied on the powers of social science research, thought the country should know how many vets returned as addicts. This was in response to an outcry from Americans who seemed to regard all returning veterans as junkies. The director of the study, Dr. Lee Robbins of Washington University, had a large sample to draw on. She chose those soldiers returning to the United States in 1971. Of the 13,760 Army enlisted men who had returned, 1,400 were found to have urine that tested positive for drugs (narcotics, amphetamines, or barbiturates). In short, these 1,400 men were unquestionably drug users. Of that sample, she retested 495 men eight to twelve months after their return home. The results were crystal clear. Only 8 percent of the men who had been drug positive in their first urine test remained so. Therefore, 92 percent of those using drugs upon their return home simply quit, walked away from dependence on the substance they enjoyed in Vietnam. It was the remaining 8 percent that were making their way to the rehab facilities—the hard-core addicts.

This finding is staggering in its implications. Virtually every study and every statement made about human addiction is based on the image that heavy drug users are victims of their substances. Yet Schachter's work suggests that the vast majority of humans are able to walk away from a drug should they choose to do so. Those who cannot are not so much victims of a ravaging physiological need as they are of a certain psychological character. That psychological profile, no matter how it might be characterized, is what is at issue—not the substance abuse. As we explore the matter more deeply, we shall see that much of this profile can be attributed to the mind of the addict.

The Effect of Drugs

Drugs, of course, are the stuff of the "hard" addictions. Drugs do not require six months of planning to produce the rewards that lead to the "soft" addictions. The martini, the joint, any mind-altering substance is quick and, for the most part, cheap in our culture. It can be experienced once, twice, three times daily and still be within the realm of social acceptance. Drugs offer a speeded-up version of experience. They overpower some people and send them into a downward, unhealthy spiral. Some of these substances will create a physical dependence. Yet, when that dependence is remedied, the cold reality of the psychological addiction becomes apparent. In order to realize the depths of the psychological habit, it is necessary first to understand the relationship between addictive behavior and real physiological dependence.

The American Psychiatric Association defines addiction as "dependence on a chemical substance to the extent that a physiological need is established. This manifests itself as withdrawal symptoms . . . when the substance is removed." This narrow definition raises the issue of physiological dependence. It has come to be believed that addicts are tied to a physiological process, and that bodily need drives the addict to continually seek the drug. As I have said, nothing could be further from the truth.

When an addict phases out his use of a narcotic or alcohol, there is an immediate but medically controllable period when his body must adapt to the absence of the substance. Cellular changes go on, but there is little understanding of what they are. Yet the effect of the drug's removal is visible. For the first twelve hours after stopping heroin, for example, muscle pain, sneezing, sweating, tearing of the eyes, and yawning can occur. From about thirty-six to seventy-two hours after, more severe and uncontrollable muscle spasms occur, along with cramps, restlessness, increased heart rate and blood pressure, sleeplessness, vomiting, and diarrhea. These symptoms gradually decrease over five to ten days. While it sounds awful, it can be no worse than a bad case of the flu. Yet, once the drug has been gradually removed and the physical dependence on it is no longer a factor, 90 percent of addicts will return to their old habit, as we have noted. Their bodies do not crave the substance; their minds do, and mind problems are the most difficult to solve.

There is one physiological phenomenon that bears on the addictive process, and that is the development of tolerance for a drug. Tolerance is loosely defined as the adaptation of the nervous system and other bodily organs, such as the liver, to a set dose of a substance. The net effect of the building up of a tolerance is that it takes more and more of a drug to produce a given mental state. Again, the first assumption is that we are dealing with a purely physiological phenomenon. With alcohol, for example, the liver becomes more efficient at metabolizing the substance, thereby creating the need for more to be consumed in order to achieve a high. This is referred to as metabolic tolerance. There is also something called pharmacodynamic tolerance, where it appears that certain cells in the brain become adapted to a drug's presence and as a result do not respond as vigorously.

Yet even with tolerance there is a psychological factor, in that learning also plays a role. In one study, a group of rats trained on a maze were injected with alcohol *before* each practice session. Another group trained on the same maze, only they were injected with alcohol *after* each session. On what was called a test day, both groups were given the alcohol before the test session. The rats that had had alcohol before the daily practices performed far better than the group that had been given alcohol afterward. In short, tolerance is a complex phenomenon that ties together physiological and psychological processes. Nowhere is all of this more evident than with heroin.

Heroin

The closer heroin addiction is examined, the easier it is to see both physiological and psychological factors in it. Consider Sam J., who fell into heavy narcotic use in New York City. There it is easy to develop addictive behavior, not just because of the city's complexity, the stress of living there, and the level of poverty in some quarters, but because of the availability of drugs. Obviously, availability is the necessary first pitfall.

Sam started using heroin, the choice of many heavy abusers. He had taken the drug on a dare one Saturday night and had not been impressed. It had made him feel dizzy and nauseated. A few weeks later, the same group of friends dared him again. This time Sam felt the euphoria. Heroin, which the body quickly breaks down into the mind-altering substance morphine, had done its damnable trick. Sam was hooked, but he thought intelligently so. He was sure he could be a Saturday night user only. Unhappily, however, Sam turned out to be one of the 10 percent of people who, after being exposed to a substance, have a very difficult time using it in moderation or dropping it altogether.

After several weeks, Sam began to seek heroin more often. He gradually lost interest in his job. He couldn't fund his habit easily, and Sam, once a respected high school teacher, began his career as a mugger. His life took a downward spiral until, by good luck, he was able to take part in a new drug program at Rockefeller University in New York. The program did not make sense to him. Another narcotic, methadone, would be given to him free, and he would have a free room at Rockefeller Hospital. The doctors held out hope that this would control his appetite for illicit drugs and allow him to return to a functioning life.

Sam is a composite addict, the sort of prototypical patient we all have images about. However, the Rockefeller program, under the direction of Dr. Vincent Dole, was real. Dole, realizing there was no known mechanism of addiction, or tolerance, or dependence, reasoned that the problem should be dealt with clinically in a pharmacological setting. It was a solution geared to the physiological problems of addiction only: vary the narcotic and see if the patient is better off. The springboard for methadone therapy came from work done in Kentucky showing that narcotics of all kinds have different effects on the nervous system. That is, they act at different sites with different durations. Dole hoped to find a drug that would satisfy the body's physiological dependency only and leave the mind alone enough so that the addict could participate psychologically in society.

Dole took the dispassionate, biological view that the body needed chemicals in these dead-end cases of addiction. Supplying those chemicals seemed highly reasonable and allowed for the possibility that the person, even though continuing to be drugged, could still function. From the start, his idea was not exactly in the mainstream of thought on how to "help," but in retrospect, his work has illuminated many of the problems of the addict.

After a couple of false starts with inappropriate narcotics, Dole hit on methadone. He was up against the problem of tolerance for heroin in the addicts he was trying to help. If 10 milligrams of heroin is injected into an addict and a nonaddict, the blood concentration of the narcotic over time will be identical for both. The difference is that the addict has built up a tolerance, and his euphoria lasts for a shorter time. And after an identical single dose is administered, the addict will go into withdrawal within a couple of hours, whereas the nonaddict may not experience withdrawal at all. What Dole figured out was how to adjust the dose of methadone so that it was above withdrawal level for the addict at all times. Because he was not in withdrawal, he could function.

Methadone does not produce withdrawal symptoms because of the way it is metabolized in the body. Addicts are given between 50 and 100 milligrams per day. The drug is administered orally, causing absorption through the intestines and the liver, which essentially buffers its action. After methadone reaches the intestine, it is taken by the blood to the liver, which, on the first pass-through, retains approximately 85 percent of the drug. Then, each time blood circulates through the liver, more drug is released from storage. Thus, methadone enters the bloodstream slowly—just like a time-released cold capsule. This gradual input is important, since the effect drugs render on our consciousness comes most easily when there is a quick rise in the blood level of the drug. The brain seems to need a shock, which could sensitize it in some way to the next dose. But with a chronic, low-level change by means of an agent such as methadone, the psychological effect seems much less intense, if it is present at all.

As already mentioned, the psychological reaction of addicts to methadone is completely different from the reaction to heroin. In a period of a few weeks, they stabilize and begin to live productive lives. They are still on a narcotic but not one that produces euphoria. Their craving for heroin stops. Actually, most of the outpatients in the Rockefeller program did try street heroin after the methadone took hold, but once or twice proved enough. The heroin no longer had a euphoric effect and had little psychological value. With the high doses of methadone in place, their tolerance for narcotics in general was high enough to render the shot of heroin ineffective.

It almost goes without saying that the methadone solution

engendered much criticism. There were claims that methadone didn't work as reported; that the addicts returned to the streets to find other drugs that produce a high; that they were selling narcotics at the methadone clinics. It is fair to say there were numerous examples of each of these failures. There was also the serious problem of stopping methadone addiction. While withdrawing from heroin is a week's trauma, coming off methadone can take months and is usually compounded by several relapses into heavy narcotic use. In fact, in one major follow-up study, while there was markedly reduced criminal behavior and illicit drug abuse on the part of those patients carefully maintained on methadone, those who went off fared poorly. Still, at this writing it is one of the only ways known to be successful in controlling the problem of the committed heroin addict. A 1985 study showed that if a support system is part of it, the methadone treatment is highly effective in removing these addicts from a life of crime and uselessness. This is not a perfect world.

The methadone-stabilized patient exemplifies the range of psychological variables that make up an "addicted" patient. In reviewing this scenario, we must remember that the vast majority of heroin and other drug users walk away from heavy use. Those who end up as part of the 10 percent who become addicted are a special subset of the general population. Dole reported that there were all types in the group he assessed after the patients were stabilized. They tended to have similar attitudes about life before entering the treatment program, but once controlled, the still-addicted patients were as diverse as the cured, nonaddict group.

Other observers disagree with this appraisal and instead report that addicts tend to be the type that seldom admit they have a problem. They have lots of rationalizations for their habit. For example, they maintain that what they are doing is entirely pleasurable, and that everybody needs some form of release. They reason that there is nothing wrong with getting high now and then. Their reasons for not facing reality are endless, and they always maintain that no problem in their lives is of their own making. If the car breaks down or if the court takes away their children, it is someone else's fault, never their own. There is in the addict no sense of personal responsibility. To the extent such evaluations are accurate, they raise the question of whether the addict is one who forever sees the world as beyond his control. The environment makes things happen to him; he can't make things happen in the environment. Given that outlook, he sees the effect of drugs on him as only one more piece of evidence that he is merely a pawn in a preordained scheme of things.

Alcohol

Most of us are fortunate enough not to have to deal with the problem of heavy drug use. The main addiction of the American middle class is alcohol. After years of denial, we have finally recognized it as a major problem. To this day, the New Englander arriving at the emergency room with an alcohol-related injury and in an obvious state of inebriation will deny he has had a drink. Even today, drinking is not viewed as acceptable in New England, although everybody does it. At the same time, the New Yorker in the same situation at Bellevue doesn't have this social constraint and freely admits to drinking.

Americans like to drink. It accounts for about 3 percent of their personal expenses and is a pattern that starts early in life. It is estimated that over two thirds of males and females drink, and the heaviest drinking is done between the ages of sixteen and twenty-five. The chances of finding a drinker, as opposed to an alcoholic, in any age group are higher among the more affluent, the more highly educated, and among Italians and Jews. More interesting, the drinking pattern of youths, which shows a high frequency of drunkenness and alcohol-related absence from school or work, in no way helps predict whether or not they will become alcoholics. In short, in the early years, novices, future alcoholics, and social drinkers all can behave the same. As is the case with sinister drugs like heroin, exposure to and use of alcohol does not mean addiction will follow.

For all those who start drinking early in life, approximately 5 to 10 percent continue and become alcoholics. The highest rates are for thirty- to fifty-year-old men, and there is a greater incidence among lower socioeconomic groups and among Catholics, especially French and Irish. The toll for this widespread alcoholism is seen everywhere. In general medicine and surgery, for example, upwards of 35 percent of all cases are alcoholics. But here again, one has to be cautious in interpreting what this means. Alcoholics may have a host of other problems, including abnormal mental states, and it is these other factors that contribute to their higher medical risk.

Alcohol is a depressant drug. In social situations it is frequently used to loosen one up, to act as a stimulant. In fact, however, the alcohol is assumed to have an anaesthetic effect on some part of the brain, thus allowing for the release of inhibitions. At present, the actual mechanism by which alcohol produces the psychologically stimulating effects associated with its use is not known. One of the current theories suggests that alcohol produces morphine-like substances in the brain of some individuals, and that these substances give rise to more intense sensations of pleasure, resulting in a greater probability of addiction. This promising lead of tying alcoholism to opiate systems remains to be confirmed. It is known, however, that a genetic factor exists in alcoholism, thereby suggesting that some people are more susceptible to such bodily chemicals than others. Studies of adopted children reared apart from their alcoholic parents show that they are five times more likely to become alcoholics than are adopted children of nonalcoholic parents.

Another aspect of alcohol abuse is that it does damage throughout the body—notably to the liver, where it can result in cirrhosis, and to the esophagus, which can lead to esophageal carcinoma. Recent research also links it to brain damage. Rats that have been exposed to chronic alcohol use show marked cellular changes in their hippocampus, the brain structure that is crucial to memory. There is evidence that some degeneration of the cerebellum, which manages motor control, is possible in the seventh decade of life. Also, some heavy drinkers of Italian chianti contract a disease that attacks the corpus callosum, the nerve cable between the two cerebral hemispheres.

There are other brain abnormalities that may develop with alcohol use, and these are the result of improper diet. If the brain does not get sufficient vitamins, severe damage can occur. Korsakoff's syndrome, a disease that afflicts heavy beer drinkers, is common in Boston and in Ireland, but not in London. Supposedly, this is because American and Irish brewers pasteurize their beer, which kills the vitamins. One wonders how well a vitamin-enriched beer would sell in the United States.

Theories about the causes of alcoholism are many. In addition to the evidence for genetic influences, deficiencies in the metabolism of certain enzymes have been proposed, and there is evidence that some personality traits are associated with alcoholism. Whatever the cause, treatment theorists agree on one point: once an alcoholic, always an alcoholic. To some extent, they are totally apart from other drinkers. While most social drinkers have a drink every night, alcoholics drink in spurts. They go on a binge and then abstain for days or weeks at a time. Only about 30 percent of them spontaneously seek help for their problem.

Alcoholism is difficult to treat because of the social acceptability of drinking. The alcoholic faces temptation every day, everywhere. For this reason, many alcoholics are not treated until the stage when they begin to hallucinate and become delirious. The treatment itself is entirely psychological and must be actively continued throughout the life of the alcoholic. A list of treatment options from the National Institute of Alcoholism emphasizes the psychological aspect with great clarity. Group therapy, fam-

ily therapy, educational counseling, and behavior modification
are but a few of the avenues open to the alcoholic. It is a long
path to recovery, a path full of potholes, and the fifty-billion-
dollar-a-year liquor business does not seem threatened by the
rate of rehabilitation of hard-core alcoholics.

Cocaine

In recent years, attention has turned away from alcohol and
has centered on cocaine. The current euphemism is that it is a
recreational drug that every self-respecting yuppie should have
as part of his weekly experience. When originally popularized,
it was cited not as addictive but as energizing and imparting a
heightened awareness. Cocaine has been the mind-altering substance of choice starting in the late 1970s.

Cocaine is a stimulant with a history of being in and out of
fashion. It was introduced in Europe only after a method had
been developed for isolating cocaine from the coca leaf in 1855.
Prior to that, its importation did not result in significant use,
in part because the coca leaf does not travel well. In 1880 a
Russian nobleman and physician working in Germany reported
that it was an effective anaesthetic. By the turn of the century,
physicians thought it would be helpful as an antidote to narcotics
(like morphine) and alcohol. Sigmund Freud, then a neurologist
in a Viennese hospital, picked up the lead and tried it on his
alcoholics and drug abusers. He also tried it himself. He was
so impressed that he wrote a highly influential review article
called "On Coca." He became an avid user of cocaine and
wrote another paper about it, "Song of Praise." None of this
was lost on the Coca-Cola company, which added an extract
of the coca plant to its product between 1896 and 1906. Coke
was truly "the real thing."

Cocaine has a chemical structure close to that of the local
anaesthetics lidocaine and procaine, which are commonly used
in dentistry and surgery. These drugs act as anaesthetics by

somehow changing the membrane of peripheral nerve cells, making it more difficult for them to discharge and therefore to impart their messages to the brain. Here's how scientists think the mechanism works. Nerve cells have a sheath of lipid (fat) around them. When a nerve starts to discharge, channels in the lipid membrane open up to allow sodium ions to flow from the outside of the neuron to the inside. This triggers an electrical current to travel down the nerve. Lidocaine, procaine, and, presumably, cocaine bind with the lipid to somehow block the sodium channels and thereby prevent the nerve from firing. The similar action of the three chemicals suggested that, in addition to cocaine, one of the local anaesthetics might also produce euphoria if administered to the brain, which has turned out to be the case. Snorting lidocaine gives effects similar to those experienced with cocaine.

When introduced into the brain, cocaine primarily affects the sympathetic nervous system. Cocaine use causes an immediate increase in heart rate and blood pressure, and in large doses raises body temperature and causes dilation of the pupils. These palpable effects go along with what seems to be increased mental activity, euphoria, sexual desire, and an overwhelming sense of self-confidence and well-being. The drug does not impair the memory system, which means that when it wears off and the taker reassesses matters, he can suffer a depression that comes from realizing that the same imperfect person is once again housed in the same imperfect body.

There is no clear understanding of how cocaine causes the grand effects. Other drugs that alter the sympathetic system do not produce the euphoric state. What is known of the behavior of cocaine in the body is reminiscent of the observation about narcotics. The euphoric effect is created by the sudden change in blood level of the drug. Thus, injecting cocaine intravenously or smoking cocaine paste causes a faster and fuller sensation of euphoria than does taking it orally or snorting it. As with the narcotics, the overall blood level of the substance can remain

high while the euphoria disappears. In order to regain the euphoria, another blast is called for.

It is still too early in this culture's experience with cocaine
to know all its effects. We do know that chronic snorting can
cause damage to the nasal septum. It can induce hallucinations
and psychotic symptoms, anxiety and irritability and stroke.
And it can drive you to the poorhouse. Yet it is everywhere.
In 1980, U.S. Customs officials reported seizing sixty-five hundred pounds of cocaine, while in 1960 they confiscated only
eleven pounds. Currently, it is estimated to be a thirty-five-
billion-dollar cash business in the United States alone, which
would make it our sixth largest industry.

The social reinforcements to cocaine use also contribute to
its popularity. In American society, the effects cocaine produces—alertness, increased mental activity, decrease in appetite—are all very appealing states of mind. It sounds as if it
were designed for the middle and upper classes, all of whom
cherish such indulgence. Consider the Wall Street trader who
is working in a highly stressful and frenetic atmosphere. He is
a perfect candidate for the cocaine lifestyle. He makes plenty
of money and so can afford the drug, and he has every reason
to take a stimulant that will keep him alert on the trading floor.
At night, coke has the social acceptance of the business community. It keeps them awake to party after a long day at the office.
But quickly the routine turns vicious. Sleep becomes almost
impossible, causing greater fatigue and then greater cocaine use
to stay awake. Eventually, such individuals must submit to
careful medical observation and be brought down with sedatives.

Is cocaine addictive? Undoubtedly it is, although the effects
are surprisingly varied. Until relatively recently, it was widely
believed that cocaine was not addictive in a physiological sense
and that the user did not develop a tolerance for it. Proponents
had maintained that repeated doses of the same amount of the
drug had the same psychological effect, but it is now known
that heavy users must drastically increase their dose to achieve

similar psychological highs. Whereas the average dose for an occasional user is only 25 milligrams, some people can take up to 10 grams per day, according to reports. For a novice, such a dose could result in convulsions and even death. At present, the tolerance is thought to be largely metabolically based. Cocaine, when first used, stays in the blood in a potent concentration for approximately one hundred minutes. With repeated use, it stays in the blood only fifty minutes.

Some people respond in quite the opposite way and find that, with continued use, it takes less and less of the drug to produce the desired high. This points up a number of interesting aspects of drug use. First, there is tremendous individual variation in how people respond to drugs. Many scientists assert that cocaine somehow prevents the reuptake of the brain neurotransmitter dopamine. As a consequence, the cells that dopamine innervates remain "turned on" for a longer period of time. Another proposal is that cocaine produces a "kindling effect" in crucial brain structures associated with mood changes. The kindling effect is a concept borrowed from epilepsy research, where it has been shown that slight electrical stimulation of the brain over a long period of time eventually becomes effective in producing seizures. As applied to cocaine, this theory proposes that there is some kind of pharmacological kindling going on where the drug has established an active center in the brain. With chronic cocaine use, the brain center fires off with only a small trigger from the new intake of the drug. This is only hypothetical for now. What is not doubtful, however, is the variation in response seen with chronic use.

Cocaine is psychologically addictive. It is habit forming, and for those who take it intravenously or smoke it, it can be extremely destructive. In addition to damaging the pulmonary system, it can produce drug-seeking behavior, which prevents the addict from functioning in society. There is no doubt that the Saturday night or occasional user can easily survive the cocaine experience. On the other hand, the heavy user is in

for a long struggle with life. Cocaine addicts are now the majority of clients at any drug rehabilitation center. In 1975 they
were small in number. Starting in 1986, cocaine was modified
and sold in a raw form called crack. Unlike traditional prepara-
tions, it can give a powerful and quick high when smoked,
like the effect of the intravenous blasts that used to be favored.

Marijuana

Marijuana, or *Cannabis sativa,* is another drug that is considered psychologically but not physically addictive. Marijuana
was barely available in the United States until Prohibition in
1920, when working-class people began growing it or smuggling
it in as a substitute for alcohol. In 1937 it was outlawed in the
United States. In the nineteenth century, Baudelaire, a heavy
user of hashish in Paris, wrote about the effects of the drug in
terms that correspond with more modern experience. He described the euphoria, uncontrollable laughter, paraesthesia and
weakness, perceptual disorders of time and space, and mental
confusion and incoherence that can accompany its use. Psychiatrists at that time commonly recommended the drug to their
students, so that they could gain insight into mental disorders.

Marijuana was the drug of the 1960s. It fulfilled all the needs
of the Vietnam years. While much of youth was upset about
the war, they wanted a drug that was a thorn in the side of
the older generation. Marijuana did the trick. It was illegal,
which meant it was fun to deal in. There was some risk involved,
some form of rebellion associated with its use. Smoking it then
became a cause in itself, and all the usual arguments were trotted
out to support its legalization: it is not addictive; every culture
has its mind-altering drug, so let us have marijuana; pot is
simply our generation's equivalent of a worse drug—alcohol.

The arguments were partly true. Marijuana is not addictive
in the physiological sense. Some claim that for heavy users it
takes less and less to achieve the same psychological effects. In

the late 1970s, however, new studies by the National Institutes
of Health demonstrated that over the long term its use produced
changes in brain chemistry. Julius Axelrod, a Nobel laureate,
took time out from his usual work and studied what happened
when tetrahydrocannabinol, or THC, the pharmacologically
active chemical in marijuana, was consumed. The compound
was "labeled" with a radioactive tracer and injected into rats.
Axelrod found that even a slight dose could be detected in the
brains of these animals six months after the last use of the
drug. It was binding to some receptors in the brain and was
not being metabolized out. In that sense, it is worse than alcohol,
which is removed from the body within hours.

In any case, marijuana lost its social attraction, became commonplace, and fell out of favor. The young have largely returned
to alcohol, and if they can afford it, they use cocaine. The ebb
and flow of interest in drugs is tied to social events. People
don't want to drop out and be aloof (marijuana). They want
to be productive and successful (cocaine). The psychological
attributes of substance use and abuse always tell most of the
story.

As a final note, it is worth considering the problem of drug
use in its wider context. The United States government is pater-
nalistic. A large number of our laws are directed toward protect-
ing us from harmful substances. Citizens must be told what is
good for them. This attitude explains in part why most drugs
in the United States are sold by prescription only. At one level
it appears reasonable—but is it?

In most European countries, the vast majority of drugs are
obtainable without a prescription. It is assumed that their citizens
are not prone to consuming substances of which they are ignorant or that they had not been advised to take. The European
system works well, although errors certainly do occur; it assumes
an educated person will act reasonably. In short, the Europeans
already knew what Schachter discovered: that most people are

reasonable and react intelligently to addictive drugs. Most people can have a drink; only a small percentage become alcoholics. Most people can have a joint; only a small percentage become addicts. Those who surface out of control appear to have a genetic disposition for a particular kind of substance abuse. They are victims of complex biological and psychological forces that make them reluctant or unable to change. They are a special class of people who will always be around, no matter what their society's rules for dealing with mind-altering substances.

In this light, the question must be asked: is it worth the effort, cost, and, ultimately, failure of trying to control the availability of illegal drugs? Currently, drugs are supplied to the public by organized crime. They arrive in the hands of the street peddler through a network of corruption, and both government officials and private-sector employees are part of the corruption. Yet one fact is lost in our perception of the drug traffic. Most of the drugs go to the middle class for recreational use. Only a small percentage of the total volume is for the addict. Organized crime exists because the middle class uses it for certain functions, one of which is the delivery of illicit drugs. The cocaine-snorting Wall Street broker may vote for Reagan, who inveighs against organized crime, yet that same broker is largely responsible for the existence of the crime structure, with all of its horrid power beyond the drug business.

The question becomes: should our culture allow for self-abuse, or is it society's duty to protect its citizens from the risk of poor health and a damaged mind? The question is complex and confounded from the start. Should society incur all the expenses of fighting corruption in an effort to prevent just a small percentage of its citizens from abusing themselves with drugs? A strong argument can be made that it should not. The legalization of such substances might go a long way toward repairing many inconsistencies of our culture.

Here's the scenario. Cocaine may be purchased at Bloomingdale's, at restaurants, wherever. It is taxed just like liquor. Its purity is regulated by the government. The private manufacturer of cocaine is taxed handsomely as well. The budget deficit would be considerably reduced, not only because of the new tax but also because of the hundreds of millions of dollars saved, since we no longer need to pay drug enforcement personnel. Organized crime would be dealt a severe blow. And approximately thirty-five billion dollars would be removed from the underground economy and placed in the taxable economy.

The suggestion is not new, yet it has never received a full public discussion. No one can take pleasure in knowing that some members of our species will find a way to abuse themselves. The central question is, however, whether it is really worth the price to try to stop an event that will inevitably occur anyway.

9

Love

Love undoubtedly has more variety and complications than any other human emotion. It ranges from a child's love for parents to adolescent infatuation, followed by states of caring, passionate love, and finally companionate love—and all raise the question of how much of this most tender emotion is biologically inevitable and how much of it is culturally based. The strong sensation of love for one's parents, which abounds early and normally continues throughout life, argues for a primarily biological factor. That love seems inherent and spontaneous. Yet much of what we perceive as a profound, biologically based response is frequently culturally driven. What is biological in love are the states of arousal that occur in all love relationships; what is cultural is how we interpret these states. The brain's interpreter, drawing on cultural mores and beliefs, assesses the aroused state and gives it a psychological context. In our culture this psychological context is called love.

Knowledge of the psychological and societal role that love plays is, nevertheless, often shunned in America. Starting in the 1960s, psychologists systematically examined the subject of sexual love. Two of the major researchers, Ellen Bershied and Elaine Walster of the University of Wisconsin, tackled the problem and soon discovered that it ranked almost as a taboo.

Senator William Proxmire of Wisconsin publicly reprimanded
them after they had received an $84,000 grant from the National
Science Foundation to study passionate and companionate love:

> I object to this not only because no one—not even the
> National Science Foundation—can argue that falling in love
> is a science; not only because I'm sure that even if they
> spend $84 million or $84 billion they wouldn't get an answer
> that anyone would believe. I am also against it because I
> don't want the answer.
>
> I believe that 200 million other Americans want to leave
> some things in life a mystery, and right at the top of things
> we don't want to know is why a man falls in love with a
> woman and vice-versa. . . .
>
> So National Science Foundation—get out of the love
> racket. Leave that to Elizabeth Barrett Browning and Irving
> Berlin. Here if anywhere Alexander Pope was right when
> he observed, "If ignorance is bliss, 'tis folly to be wise."

The uproar was boisterous, and the NSF actually backed
down. To everyone's surprise Senator Barry Goldwater came
to the defense of the project, finding himself in concert for
once with the *New York Times!* Walster and Bershied prevailed,
however. Walster and her husband went on to summarize the
research in a delightful book called *A New Look at Love,* which
has a consistent capacity to inform with good humor and solid
fact.

Attempts at understanding love in our species did not get
off to a fast start. But since it is such a pervasive emotion, it
has caught the attention of just about everyone through the
years. One of the first theories about love and its function in
our lives comes from Plato. In the fifth century B.C., Plato
wrote in *The Symposium* that in the beginning there were essentially three kinds of people: men, women, and an androgynous
third sex. The third sex was a union of two; it was round,

with one head but two faces, two "privy" members, four ears, four eyes, four hands, and four feet. Zeus felt threatened by these creatures and decided to cut all three groups in half. This left the once-complete man looking for his other half and represented the homosexual class. Similarly, the once-whole woman had to search for another lesbian woman. Finally, the androgynous beings were divided to make up the new heterosexual class, the male half looking for a female and the female half for a male. Plato came up with this idea to round out his theory of the role love played in human life. Humanity, he felt, has been longing for completion ever since Zeus carried out his cleaving act.

The myth Plato reports in *The Symposium* is attributed to Aristophanes, who was a writer of satiric comedies. Scholars are not sure that Plato took it seriously, but his is simply a Greek version of an old myth from India. In the Indian tale, primeval man looked around and found only himself. He then willed himself to fall into pieces because of his loneliness, and from these pieces husband and wife were born. The wife reacted to this by saying, "How can he unite with me after engendering me from himself? For shame! I would conceal myself." She therefore became a cow and he a bull, and from their union came all the cattle.

The Greeks clearly wanted the myth to explain more than just loneliness. Plato's primeval man developed *hubris* and threatened the god Zeus. The cleaving and the subsequent need for completion, love, was viewed as punishment for this *hubris*. As we have said, not exactly a fast start for the concept of love.

Though poets and philosophers wrote endlessly about it, love was ignored by scientists until Freud gave it a little attention. His view was consistent with the conventional idea that all types of love are sexual in origin. According to Freud, the young child starts off with the narcissistic view that all love is directed toward himself. Gradually, through many processes, it is directed to one of his parents. Finally and reluctantly, the love is transferred to another adult, a member of the opposite sex. Freud felt that love was always disappointing, since the true instinctual desire is to love only one's parent of the same sex. The normal person represses this in pursuit of a mate of the opposite sex, but as a result never quite achieves completion. When you think about it, this idea is just as bizarre as Plato's. And at another level they are not that much different.

Love and Culture

New Guinea is perhaps the best ground for testing whether any particular belief about an aspect of human behavior is determined by culture or biology. Amazing stories about the different folkways of that society have filled books. The New Guinean attitude about children is a case in point. Carleton Gajdusek, a Nobel laureate and the scientist who discovered the mechanism of kuru, the dementing, deadly, slow virus infection of the brain in cannibals, is also a practicing anthropologist. He made his medical discovery in New Guinea and, in the course of spending years in the bush, also learned about kinship attitudes. In one of his accounts, a mother is relaxing at the sea with her new baby girl. Her other children are playing nearby. Off a boat comes a relative from another island. They exchange greetings and the relative says in passing that she wishes she had a baby girl—all she has are boys. The mother, with no hesitation, offers her the girl in exchange for a two-year-old boy. They trade pleasantries and life goes on as if dolls had been swapped. Yet ask the New Guineans about love, and they will talk in the same glowing terms as a Westerner. How love is interpreted is what is different. Cultural values and personal beliefs and presumably states of arousal common to love in all cultures are so interlinked that it becomes impossible to talk about one without talking about the other.

Getting Started:
The Process of Attachment

Under normal family circumstances in Western culture, our first love affair is with our mother, no matter if we are male or female. She doesn't have to be a biological mother but a mother figure in any case. It can be a nanny or a nine-to-five institutional nurse. What is important is that she be perceived as consistent, affectionate, and kind. Children raised without such a person suffer poor physical and emotional development. It is somewhat controversial as to whether or not the consistent, kind, and affectionate figure can be changed during the first six months of life. After six months, however, there is little doubt that attachment is directed toward one person. When the person (usually the mother in our culture) leaves, the baby is anxious. When she returns, the baby rejoices and moves to get close to her. This gradually changes, and, over the next year, other attachments are formed, including one with the less frequently available father—or baby sitter or grandmother or brother and sister.

This time frame for attachment correlates with several ongoing brain processes. One of them is the development of the brain mechanism responsible for visual acuity. The acuity mechanism is highly dependent on the development of the cerebral cortex and, in particular, the visual system of the brain. At the age of six months, humans show major changes in this structure and a resultant increase in powers of perception. Prior to that time, the image of a face cannot be decoded a short distance away. By six months, visual acuity is sufficiently developed to allow for the easy distinction of particular faces from three feet away. Presumably, this must happen before the child can form attachments to individuals.

Imprinting is another important event that is clearly seen in animals and may also be a factor in human childhood attachments. It occurs during a critical period when any young offspring becomes attached to its mother. Konrad Lorenz, the famous ethologist, showed that the attachment could be to any-thing—a piece of cardboard, for instance, or in some cases the experimenter himself. When Lorenz was the first thing a set of ducklings saw at birth, they appeared to be attracted to him above all other objects and blindly followed him around as a child would follow his or her mother. This form of instant learning is correlated with transitory brain states that occur only during the critical period for imprinting. Certain brain chemicals are present then that are not at other times. There is not, however, enough evidence to show whether this is also true for humans.

Although in imprinting the object of attachment can be arbi-trary, for the child the attributes of a mother figure are not. Harry Harlow of the University of Wisconsin years ago made classic observations about the importance of warmth and cud-dling versus food. He raised monkeys with surrogate mothers, funny-looking icons constructed of wire. One surrogate was wrapped in terry cloth and a light was placed beneath it to make it warm. The other supplied milk but lacked the cuddly, warm terry cloth; rather, it was made out of bare wire with a nipple at one end. The monkeys preferred the cuddly surrogate and would go to the other for feeding only. If a loud noise occurred, the monkeys always jumped on the terry cloth object. Clearly, the warm, soft mother substitute produced a "security" response the other could not.

Researchers at the University of Virginia have taken Harlow's observations into the human setting and watched the long-term impact of different motherly responses on a child's adjustment. Mary Ainsworth noticed three different styles of attachment in her laboratory studies of one- to two-year-old children. One group of babies used their mother as a secure base from which to operate when playing. When the mother left the room, they would show distress, but when she returned, they would be reassured and again explore, keeping close to her. Ainsworth called these the "securely attached." Another group appeared extremely distressed when their mother left, but upon her return they seemed oblivious to her. These were called the "insecurely attached." Finally, the "avoidant attachment" group seemed to avoid their mother and had no interest in her going or coming.

In follow-up studies, Ainsworth discovered that the interactions observed in the laboratory could also be found in the home. For instance, longitudinal work indicated that the securely attached babies had mothers who did not always pick them up when they cried but nevertheless showered affection on them. Those mothers would also pick them up just to have fun, not always at eating time. In contrast, mothers of the insecurely attached and avoidant babies were inattentive to their babies' cries and, when they did respond, frequently gave little comfort. It is interesting to note that the securely attached babies had fewer disciplinary problems later in life than either the insecurely attached or avoidant babies. Clearly, nurturing is important, and the brain seems ready for it during these early years, with adverse long-term consequences if it does not occur.

Research also shows that the mother is not in full control of how she responds. Although the mother may be loving, a difficult and fussy baby that cries continually can change matters, and the mother can react with little patience. After a while, the difficult child will not often find a warm response. Having exhausted herself on previous occasions, the mother simply can't offer more reassurance. The baby then becomes a member of the insecure category. The dynamics of interpersonal relationships, of the mutual exchange of rewards and punishments, starts early with important consequences for all.

During our first years, our brain is aswirl with cellular and chemical changes. Neurons are growing and retreating. Learning the relationship between events and their possible rewarding value or lack of it occurs on a minute-by-minute basis. It is most likely that the young child is not conceptually involved in love or loss of love at an early age. What the parent perceives as the child's love is really an adult's view looking back to the later childhood years when the older child could appreciate love as a concept and offer it in return. Remember the eerie pictures of President Kennedy's funeral? John-John was waving and whimsically saluting, while his older sister, Caroline, looked somberly straight ahead, more aware of lost love. The younger child responds to simple contingencies of reward and punishment, which are vastly important in normal development. He or she has not yet labeled or interpreted simple attentive behaviors as love. Nor can the child grasp the implications of death and corollary loss. The simple, conditioned behaviors of the young child seem to be supplying crucial brain systems that need some kind of feedback and soothing so as to quell the aroused state the brain is signaling. Only later is all of this important behavior interpreted as love.

Sexual Love

With the body chemistry settled down and child-parental relationships finally established, along comes puberty. The child suddenly feels new stirrings, new awakenings. Members of the opposite sex, as a rule, begin to incite a new kind of desire. Soon, inanimate pictures do the same, and the child, emerging into adulthood, is confronted with sexually driven, romantic love. The process moves from indiscriminate interest to particular infatuations and finally a "serious" relationship. At this stage, most of us consider the event unique and vastly important. It has never happened to anyone quite this way before. It is a time of such disturbing and forceful emotion that writers and philosophers through the centuries have tried to characterize what goes on inside us as we discover love.

Until recently the topic of sexual love has escaped the methods of science. Now, however, the psychological analysis of love is rich with insight. There is even some knowledge about how the brain produces the sensations of love. Taken together, the facts spell out a story that helps bring understanding of the many shapes of love and of the inevitable move away from passionate love to companionate love that takes place over time. Although some, like Senator Proxmire, complain that the topic of romantic love should be left unexamined because of its personal qualities, others feel that by understanding it more fully, we will be better equipped to deal with its tricks and pleasures.

The Attraction Process

Passionate love starts with contact. If there is immediate physical attraction, the process of getting to know someone is quick. If the other person is not attractive at first glance, there is a good chance he or she may soon become so. The remarkable fact is that the more you are near someone, the more positively you come to feel about that person. Propinquity is a powerful draw. Robert Zajonc showed a series of faces to students. The test group viewed certain faces once or twice, while they saw others many more times. The more frequently a face was seen, the more the students liked it.

In an earlier, classic experiment, Leon Festinger, the father of modern social psychology, showed the effects of social contact on liking. He studied the development of friendships, a basic ingredient of love, in a dormitory complex structurally designed to encourage contact for some new residents and reduce it for others. The apartments were U-shaped. The people who happened to live on the ends were more isolated and never struck up friendships, while the people in the center of the U, who were constantly bumping into one another, became friends. Even several courtships began. Festinger also noted that relationships sprang up more frequently between next-door neighbors than those living just one or two apartments away.

Once the liking process has started, it is easy to detect. Normally, two people gaze at each other very little, but when attraction begins, they are always stealing glances at each other. It is an unmistakable sign. Another cue is how close together they stand. In one study, students were sent out on a blind coffee date for thirty minutes. Afterward, when the couples returned to the psychologist's office, the distance they stood apart was noted and compared to how each student rated his or her partner. The more the two liked each other, the closer they stood.

In the initial stage of a relationship, there is a "courtship readiness" ritual. Grooming begins, with women fussing with their lipstick and men combing their hair or cleaning their nails or whatever. Different postures are adopted in an effort to look the best to the prospective mate. The body language part of the attraction process is real and to be taken seriously.

How does one person know when the other is truly ready to make a move? Some years back, Eckard Hess of the University of Chicago studied the relation of the pupillary response to the attraction response. He reasoned that when a person is aroused, the size of his pupils should change, since the pupils are controlled by the sympathetic nervous system, which is involved in arousal. Hess believed that a larger pupil size could be detected by another person and thus serve as the cue that the attraction process was going well. He showed several men photographs of a woman with normal-size pupils and then compared the pupillary response of these males to the same photograph that had been subtly touched up so as to make the woman's pupils larger. The men gave a dramatically different response to the two pictures. At the same time, they were unaware of why they felt aroused. They were not conscious of the difference in pupil size in the two pictures. But their brain was.

The human aspects of attraction are really not exclusively human. Biologists and psychologists working with animals have made many observations similar to those made with people. Monkeys and porcupines, for example, will copulate only with familiar females. Dogs and cats become aroused most frequently in familiar surroundings where they have had sex before. This picture changes with too much exposure. When rats were allowed to copulate to the point of exhaustion, the male retreated from normal sexual contact for fifteen days afterward. Female rats were always willing to continue. If, however, the exhausted male was presented with a new female rat, he immediately became aroused again and performed with vigor. This has come to be known as the Coolidge effect. It seems Mrs. Calvin Coolidge visited a chicken yard and marveled at one rooster who kept performing with all the hens. She asked that the rooster be pointed out to her husband. When the President arrived, he was shown the rooster and was told that Mrs. Coolidge had requested that the President's attention be drawn to him. Coolidge thought for a moment and said, "Tell Mrs. Coolidge that there is more than one hen."

Sexual Arousal

The arousal of passionate love is a pervasive aspect of the bigger process of love and one that fits neatly into data about the brain because it can be experimentally examined. In one study, students of both sexes were shown erotic pictures and were duly aroused. A less fortunate group was exposed to slides of geometric shapes. Both were then told to go to what they thought was an unrelated interview. Recordings were made of their responses to the interviewer. The aroused males made advances to the interviewer if she was a female and avoided eye contact if the interviewer was male. Aroused females made advances toward males and to some extent toward female interviewers as well. None in the group that had seen the geometric shapes responded unduly at all during their interview. This is like the cocktail party effect. When two mates go to a cocktail party, one of the objectives is for each to talk and flirt with others. With success, the mates leave the party in a somewhat aroused state, which then pays off in their own relationship.

The role of arousal in the desire for sex is a very real phenomenon and is easily demonstrable in experiments. In another study, students were asked to view three different films. One was a horrifying automobile safety film that pictured grotesque accidents, another a neutral film about Nova Scotia, and the third an erotic film. The order of the films was varied and shown to a group of women. When the safety film was shown first and the erotic film second, sexual arousal was intense. When shown the other way around, the building sexual arousal was arrested by the safety film. In short, the sexual response can be enhanced by a prior arousing experience, even if that experience is distasteful.

Fear works the same way. In another study, men and women were asked to participate in a learning experiment. The men soon discovered that their partner was an outrageously beautiful coed. Some of them were told the experiment would require an ever so small shock, while the other group was told a substantial shock would be delivered to them. With that bit of frightening information running through their head, they were asked to evaluate their gorgeous partner. It was the group with the severe shock supposedly in store that rated the woman as especially tantalizing.

In a related experiment, men had to cross one of two bridges in Vancouver. One was a 450-foot-long, 5-foot-wide bridge that swung and swayed over a gorge with a 250-foot drop. The other was a stable, solid bridge upstream from the other. Meeting the men at the other end of each bridge was a woman who maintained she needed a questionnaire filled out for a class project. She said she didn't have time then to explain the project in detail and gave her phone number. Guess who called?

These consistent findings of the role general arousal plays in sexual attraction and enjoyment suggest that the couple who fight before lovemaking may be sliding into that pattern of behavior because of its delightful aftereffects in bed. The process may not be consciously perceived, yet the body and brain know what is happening. And it works only in a delicate balance. Other research has shown that lasting relationships must consist of a mixture of emotions. In one study, three groups of dogs were raised in either a totally loving environment, a totally hostile environment, or a mixture of the two. The dogs that were dealt with inconsistently were the most attracted to and dependent on their trainer. The balance, the unpredictable, keeps the arousal level high, with consequent satisfaction.

Sensation Seeking and Arousal

Tied very closely to arousal systems is the issue of sensation seeking. Do people who are aroused more quickly and easily than others have a different brain chemistry? Sensation seeking is a very important trait in humans, and much work has been carried out over the last twenty years on the identification of this very real aspect of our emotional lives. It turns out that people who are sensation seekers have love patterns different from people who aren't. This fact, more than any other, may link these subtle emotional processes to brain mechanisms active in the process of sexually driven love.

Marvin Zuckerman at the University of Delaware has developed a simple twenty-two-point questionnaire that sorts people into categories of high and low sensation seekers. Examples of the alternatives offered a subject are as follows:

1. A. I prefer people who are calm and even-tempered.
   B. I prefer people who are emotionally expressive even if they are a bit unstable.
2. A. I dislike all body odors.
   B. I like some of the earthy body smells.
3. A. I can't stand riding with a person who likes to speed.
   B. I sometimes like to drive very fast because I find it exciting.

This Sensation Seeking Scale reveals a profile. People who choose the more unsettling of the alternatives tend to be more experimental in their interests. They try drugs, they try hypnosis, they try new and spicy foods. Heterosexuals claim to have much sex and many partners. Married couples say their sexual activities are highly active and varied. All of this seems to suggest that some kind of arousal system is the basis for much of our behavior. The question is whether or not those who seek sensation have different *brain* arousal systems than do non–sensation seekers. Zuckerman claims they do and offers some support for the idea.

Studies of twins show a substantial genetic component in the degree to which a person responds to an arousing sensation. An analysis of over 420 pairs of twins also reveals that the trait is managed by several genes. This evidence for a biological factor is bolstered by an examination of the biochemical profile of the sensation seeker. Sensation seekers have different plasma and cerebrospinal fluid levels of a number of metabolites that are related to dopamine, noradrenaline, and serotonin. In short, these brain chemicals, which appear to be involved in arousal, seem to be altered in the sensation-seeking adult.

This biochemical story has led to the view that sensation seekers suffer from an abnormally low level of arousal, and thus the high–risk behavior that they indulge in is a compensatory activity that allows them to achieve the same level of arousal a non–sensation seeker normally experiences from a far less risky behavior. Several investigators believe that rewards or gratification is reflected in the activity of the neurotransmitter norepinephrine. In this context, risky behavior is viewed as fear provoking in the sensation seeker, which causes greater production of norepinephrine, which in turn produces a gratifying response.

Zuckerman's theory evolved into a frequently advanced idea that the human species seeks to maintain an optimal level of feeling. This optimum is supported by several different arousal systems in the brain that in turn are controlled by several different types of neurotransmitters. These systems operate in delicate balance and, when disturbed, provoke behaviors that try to bring them back to the optimal level. Marked imbalance of the brain systems can produce pathological states, and restoring them to optimum requires outside intervention and pharmacological therapy. The idea has a lot of intuitive appeal and evokes the classic biological principle of homeostasis—a steady state of harmony in the whole bodily system—perhaps the strongest mechanism in living tissue.

The famous Berkeley psychologist David Krech once made the observation, "There is no phenomenon, however complex, which when examined carefully will not turn out to be even more complex." Nowhere is this truer than in studying human emotions and the brain systems that support them. Other researchers have described several problems with the optimum level theory, the rather specific notion that the catecholamine arousal system is crucial for the variety of emotional states it is supposed to support.

Much of the work supporting this idea comes from brain stimulation experiments. It has been known for years that when electrodes are placed in various brain areas of animals, they will stimulate themselves, sometimes to the point of exhaustion. Other studies revealed that these brain areas contain specific neurotransmitters. From this we can infer that certain brain chemicals are active in producing particular states of pleasure (reward). As we have already described, supporting evidence comes from looking at other biochemical markers that in human populations can be obtained from blood, cerebrospinal fluid, urine, and so on. The problem is that after the critical chemicals are identified and then eliminated by various methods from the brain areas thought to be involved, there is no change in the animals' behavior! This negative finding suggests that the reward mechanisms of the brain are highly redundant and one can compensate for another. These findings do not refute the optimum level theory. They merely illustrate how incredibly complex the brain environment is in supporting our psychological states of mind.

Love's Pain

The painful part of passionate love is when it stops abruptly or is never realized. Donald Klein at the New York State Psychiatric Institute has reported that people who are passionately in love secrete a chemical called phenylethylamine, which produces an amphetamine-like high that is interpreted as "being in love." It also has certain addictive qualities, and Klein suggested that when love is spurned, the victim can go into a state of withdrawal, which in a psychological sense becomes the broken heart. He also notes that people in this state of mind frequently crave chocolate, a food that is high in phenylethylamine!

The Inevitability of Companionate Love

Passionate love gradually dwindles down to companionate love, and it comes none too soon for some. Others lament the change, which is best summarized by the cardiologist's rule: if you are middle-aged and have had a heart attack, you may have sex with your wife but not with your mistress! In one study, out of thirty-four male deaths during coitus, twenty-seven of them occurred with mistresses. The arousal level was simply too high.

The end of passionate love finds two kinds of responses. It also happens at a time when the sexual habits of men and women are quite different. Several investigators of sexual patterns, ranging from Kinsey to Masters and Johnson, have shown that for our culture, males start their sexual activity early, at about the age of fifteen. This activity can take the form of actual intercourse or masturbation, and it occurs approximately three times per week until the age of thirty-five, with a peak at the age of thirty. Sexual activity then gradually drops off to about once a week at sixty, and less after that into the seventies and eighties. Females, on the other hand, start slow. Young women rarely masturbate and on the average do not become sexually active until their twenties. Between thirty and forty, females are most active, with sex occurring two times a week. They drop off to less than once a week by the time they reach sixty. Thus, throughout the life span, males are more active.

The intensities of passionate, romantic love, triggered by powerful brain states, evolve into companionate love. Sometimes this change takes place quickly and is almost desired. Professional couples frequently find rewards in their jobs and want a peaceful, tranquil life at home. The problem with this quick move into companionate love is that it is dangerous in the long term. Studies have shown that while wives tend to be very satisfied in the early years of marriage, after twenty years many feel a dramatic loss of love and compatibility. This state of mind increases the likelihood of extramarital affairs, through which a man or woman can rediscover passion. Although Kinsey found that an affair did not increase the chance of divorce unless the spouse found out about it, one study of a wonderful, self-serving response showed that spouses did not believe their extramarital activity contributed to their divorce. At the same time, they felt strongly that their spouse's extramarital affairs did contribute to the divorce!

Love's Pathologies

Love in its simplest and most direct form can be described as someone's psychological reaction to biological arousal by another person. That leaves the question of what the brain's interpreter does when the object of love arousal is physically remote—or even quite theoretical. In such cases, we can observe phenomena that may be either harmless and normal or pathological. Teenagers commonly swoon over movie stars or rock idols and put up their pictures in their rooms. The intensity of feelings about these far-removed characters can be quite remarkable, very real, and perfectly healthy.

In the pathological state, a delusional lover may take on central importance. This response has a variety of forms. It occurs most frequently in women who create a totally phantom lover— someone who does not even exist—or who attach themselves to an image of a strong man they might have met once. In de Clerambault's syndrome, a young woman might imagine that a dominant, delusional lover is actively trying to seduce her. When these symptoms are persistent, the patient is considered schizophrenic. Others experience the delusion recurrently and are not considered mentally ill, although they may be under psychological care. Clearly, developing delusions in response to a strong emotion emitted by a powerful brain mechanism is one way this kind of person makes sense of the strong feelings. It is an extreme response, but it may be the clue that helps us understand the normal mechanisms of self-perceived romantic love.

Love. It is very real at a psychological level, especially for adults. In young children it takes the form of attachment, a strong biological event that is guided by both endogenous factors and rewards and punishments coming from external sources. Only at a later age does the child interpret the attachment as love. Romantic love, on the other hand, appears to be initially fueled by an interpretation of aroused brain states. What triggers the arousal?

The brain's arousal system is influenced by a number of factors. The issue for humans is: why does person A become aroused and person B does not? This, of course, postulates that arousal comes first and the interpreter follows. Joseph Le Doux, who has been fascinated with this problem for years, has recently shown in work with animals that stimuli—which is to say, images—from the outside world are analyzed apart from conscious awareness. Depending on the outcome of that analysis, arousal does or does not take place. The analysis calls upon old memories buried deep in the brain, certain genetic factors, and most likely many other elements. Once the arousal is triggered, the interpretative brain takes over. Le Doux has actually traced brain circuits that are crucial for triggering this kind of arousal. He can lesion them and his animals no longer are aroused by certain stimuli. In short, neuroscience is in hot pursuit of the brain mechanisms of our subtle emotional life. But to dissect thus in no way diminishes our appreciation of the state of mind we call being in love.

10

Sleeping and Dreaming

If ever there was an easy-to-identify altered state of consciousness, it is sleep. This unique brain state produces richly different mind states called dreams, psychological events that have always fascinated mankind. Scientists have tried to explain the sleep state, to analyze it, bringing to bear all the modern techniques of electrical and chemical analysis, and yet sleep remains deeply mysterious. Why the body needs sleep is still not known. Most studies simply report the various physical changes that correlate with the sleep state. Yet sleep holds the key to many other insights. We dream when we sleep, and dreaming is crucial for humans and is presumed to be just as important for animals. When prevented from sleeping, people can die; animals do die. "To sleep, perchance to dream" is a set of processes that give the researcher a view of how our brain and mind unite to form powerful interactions, where psychological states guide brain states and vice versa. Let's start by considering the brain state of sleep.

Types of Sleep

Much of what is known about sleep in humans is largely credited to William Dement and Nathaniel Klietman, who in the late fifties described two distinct stages of sleep. Their basic research tool was the electroencephalogram (EEG), the record of brain activity as summarized by an array of electrodes placed on the skull that are sensitive to small electrical potentials of the underlying brain tissue. Dement and Klietman noted that during one stage of sleep rapid eye movements (REM) occur. This stage has come to be known as REM sleep. REM sleep takes place every ninety minutes during the normal sleep cycle. These eye movements appear in the context of massive physiological change. As the EEG shows, brain waves slow down, heart rate increases, blood pressure drops, muscles (except those in the eye) lose their tone, body temperature tends to match the temperature of the surrounding environment, snoring stops, and all gastrointestinal movement ceases. Additionally, in males REM sleep commonly results in penile erection, a response that occurs in infancy and on into senility. (Even though the erection is not associated with sex-oriented dreams, its presence can frequently help sex therapists to determine whether impotence is physical or psychological.)

There are obviously some major biological processes kicking into action during REM sleep. Yet no one knows exactly how or why the brain shifts into this state. And it is during this state of suspended animation, with heart racing and body unable to move, that we dream our most vivid dreams. REM sleep is important for something, but it remains difficult to say what. Michel Jouvet, a noted French researcher, believes that clues can come from animal studies.

For Jouvet, REM sleep is the period during the day when behavioral patterns needed for survival are rehearsed. He observed that monkeys as well as cats, dogs, rodents, and other warm-blooded animals all had sleep patterns and EEG activity that resembled those seen in humans. He also noted that cold-blooded animals, such as reptiles and snakes, did not have such patterns. In searching for an explanation for what this all meant, he found that destroying the locus ceruleus, a part of the brain of warm-blooded animals, prevented the motor inhibition during REM sleep and unmasked amazing behaviors peculiar to each species. He reasoned that the animal equivalent of the human dream state was a rehearsal of essential, genetically driven response patterns such as those used by the animal in fight or flight responses. Animals when awake are able to carry out such patterns smoothly because they have been carefully rehearsed during REM sleep. Because REM patterns are not seen in cold-blooded animals, Jouvet felt that REM sleep is a late arrival in evolution and somehow relates to important psychological and behavioral functions. Whether or not this explanation is correct, it gets high marks for inventiveness.

The other sleep state is called non-REM sleep. REM, or stage 1, sleep is interspersed between non-REM sleep intervals several times each night. The non-REM phase consists of three different stages. This overall phase of sleep is at its deepest stage at the beginning of the sleep cycle. As the night progresses, the REM periods of sleep become longer. However, non-REM sleep continues to interrupt the REM mode and makes up about 75 percent of the total time spent in sleep. About 50 percent is spent in what is called stage 2 sleep, and the rest of the time is spent in the deeper stages of sleep, stages 3 and 4, which are referred to as slow wave sleep because of the kind of electrical activity the brain produces during this time.

Non-REM sleep has not been studied as much as REM sleep, and some researchers don't think it is as important as REM sleep when considering mental phenomena such as dreaming. However, several findings suggest that dreaming can occur during both phases of sleep. Although it is true that most people say they have dreamed only when awakened during REM sleep, some 15 to 20 percent report dreams during non-REM periods. Moreover, people may underreport their dreams during non-REM sleep only because their memory system is not working well during that phase. Sleepwalking, anxiety attacks, and night terror also occur more often during these slow wave states of sleep. Here again, the episodes are usually not remembered the next day. There can be little doubt that the brain is rich with mental activity during all phases of sleep.

These observations on sleep patterns amount to no more than a description of brain activity during sleep. They offer no insights into what sleep is and why we need it. Furthermore, no explanation is offered for how the different electrical patterns reflect underlying brain chemistry. Indeed, measures of the brain's metabolic activity during sleep have revealed only that brain metabolism is above normal during REM sleep and slightly below normal in non-REM sleep. Overall metabolic activity in the brain changes very little during sleep. At first pass, it is hard to think the brain needs sleep to rest and conserve energy when metabolism remains so high.

Life Cycles, Sleep Cycles

The human sleep cycle changes during childhood and with age. Awareness of the changes and the importance of sleep comes to most of us during our early parental years. Babies need much sleep, but they take it in a damnable pattern! Babies can sleep up to twenty hours a day, whereas a four-year-old needs only nine to ten hours. During the first year of life, there is a high degree of REM sleep—approximately 80 percent of total sleep time—which quickly drops to about 35 percent by the age of two. This dramatic change is thought to reflect maturing brain systems, particularly parts of the cortex that are adding their neural sheaths during this period—a process called mylinization, which is very active during the first two years of life and is presumed to make communication among neurons more efficient. Why REM sleep would contribute to that process is not clear. Nonetheless, by young adulthood, the need for sleep drops to an average of seven or eight hours, with REM occupying only 25 percent of the time. Sleep time remains at that level throughout most of the rest of life. After the age of sixty there is a further slight drop. More important, aspects of non-REM sleep drop way off and sometimes disappear; the decline of this phase of sleep correlates with an increase in the number of spontaneous awakenings that occur in the elderly.

But sleep statistics are only averages. Individuals vary tremendously in their need to sleep. Some active people need only four to six hours a day throughout their lives, while others need closer to nine hours. Studies have noted that those needing less sleep show no drowsiness or fatigue during the day. Their brain and body must somehow be different, but no one knows in what way.

Sleep Cycles, Body Cycles

Sleep is part of a cycle, a circadian rhythm. Everything from algae to humans functions on a twenty-four-hour clock. There are several bodily functions that tend to move together, such as body temperature and the secretion of urine and cortisol. It has been observed that when the sleep cycle is extended to thirty-three hours, these other bodily rhythms do not change. In fact, while humans have clicked into the twenty-four-hour cycle, the more natural one is twenty-five hours, which is still manifested in some people. It is not known why people, when removed from all the cultural cues to keep on a twenty-four-hour cycle, prefer a twenty-five-hour cycle.

Since most sleepers are on the twenty-four-hour cycle, the twenty-five-hour tendency was discovered by placing people in a windowless room in which no cues for daylight and darkness or other markers of time were available. When living in this kind of environment, people will tend to go to sleep and get up one hour later each day. Some people living in their everyday environment keep to this natural twenty-five-hour cycle and seem unable to change to the twenty-four-hour cycle, even though they are out of sync with everybody else. This inability can be very disruptive, and such people are hard pressed to maintain a nine-to-five job. Every day their wakeful cycle notches forward, leaving them more and more dazed as they try to fit into the established twenty-four-hour sleep/wake cycle.

The discovery that a sleep/wake cycle is maintained even in the absence of light still leaves open the questions about how brain mechanisms in most people link the sleep/wake cycle to the light/dark cycle. It turns out there is a small structure at the base of the brain called the suprachiasmatic nucleus (SCN), and it receives some information directly from the eye. When this structure is destroyed in animals, the twenty-four-hour cycle drifts away from being locked into the light/dark cycle, just as it does when animals are reared in environments with constant illumination. Other studies have shown that when a radioactive metabolic tracer or marker is given to normal animals, their SCN shows metabolic action during sleep but not during waking hours, thereby suggesting it is very active during the sleep cycle. Taken together, these results hint that something very important occurs in the SCN that helps guide this grand cycle of sleep and wakefulness.

In a related set of observations, it was found that most blind people run on the twenty-five-hour cycle, just as do subjects in constant-illumination experiments. Presumably, their SCN is not getting the critical input needed to synchronize them to the light/dark cycle.

These rhythms play an important role in our overall health. Consider a graphic example of how cycles have an overriding influence on body states. When rats were given a poison, *E. coli* endotoxin, at three in the afternoon, 85 percent died. When the same dose was given at midnight, only 4 percent died! In other experiments, mice exposed to loud noises at one time of the day experienced fatal convulsions, while at another no ill effects were observed. In humans, there can be a 30 percent difference in blood pressure between day and night. In some cases of hypertension, a patient standing up at seven in the morning will faint. The same act at three in the afternoon will produce no strain. Likewise, a medication appropriate for the morning could be disastrous at night. Even though these differences are well documented, modern medical practice tends to ignore such considerations when prescribing drugs. Doctors maintain that it is hard enough to get patients to take their drugs daily.

Theories of Sleep

The main theory until the time of Dement and Klietman's work was that the brain fell into sleep passively. This notion, derived from European research, held that sleep resulted from lack of stimulation. But later experiments radically changed this concept of sleep as a more neuroscientific approach was adopted.

The stimulation story starts in Belgium, where Frederic Bremer first studied cats whose cortex was disconnected from the rest of the brain. Bremer, one of the pioneers of modern brain research, made his lesions by simply sectioning the brain through the midbrain, which sits on top of the spinal cord. This surgery left the cortex intact with all major blood supplies and body chemicals, but severed *all* peripheral neural inputs. These cats slept chronically. Nothing woke them up. He then took another group of cats and made the same brain lesion but a bit lower, thereby allowing sensory input into the cortex. This group of cats now had a normal sleep/wake cycle. He then cut the peripheral nerves that provided the sensory input these cats had access to, and quickly they, like the others, slipped into chronic sleep. This work provided strong support for the claim that sleep occurs from lack of outside sensory stimulation.

Several Italian researchers didn't believe the conclusion of these studies, probably because they realized that one can sleep in Rome even though all hell can be breaking loose at all hours outside the window. Giuseppe Moruzzi, who worked for years in a beautiful garden laboratory in Pisa, refined the size and location of the disconnecting lesions first made in Belgium. This was an important and crucial advance. Working with an American, Horace Magoun, he discovered that it was not the interruption of the sensory fibers from the eyes, ears, and skin surface that prevented arousal. Rather, Bremer's large lesion had also interfered with another structure called the reticular formation, and that produced problems for arousal. The reticular formation is more in the midline of the brainstem, and it feeds fibers up and throughout the entire cortex. When it alone was surgically lesioned, sparing the sensory inputs, the kind of stupor and sleep patterns seen in the much larger lesions made by Bremer resulted. The Italian research refined Bremer's original and seminal observations, and a new structure that was crucial for understanding sleep mechanisms was identified.

There was other evidence against the lack-of-stimulation theory. Using techniques different from those adopted by Bremer and Moruzzi, other scientists demonstrated that stimuli from the periphery did make their way to the brain during sleep. Using sensitive electrical recording procedures, they easily showed that sensory stimuli could still evoke responses in the sleeping brain's neurons. In addition, they noted that during sleep messages were getting to the motor neurons descending into the spinal cord. This output to the spinal cord does not result in body movement because, as clever researchers also discovered, the messages are inhibited by yet another brain system before they actually reach the peripheral muscles. When all of this is considered together, it is clear that the brain remains active in sleep and does not fall into sleep for lack of stimulation.

Moruzzi went on to show that the reticular formation was divided into two different functional regions. One region was very active in controlling wakefulness and another in inducing sleep. The latter area was the raphe nucleus. When it is lesioned in animals, they go into perpetual sleep. It is loaded with cells that use serotonin, and it was first thought that this neurotransmitter was the critical chemical for inducing sleep.

The serotonin assumption was quickly challenged. Drugs that were thought to inhibit the production of serotonin were given to animals, but they experienced only a transient insomnia and then restabilized. How could this be? Scientists originally hoped that one neuron produced one transmitter that served one function. According to this view, interruptions in the production or functioning of a transmitter should induce a specific loss of brain function. In recent years, this theory has fallen by the wayside with the realization that neurons can manufacture several neurotransmitters. Blocking the production of one does not necessarily mean the neuron will not function. Clearly, in these sleep experiments, the raphe nucleus continued to operate even though its serotonin system had been disrupted.

This work with the reticular formation provided an accurate description of the brain structures controlling the induction of sleep and wakefulness. Stimulate one structure and we wake up; stimulate another and sleep returns. But what biological mechanism triggers these brain structures into action?

Curiously, the idea Aristotle proposed, that sleep was somehow related to circulating nutrients, remains one of the more credible theories about what induces sleep. Results of recent experiments strongly suggest that there is a sleep–promoting substance. Scientists took extracts of blood or urine or cerebrospinal fluid from sleeping animals and injected them into wakeful animals. Of the several substances they found that induced either drowsiness or sleep, one in particular, a small protein called delta sleep–inducing peptide (DSIP), for a while looked like an extremely powerful sleep inducer. Yet other factors have been discovered that have several other effects on body physiology, suggesting that none of their actions is specific for sleep. In short, the hunt continues for a single substance that may trigger sleep.

In contrast to the theory of a sleep-promoting substance, other scientists argue that a genetic mechanism in the brain cells of sleep structures such as the reticular formation spontaneously turns on and drives the cells to action. This theory provides a way to explain the strong effects of sleep on bodily rhythms. The idea here is that to search for substances that regulate such brain structures as the raphe nucleus is fruitless. The regulation of these structures is under a genetic time clock within the nerve cells of the brain areas involved. With this view, there are no Aristotelian circulating nutrients, whether they are called DSIP or anything else.

The Why of Sleep

Why do we need sleep? There is no doubt about the need. Sleep-deprived humans quickly begin to hallucinate, become depressed, and after prolonged periods of time lose their ability to carry out any kind of mental function. Sleep deprivation can also cause death. In animal studies, rats that were kept awake developed emphysema and heart problems, and eventually died. Clearly, sleep is needed for something.

At present, the best explanation comes from the intuitive thought that during sleep the body, brain, and mind repair themselves in some way. This idea, called the restorative hypothesis, has been advanced for centuries and has much support. Moruzzi, one of the pioneers of modern sleep research, believed in the idea, although he felt that most of the restoration is for the brain, not the body, and for only those parts of the brain that are active in learning and remembering. This claim fits with dozens of studies that show memory mechanisms are critically affected by sleep. Information learned before going to sleep is retained better than information learned after waking up. Sleep somehow prevents interference with the storage of information for long-term use. More exacting studies have been carried out in animal research. Rats were trained to perform a simple task, and the amount of their REM sleep was recorded after each practice session. While the animals were learning, there was an increase of REM episodes, but as the rats mastered the task, their REM returned to normal levels. Further, as already mentioned, when the rats were deprived of REM sleep afterward, their learning was much impaired. Something very important happens during the REM phase of sleep that seriously affects our ability to remember.

More recent yet related ideas concerning why we sleep have come from none other than Francis Crick, the Nobel laureate and co-discoverer of DNA. As one of the first efforts in his newly adopted field of neuroscience, Crick proposed that sleep represents the time when the brain unlearns all of the preceding day's erroneous information. He reasoned that a vast number of episodes occur each day, and the mind makes spurious correlations between their causes and effects. These are dropped by the wayside during sleep. Since newborns would make more of these kinds of associations, they would require more sleep, as is the case. However, Crick's theory leaves many unresolved issues. His model, for example, does not account for why spurious correlations made before one goes to sleep are more accurately remembered than others made during the day.

Additional support for the restorative hypothesis comes from investigators who feel that sleep is a time for regeneration of the whole organism, and much of what is accomplished for the organism during sleep happens in the body in general. Sleep, in this view, is secondary to other, more important events. Ian Oswald, for example, argues that during sleep there is a tremendous amount of tissue restoration going on. In all mammals, there is more brain protein synthesis and body cell duplication during sleep. These are obviously crucial activities for good health. In humans, more of our critically needed amino acids are secreted in urine during our waking hours than during sleep. Also, when a mammal is deprived of sleep, the body makes a shift to destructive metabolism, a process that expends cellular energy reserves. However, during sleep there is a greater secretion of growth hormones—corticosteroids—substances that lead to constructive metabolism. Interestingly, people who go on severe diets begin to sleep more, perhaps an attempt by the body to help conserve proteins.

Sleep Disorders

What does it mean to sleep abnormally? Americans request twenty-one million prescriptions for sleeping pills a year. Yet the insomniac functions perfectly normally during the day. At the same time, the sudden onset of insomnia may well reflect something wrong with the body or mind, and that kind of insomnia can be treated. However, it should be kept in mind that people are somewhat prone to exaggerate incidents of insomnia, often overreporting rather slight sleeping problems. Insomniacs frequently overestimate how long it took them to fall asleep. They tend to attribute certain of their everyday problems to lack of sleep, when in fact they always have been light sleepers. In this regard, some experts assert that insomniacs are born, not made. Careful clinical histories reveal that insomniacs were never good sleepers, even in childhood. This finding suggests that the factors regulating the sleep and wake centers in the brain may be overly sensitive to outside stimulus. But most important, especially in light of the restorative hypothesis, which suggests that sleep is a necessity rather than an option, insomniacs do sleep. It is the pattern of their sleep that is erratic.

A very common occurrence with aging is the development of sleep apnea, a condition in which the sleeper stops breathing. It can last for fifteen to thirty seconds, and during that time there is a change in the levels of oxygen and carbon dioxide in the blood, which ultimately shocks the person awake. He takes a massive gulp of air to charge the lungs with oxygen once again and quickly returns to sleep, largely unaware of the entire event. Sleep apnea starts after the age of forty, and, remarkably enough, it can occur hundreds of times per night, and the only person who may be aware of it is a sleeping partner. It is a startling sensation, and some have suggested that the brain mechanism, which must somehow be suppressing the respiratory response, may also be the one that goes awry in sudden infant death syndrome.

Of course, a host of factors can affect sleep. Jet travel to other time zones can be very disruptive to body time. Too much alcohol or drugs or stress or whatever can play a role in disrupting normal slumber. When these are ruled out as causes of sleep disturbance, the more serious problem of mental illness emerges. Depression and, for older people, dementia can both be very disruptive to sleep. Sleep changes in these severe forms deserve medical attention. In short, an abnormal sleep pattern is one of the brain's wonderful signals that things are not quite right.

Dreams and the Mind

Now we know that the mind is not asleep during bodily sleep. It seems active indeed, and at last we come to its product, dreams. Dreams are powerful images in our lives, and most of us believe dreams have changed what we do and who we think we are. Robert Louis Stevenson said that the plot of *Dr. Jekyll and Mr. Hyde* occurred to him during a dream. The dream state seems to offer a window into our mental lives. But does it? Or do dreams simply represent the random collision of memories activated by chance during sleep even though the interpreter tries to attach a meaning to them? In short, if three truly unrelated facts come into our sleep consciousness, the interpreter's attempt to make sense out of them might well produce the kinds of bizarre images we frequently experience when dreaming.

Freud, with his typical genius for describing a plausible reason for a mental state, welded certain concepts into the Western mind that may or may not be true. As with so many of Freud's ideas, an assumption is made that there is something in our personal life history that is out to get us. Freud believed that dreams were hidden anxieties or desires slipped into consciousness. He maintained that dreams had a manifest content (the actual content) and a latent content (the true psychological content). Something called dream work transformed the one into the other. Freud believed this was necessary because the raw message might be unbearable for the sleeper. In nightmares, Freud maintained, the manifest content is not sufficiently transformed, with the result that the sleeper springs awake in horror. However, Freud believed the purpose of the everyday dream was to realize some instinctive impulse, to have what he called wish fulfillment. For Freud, dreams exist because they must.

The modern analysis of dreams points to a less metaphorical hypothesis. First, although dreams that are high in visual content occur during REM sleep, other dreams take place during non-REM sleep. What is interesting is the difference between the kinds of dreams that occur during these two phases. The frequent, REM dreams are violent, emotional, and vivid. The less frequent, non-REM dreams tend to be rational, less vivid and visual, and more pleasant. In one study of over ten thousand dreams, researchers ascertained that of most dreams that were recalled, 64 percent were associated with sadness, fear, or apprehension. Only 18 percent were happy and pleasant, and a meager 1 percent dealt with sexual feelings—percentages that are consistent with the frequency of dreaming during the two main phases of sleep.

Other facts about our dreams are useful to consider. It turns out that blind people do not have visual dreams. Theirs are filled with auditory images. Additionally, people slowly losing their sight gradually lose the visual quality of their dreams! This suggests that either visual systems in the brain participate in dream formation or what we dream about is closely related to the previous day's experiences. If those experiences are encoded visually, and most are, they appear in our dreams. If vision is not available, the mind's natural strategy is to use auditory images, as the blind do.

Dreams reflect long-term brain activities and represent ongoing interpretations of the events being entered into sleep consciousness. Dreams are not reconstructed at the last moment before waking up. They also are susceptible to learning patterns that can be established to control them. In one study, a therapist took patients who had particular recurring but unpleasant dreams and helped them learn how to change the discomforting endings. A woman, for example, kept dreaming of meeting her ex-husband, and as they were about to kiss and make up, she would suddenly wake. Through a simple conditioning paradigm in a sleep lab, this patient was awakened during a REM stage and told to change her dream. After many such trials, she—like many other similarly trained patients—reported that the dreams ended in a more positive way: she introduced her ex-husband to her new husband!

Children's dreams are largely pleasant and develop in predictable ways. At first, children do not understand what is being asked about when queried about their dreams. In a second stage, they believe their dreams are as real as life and expect that a visitor to their bedroom would be able to witness the dreams. Later on, they realize that a dream is an imaginary event. Finally, they arrive at the adult perception that dreams are a part of our mental life. This sequence demonstrates how mental functions develop in the child. The interpreter, the hypothesis-generating system of our mind, is gradually liberating itself from the purely personal, egocentric view of the world. The distinction between private notions and public theories of the world comes slowly for the child. Apparently, this is also reflected in the perception of their dreams.

When research on the brain's arousal systems is considered together with the mental phenomenon of dreams, we once again see how the interpreter constructs a theory to explain changing brain states. The arousal system appears to activate memories. These memories may reflect current concerns or simply the most memorable events of the preceding days. They appear in sleep consciousness in no particular order. If the sequence of memories is sensible, a simple hypothesis is generated to explain their presence. If the order is jumbled and compounded with unrelated thoughts or concerns, the resulting hypothesis or dream is bizarre. This view goes a long way to explain the content of dreams. And, once again, we see how mind and brain are intertwined.

Sleep is wonderfully rewarding. When all is well with life, it is usually a time for pleasant dreams and a time when restorative activities of some hard-to-define kind are going on in the brain. When someone's sleep pattern begins to change, it is a pretty good sign of possible psychological problems. If left unattended, these disturbances can grow into major illnesses. As will be seen in subsequent chapters, an overaroused system—which is to say, a brain that is not sleeping—can influence the immune system, with consequences for the capacity to heal. Likewise, the underaroused system that accompanies sleepiness can also affect immunity. Sleep reflects brain states and needs that in turn reflect mind states. It is like an indicator light on a control panel: if it lights up, check out why.

11

Stress

A few years back, the problem of persistent stress on the job was in the news as the reason why air traffic controllers should be paid more money. It was an appealing idea, and it seemed to make sense. Their job appears intricate and fatiguing, and if they make a mistake hundreds of people can die. There was only one fault with the argument: air traffic controllers from other countries did not complain of stress. Either the concept of stress was being misused by those union officials who were interested only in promoting better wages, or stress occurred as a result of the controllers' personal, cultural, and psychological view of the world.

Then there is the case of the overworked executive, perceived by others to be burdened with the well-being of his company, not to mention his responsibility to his stockholders, wife, kids, and dog. "Don't bother Mr. Smith. He's very stressed today." Actually, Mr. Smith is quite happy and thriving doing what he likes to do, but he finds it convenient to let people think he is overworked and under pressure. He is therefore left alone, and others around him work harder to help relieve his condition. Here we have the concept of stress as a social tool.

The use and misuse of the concept of stress should not mask

the awful truth that true psychological stress abounds. Consider the disintegrating marriage, where one spouse has taken a definite dislike to the other, or it's mutual. Necessity dictates that they still live together for reasons of religious belief or money or indecision. Every time spouse A says something, it grates on spouse B, and B's blood pressure goes up. Locked into the relationship, they let the back-and-forth irritation build, and with each day the body experiences greater stress.

Or, a mother is pregnant and the husband is not supportive. The other children are being difficult. The husband announces he has been fired with only two weeks' severance pay. The mother's father calls with the news that his wife has fallen very ill. This bad situation continues for months during the woman's pregnancy. She has taken a college course in psychology and learned that when female rats are put under stress during their gestation period, there is a pronounced effect on the gender of her offspring, with male rats becoming feminized and females behaving more like males. Could the pregnant woman be adversely influencing her child's whole life? A friend agrees that might be the case, and she adds this idea to her bubbling stew of stress.

Stress is one of the most abused yet important topics in public health. Attention to stress levels is fundamental to good health management, since stress is a very real bodily state and influences everything from our memory capacity to our weight and to our ability to fight off disease. When it is too severe it can be deadly. At the same time, it is also important to realize that stress can help as well as harm us. Stress can be a life saver.

The reality of stress is as follows. An event perceived as threatening occurs. The event can be external or internal. Sheer physical exertion (internal) can elicit the stress, as can a trying argument with the boss (external). Whatever the trigger, it sets off a complex response that involves more than fourteen hundred physiochemical reactions in the brain and body, and all of these changes are mainly orchestrated through two main systems managed by the brain: the autonomic nervous system and the neuroendocrine system of our body.

The Autonomic Nervous System

The autonomic nervous system functions largely outside conscious control. What that means is that once triggered to action by either conscious or unconscious processes, it runs by its own set of rules, uninfluenced by the conscious mind or simple rules of learning. More specifically, current knowledge suggests that both conscious and unconscious processes have their effect on the autonomic response through the hypothalamus, a small, powerful brain structure that sits at the base of the brain and receives messages from any of a number of "higher" brain structures. The hypothalamus has direct neural connections to the sympathetic and parasympathetic nervous systems, which are best thought of as a network of fibers that innervate most of our bodily organs and allow for response. The two aspects of the autonomic nervous system work to keep bodily organs under a dual control, ready for extreme action (sympathetic) and also for restoration (parasympathetic). Consider the heart's response to stress.

The sympathetic system, using the neurotransmitter noradrenaline, sets the heart up for harder work. The cardiac muscle finds noradrenaline a stimulant, and with the heart working harder, the body is ready for greater exertion. But before the heart runs away with itself, the parasympathetic system begins to modulate the cardiac muscle by secreting the neurotransmitter acetylcholine, which causes the heart to decrease its rate of response. These tradeoffs, which are critical for pacing a muscle system, are managed by neurons in the hypothalamus, which in turn is subject to a wide variety of influences. The hypothalamus is the brain's and mind's gateway to bodily health.

The Hypothalamus and Hormones

The hypothalamus is exquisitely sensitive, and it mediates dozens of influences on the other messages it ultimately sends out to the heart and other organs. For example, it also controls the release of hormones, which exert influences that ultimately feed back to it. The hypothalamus is, then, the brain connection for hormones produced in the body, and it constitutes the second major axis of overall bodily response during stress. Both these response mechanisms, the hormonal system and the autonomic nervous system, are excellent illustrations of how mind states might well affect health states.

When the body is under stress, the sympathetic nervous system, controlled by the hypothalamus, is called into action. Upon activation by this system, the adrenal gland secretes adrenaline, and the blood quickly distributes this powerful stimulant. This hormone also feeds back to the hypothalamus and tells it to keep sending down signals for continued secretion. Meanwhile, however, as if the body had read Montaigne's essay *On Moderation,* the hypothalamus has also sent out a signal to the pituitary gland to release yet another chemical, ACTH. This substance travels down to a different part of the adrenal gland and commands it to secrete another hormone, cortisol. Cortisol feeds back to the pituitary and to the hypothalamus, telling it to shut off all of the stimulant activity, thus providing the negative feedback needed to keep things in control. The hypothalamus, receiving these messages, somehow decides which to believe and how much stimulation should be sent out to provide an active response. It is the consummate dispatcher.

To some extent, the overall objective of this intricate biological circuit is to produce cortisol, the body's own wonder drug. Cortisol prepares the body for major action by altering how it will metabolize its resources. If stress has been precipitated by danger—say, a sudden challenge to personal safety like a hiking accident—there will not be time to eat before coping with the problem at hand. Under such circumstances, it is crucial to raise the glucose level in the blood in order to provide an energy source for the brain. Cortisol offers immeasurable help in the task of feeding the body and brain. It prevents glucose from being taken up by bodily tissues when it is required by the brain. It also breaks down protein into amino acids, which are the chemical elements needed for tissue repair if injury should occur. It increases blood pressure in certain vessels that for some mysterious reason is momentarily low—a condition that always follows the onset of stress—and thereby restores the system to a good functional level. In short, cortisol is the bugler that alerts the body for action. It is also an easy chemical to detect in blood and therefore serves as a good measure of the level of stress being experienced under different test conditions.

In one study, parachute trainees from the Norwegian air force were examined for stress. Their cortisol level prior to their first jump was extremely high. Once the activity became familiar, the stress response dramatically changed. For the second jump, there was no increase in cortisol level. In other studies, far less threatening events are shown to trigger the cortisol response; all it takes for some people is to get on an airplane. The stress, as measured by cortisol release, is extremely sensitive to psychological states. The connection between mind and body is never more tangible than at this junction.

Stress starts to take its toll when cortisol levels shoot up constantly and remain high. That brings on chronic high blood pressure, which is bad; protein imbalance, which is also bad; and an inhibition of the immune response, which is even worse. After extreme stress, the body is so vulnerable from all of these changes in normal metabolic activity that in some situations it cannot respond to simple infections, and death can ensue with frightening speed. Clearly, life situations leading to chronic states of stress should be avoided.

Genes and Stress: The Forgotten Story

The place of stress in our overall health is a vexed issue further complicated by the fact that susceptibility to disease has a large genetic component. That is to say, when stress is cited as the cause of an illness, it may not be the cause at all: the individual's genetic makeup may predispose him to a disease, and the environmental factors generally blamed may actually play little or no role in producing the illness. This fact, revealed by the work of behavioral geneticists, is just now beginning to gain acceptance.

There is little disagreement that susceptibility to disease varies with the individual. When a large number of people are exposed to an infectious bug of some kind, most of them remain asymptomatic while others have either mild or severe reactions. Their response may well relate to their state of stress. For example, we now know that a wide variety of life stressors—divorce, death, loss of job, or moving residence—all lead to a higher incidence of medical problems.

At the same time, the extent to which the body responds to stressors could be largely genetically determined. Once again, researchers have turned to identical twins to look for answers. Identical twins display a high concordance rate (36 percent) for falling victim to a disease organism, such as the polio virus, when it is introduced into their environment. Fraternal twins, however, show a far lower concordance rate (6 percent).

Stress, we are constantly warned, can lead to heart disease. But the facts—as they now emerge from studies in behavioral genetics—are beginning to paint a more complex picture. The genetic issues are best illustrated by the fact that the concordance rate for coronary disease is higher for identical twins than for fraternal twins. Yet the high rate in identical twins cannot easily be explained by such commonly attributed factors as high blood pressure, high serum cholesterol, or smoking habits. In one study, the identical twins who were concordant for the heart disease were discordant for these disposing factors. The genetic factor is powerful and must always be taken into account when considering how environmental stressors affect somatic systems such as the heart. The same story holds for other diseases: ulcers, asthma, and colitis.

Stress, Thinking, and Memory

The impact of stress on bodily organs and general health is by now both evident and generally accepted. Not so commonly recognized, however, are the profound effects of stress on our thought and memory processes. A vast amount of research on the topic of stress and cognitive efficiency—better known as our capacity to think—has been summarized by the psychologist Allan Baddeley of Cambridge University. He observes that stress produced by dangerous situations influences the attentional system by severely limiting its breadth. The arousal that accompanies stress narrowly focuses a person's attention on the one aspect of a situation perceived by him to be the most important. If stress is triggered when he is doing something he believes important, his efficiency in that activity will improve. There have been dozens of studies, and each makes this same general point. Stress, even stress with aspects of danger, does not, contrary to many popular views, impair performance of tasks. Thus, if in fact American air traffic controllers are under stress, they might not attend as well to irrelevant conversations going on around them, but they ought to perform better their central task of directing air traffic.

At the same time, these studies showed that if an activity carried out under stress is viewed as unimportant, performance of the task will be impaired. From this it would appear that when under stress, people fall back on a priority of values, and those activities which they consider more important get the most, or perhaps more accurately, the remaining, attention.

This can be dangerous. Suppose a tank commander is rolling along what he thinks is a quiet road and is suddenly fired upon. If he thinks praying is more important than attending to his guns, he will let his stress response direct him to the wrong means for survival. He will desert his present priorities for others that may not be useful in the immediate situation.

Facing a novel experience and thinking clearly about it, however, is a different matter. Here one doesn't have the advantage of practice. Problem solving in a new crisis situation may depend on summoning information that one has never put to use before. Thus, in such real life situations as rescue operations, a novice can perform very badly because of stress. Feeling the strong urge to help, he abandons considering the obvious danger and leaps in, frequently at the cost of his own life. The novice who is not under stress will view an identical scene with caution and figure out how to help in a much more reasonable manner. As a consequence, professional rescue workers learn to size up fearful situations in a systematic way so their attention does not become too focused on the person needing help. Their ability to control their own heroic urge is drilled into them during training by exposure to every conceivable rescue problem and by practice in recalling all pertinent information in dangerous, stressful situations. That is, stress plus good training can equal optimal efficiency.

When the aroused state impairs our ability to attend to the relevant matters at hand, we are handicapped according to the same concept of resource use discussed in the chapter on memory. The brain and the psychological system have limited resources—that is, limited energy. With arousal, the emotional state of fear takes up many of these resources, leaving fewer to be dispensed for other important functions such as scanning the environment for important data and thinking clearly. We humans do not have infinite capacity for taking in all things simultaneously. Performing one task interferes with another. The task can be either emotional or cognitive.

The effect stress has on memory may also be attributed to attentional difficulties. Not only is our ability to recall greatly impaired when we are under stress; our memory for events experienced under stress is also undermined, since, as we have just noted, stress focuses the mind on particular activities. As a consequence, under stress we should remember important activities better than unimportant ones, but the difference should be much less in nonstressful situations. That is exactly what occurs. Particular aspects of a fearful event become imprinted in the mind and sometimes haunt the victim for years. Other aspects of a fearful situation go completely unnoticed.

Some memories of stressful situations are incredibly durable. Recent research to find which brain structures respond to the hormones released during stress may explain this durability. It is now known that the hippocampus, which transfers information from short-term to long-term memory, is loaded with cells containing cortisol receptors. It may be that the hippocampus becomes highly activated in response to the cortisol arriving through the blood. Thus, it becomes especially efficient and welds into memory information that was being processed at the time of a stressful event. In this way, a person would remember what he was doing when he heard the news of President Kennedy's assassination. At the moment he found out about it, his hippocampus was processing information that dealt with his current surroundings. With the surge of stress, facts of that environment were indelibly written in the brain.

Avoiding Stress

The physiological mechanisms that produce stress are obviously delicate. If one factor in the complex bodily network that links neurons, hormones, and the mind is perturbed, the change ricochets throughout the system. One of the goals of psychological research has been to determine the factors that can lead to stress. Psychologists interested in this approach have tried to alter patterns of behavior that give rise to harmful stress, for once triggered, it is difficult to control. This research differs from other kinds of psychological studies that try to determine what to do about the stress response. The former centers on how to change one's mental attitudes so as not to trigger stress in the first place.

A key concept in the business of stress production is control. Animals and people are particularly prone to stress when they can't—or think they can't—control their immediate environment. In animal experiments, for example, two groups of rats are exposed to random shocks. One group can terminate the shocks by turning a wheel, while the other group can do nothing about them. The test cages are rigged in such a way that both groups receive exactly the same shock. Nonetheless, the studies showed that the animals that could control the shock were far better off. They developed stomach ulcers at a slower rate than the group without control.

It's easy to see how this animal model can be applied to human situations. Middle-management executives, for example, should suffer from more stress than top management, since middle managers may be powerless to solve a problem or alleviate discomfort. At the same time, top executives faced with a similar problem have the authority to change the environment and should feel less stressful. In fact, studies of organizations show this to be the case.

With findings like this in the professional literature, it is no wonder the government saw the need to monitor the psychological aspects of the workplace. Before that, in 1970, the controversial Occupational Safety and Health Administration (OSHA) was established to protect workers performing physically dangerous jobs. The National Institute of Occupational Safety and Health gave out grants to study problems in the area of mental stress.

Individual Variation in Response to Stressors

People vary tremendously in their response to stressful situations. Some people emerge unscathed after a horrendous experience such as war or after watching ten Jerry Lewis films in a row. One cannot measure stress by simply assessing the stimulus or event in and of itself. The extent of stress depends on how each adverse experience is interpreted by each individual. Much of our understanding of stress comes from trying to decipher these intervening psychological variables.

One of the variables that emerge from recent research is the distinction between constructive and destructive stress. Constructive stress is the kind that comes when a particular situation is viewed as a challenge, and the individual perceives a potential for real gain, whether material, emotional, or spiritual. In destructive stress, the perceiver tends to accentuate the possibility of loss. Thus, the constructive and destructive responses depend on the context. A positive appraisal may be evident in one setting but not in another. It is now known that these two different states of stress are associated with two identifiably different brain states.

When someone is threatened with loss, the full stress response is evident, with elevated levels of both neurotransmitters and cortisol. When someone perceives a situation as challenging, although there are higher levels of neurotransmitters, there is no elevation of cortisol. Consequently, the challenged person is not at risk from the somatic effects that can occur with increased cortisol levels. The person who lives in the midst of stressful events he takes as a challenge may well thrive, while another who sees the same events as threatening can let the stress destroy him.

Attitude Changes in Controlling Stress

Karl Marx made the shrewd observation that one of the potential risks to a capitalist culture is the way a worker may come to view his or her job. He saw the emphasis on production and profit as a process by which the worker became alienated and would ultimately lose sight of the intrinsic value and pleasure of work. The idea that work inevitably becomes boring, tedious, and devoid of personal significance, thereby creating stress and great dissatisfaction, seems to make sense until one considers the Japanese.

Emerging from a different culture with different attitudes, workers do not consider the Japanese factory a dreary place but a family center. This outlook allows for different interpretations of the environment, and, not surprisingly, stress is uncommon in the Japanese workplace. Such sociological variables demonstrate just how powerful the conditioned mind can be in controlling stress. Modern researchers have taken their lead from these cross-cultural truths and are trying to develop mental strategies for workers under stress. The current view on how best to control the physiological response to stress is to work on the mind.

How a stressful event is initially evaluated by the mind is crucial to the body's management of stress. The aim of the "cognitive" approach to stress mediation is to identify the patterns of thought that provoke or exacerbate stress. Once they are identified, an attempt is made to replace the old, destructive patterns with new, constructive ones. The method is being applied to such diverse problems as headache, divorce, job aggravation, and heart disease. How effective these procedures will prove to be is still unknown. Yet the notion that the best stress management should occur at the psychological level seems reasonable. The essential task is to train the mind not to send a triggering stimulus to the autonomic nervous system.

Coping with Stress: The Dangers and Failures of the Physiological Approach

Perhaps people who cannot cope with stress on a psychological level may learn to cope physiologically. However, physiological intervention can be very dangerous. Animal studies illustrate that baroreceptors can inhibit stimulation of the brain's reticular formation. This formation plays a vital role in controlling levels of arousal, and baroreceptors, which are stimulated by increased blood pressure, send information to the reticular formation. Baroreceptors are sensitive to the stretch produced by expanding blood vessels, and are found, among other places, in the carotid arteries at the base of the brain. When blood pressure rises, these receptors respond more vigorously, thereby inhibiting the reticular formation. This inhibition prevents arousal and creates a sedative effect. Some people apparently can learn to raise their blood pressure and set off this sequence of events. Since they would be rewarded by a suppression of the negative emotions associated with stress, such as anxiety, they could routinely use this mechanism to control their stress. Ultimately, however, the strategy would backfire: among other things, unleashing high blood pressure is not good for health.

There are other, less dangerous, and medically acceptable ways of controlling stress physiologically. Perhaps the most frequently discussed method is biofeedback. The idea behind it is very clever: teach people to control their physiological response to stressful stimuli. It sounds simple enough, yet the reality is much more complex. The basic problem is that since the autonomic nervous system is heavily involved with the physiological responses associated with stress, and since it is very difficult to influence the autonomic nervous system through learning, the biofeedback technique is almost always doomed to failure. The system responds to commands efficiently and, once triggered, carries out its activities outside conscious control. But to teach it not to respond after it has been triggered by higher brain processes is virtually impossible. In the early 1970s this view regarding the aloofness of the autonomic nervous system was challenged by a group of investigators at Rockefeller University, and strong claims were made for the possibility of conditioning it. These claims turned out to be premature and were later withdrawn. Yet the biofeedback industry exploited them, and it continues to prosper.

Biofeedback has worked in some very limited circumstances. It can, for example, reduce blood pressure under strict and exacting laboratory conditions. However, in study after study, laboratory results have not transferred to real life. The small effects noted in the lab are absent when people are functioning in the everyday environment that produces the stress they seek to relieve. The effect of biofeedback procedures on headache is one exception to this general rule. Yet even here, what transpires during the intricate biofeedback technique is not clear. One group of experimenters reversed the conditioning procedures on a group of patients suffering from tension headaches. Instead of teaching the patients to decrease tension in the frontal muscles of their head, they taught them to increase the tension. This training had the same therapeutic effect! Follow-up studies also showed that the way most biofeedback-treated patients functioned in the real world had changed after training. They avoided the circumstances that had once led to the headaches, or they became more assertive, or they evaluated more rationally why they experienced the headaches and changed their attitude. However, there was little evidence that any physiological conditioning took place. Those reporting an improvement had largely adopted more psychological coping strategies.

Stress takes its toll. Under stress, the body does not respond well to disease. The immune system is inhibited. Memory and thinking can be impaired by stress. Yet it is also evident that stress can for the most part be avoided by adopting a different attitude about the interpretation of certain life events. This is not an easy task, and someone who has spent his life evaluating experiences in a way that encourages the stress response must try to remake his response. It is most challenging.

Stress can also work in our favor in extreme situations. It alerts the body for action so that it can achieve supernormal output levels. And when people have arranged their lives and minds so they feel in charge of events, the situations that typically give rise to stress in others find these people seemingly thriving on such trials. Yet these people are *not* in fact experiencing the stress response. Their mental attitude has channeled what might be a negative, destructive situation into a perception of positive opportunity. The body then responds in a way that is not harmful to health.

Stress serves as the cardinal example of how mind, brain, and body interact. It is too important a concept, however, to be dragged out and abused. The stress response is real and must be controlled as much as possible. Its role in health and healing is immense, as we shall now see.

Healing

If you want to have fun at your next dinner party, invite a physician or two, a statistician, a historian, and a few folks who have been ill but have recovered. After the party gets going, bring up the question of medical healing. The conversation will go to splinters. The former patients will tell you about their special experience of getting better or worse while being treated. Chances are, one will say it seemed to take forever to get better and another will say he healed quite quickly. The two medics will regard the conversation as no more than Saturday night musings with the public. The public must be humored—or better, entertained—so they will trot out their favorite stories to illustrate the difference in rates of healing. The historian will comment that all recorded cases of quick healing resulting from a supposedly divine intervention—which usually resulted in someone's becoming a saint—were probably instances of misdiagnosis. And the statistician will be quietly suffering: "The numbers, please, the numbers. Give me the numbers and I'll tell you whether anything is going on that justifies all of the current excitement about variations in healing due to states of mind." The statistician makes a strong point. Unless you can give him specific data to prove something different, the most veritable explanation for most healing is that the body, somehow, does it on its own, despite the intervention of modern medicine.

Current attitudes about healing fall into two categories. The "hard," or accepted, view is that after anyone contracts a disease or is injured, the body initiates certain inevitable somatic processes that attack, isolate, and destroy the intruding microorganism or mend the physical injury. The body's vast and complex homeostatic mechanisms are designed to deal with such eventualities. The hard view takes into account that there may be variations in this healing response attributable to certain genetically determined differences in each person's somatic system. But nowhere in this dominant view of healing is there room for the mind.

The other view argues that the mind plays an important role in several kinds of healing. The mental attitude of the patient affects brain states, which in turn affect somatic responses. Hope, positive mental attitude, and depression-free states of mind are all supposed to help tremendously in ridding the body of disease and the pain that accompanies disease or injury. Conversely, the person who responds to illness and injury with despair can be expected to fall victim to the lightning speed of somatic disease responses, and recovery will be slow. Even more telling, a fatal disease will run its course more quickly. So goes the "soft" view of healing.

No wonder there was so much agitation at the dinner party. The physicians know one thing that supersedes anecdotal evidence: people under medical care die in droves, a good many of them displaying all of the positive, will-to-live qualities of mind that should ward off disease. As a result, they are weary of faith-healing quackery and exaggerated claims. At the same time, they cannot deny the common sense underlying the soft viewpoint.

Why do diseases, mild or severe, sometimes go into remission? Immunologists cannot yet answer that question, but more and more they are beginning to respect the role of the mind. One study showed that students who reported to a health service with all the classic symptoms of a cold tended to contract the cold. Other students with the same symptoms went to see a self-professed healer who, upon touching them, declared they would soon get well. The majority of this group did not continue on to develop colds. Millions of people swear by vitamin C as a cold preventive, but is it the vitamin C that does the trick, as Linus Pauling claims, or the belief that it helps? The issue of "mentally driven" healing raises intriguing questions about mind-body relations that are full of practical import. What are both the limits and the opportunities for the mind to affect bodily health? And conversely, what are the possibilities that a genetically impaired somatic system might induce in the mind a neurotic view of the world that would in turn encourage somatic disease? Once the connection between the brain and the immune system is established, the possibilities for mind-body interactions are immense. The challenge is to determine how many of them might be true.

The Immune System

The body's immune system is a marvelously intricate defense that protects us from foreign intruders. The body unleashes two main kinds of responses to unwanted substances: the cell-mediated response and the humoral-mediated response. Both generate cells and chemicals to destroy or modulate the intruders. The special cells and chemicals are produced by body processes outside the nervous system. Consequently, any effects of brain and mind on the immune response system must come somewhat indirectly. The brain must be able to trigger counterattacks against the disease by producing substances that can influence various body organs and the processes that are active in the immune response. As we saw with our description of stress

mechanisms, it has a way to do just that, through the production
of steroids like cortisol. Steroids have a big and largely negative
effect on the immune system. They can also increase the overall
amount of neurotransmitters. Neurotransmitters affect the immune cells directly by attaching to their surfaces, thus inhibiting
their normal function. In short, the brain and mind have an
avenue to reach and influence the body's immune system through
the stress mechanism.

The cells most active in the immune response are the white
blood cells, or lymphocytes, and these are in turn divided into
what are called T-cells and B-cells. Born in the bone marrow,
the T-cells migrate to the thymus gland, where they mature
into the trinity of T-cells: the helper T-cells, the suppressor
T-cells, and the killer T-cells. This group regulates the overall
T-cell response. The helper cells decide whether a substance is
foreign, and if so, they mobilize the killer T-cells to attack
the intruder. After the intruder has been isolated, the suppressor
T-cells signal the system to turn off, that the fight is over.

The helper T-cells also signal the B-cells to move their defenses
against the intruder, the B-cells having already been alerted to
the intruder and having recognized it as foreign. The B-cells
immediately proliferate and go into action. In response to the
intruder's unique molecular nature, the defenders transform into
plasma cells and then create antibodies. Finally, prodded by
the helper T-cells, they release the antibodies to fight the
disease.

The immune response is vastly more complicated than this,
but for present purposes the intricate subsystems need not con-
cern us here. The whole system is the body's line of defense,
and it is the key to managing the disease process. It must work,
and work efficiently, to attack unwanted viruses, tumors, and
bacteria. All of this is disrupted when the mind views the world
as stressful. The increased levels of steroids that come along
with stress handicap this efficient mechanism in its fight against
disease.

The Placebo Effect

The mind has many other roles to play in the management of illness, and the placebo effect is central to understanding the influence it has on somatic responses. The term refers to the response patients have to the injection or ingestion of an inert substance. In a typical experiment, for example, patients are told they are being given drug X, which is supposed to have a certain effect on their bodily state. In fact, the control group is secretly given a placebo only, such as water. Yet in virtually every drug test and in most disease treatment, there is a 20 to 40 percent positive response. Patients maintain they experienced an effect even though the inert substance administered was supposedly powerless to cause it.

Consider the placebo effect in pain research. In a typical observation, patients are told they are going to be given a drug to help kill the pain they suffer. Prior to administering the drug, the researcher ascertains the level of pain by using various psychological measures. The drug is then given to one group while the other receives the placebo. (Adhering to the "double blind" model, the scientists in the experiment are also unaware which pill they are administering; the objective is to rule out their bias, which might surface as inadvertent cues to the patient about what to say and how to react during testing.) Typically, the placebo group experiences more relief from pain than could be predicted from chance variation. The relief tends to be short-lived, and the placebo effect works for somatic pain only, as opposed to internal, visceral pain. Nevertheless, the alleviation for the cases of somatic pain is very real.

The most common theory explaining how a placebo affects pain is that an analgesic system controlled by the body's own opiates, the endorphins, is activated. Specifically, a mental state triggers an endorphin release, which in turn activates cells in part of the midbrain, thereby inhibiting incoming pain messages. Thus, the placebo effect produces real changes in the body state.

To test this idea, researchers studied normal volunteers who had tight tourniquets applied to them. How long they could withstand the pain would give a measure of the analgesia. There were two groups: one received a placebo and was told that it was pain medication, and the other group received nothing. The experimenters added another facet to the study. They divided each group into two subgroups, and one subgroup was required to take some of the drug naloxone in addition to the placebo. You will recall from our chapter on pain that naloxone blocks the pain-relieving action of our natural endorphins by attaching to the receptors of cells normally responsive to endorphins. If the expected placebo effect is due to the production of endorphins, then the naloxone subgroup should halt it. That is exactly what happened! When all the comparisons were made between the various experimental groups, the placebo group that received the naloxone fared worse in their pain relief than the placebo group not receiving the naloxone.

Other studies have found less dramatic results, and further experiments are geared to identifying all the variables involved. Taken as a whole, current research indicates that in specific instances the placebo effect has a measurable impact on body chemicals. As we will see, it can be observed in dozens of other medical situations that relate the mind and health. Among other things, this effect is probably the entire basis for the limited alleviation offered by homeopathic medicine.

The Mind-Body Connection

There are dozens of reports about how the mind plays a role in cures for cancer. Although these are largely anecdotal and/or tentative, none other than Lewis Thomas, the distinguished scientist, writer, and former head of Sloan-Kettering Institute for Cancer Research in New York has spoken persuasively on the subject. Thomas lectured on how a tough fighter from Brooklyn conquered cancer while a fragile and neurotic

Upper East Sider with the same cancer died quickly. Thomas saw no mystery here. No one would question that the state of the body can affect the mind. Why not the other way around? Thomas cited the often-noted effects hypnosis can have on reducing or removing warts to show how healing can be triggered by the mind: warts on one hand can, upon instruction under hypnosis, be made to disappear while warts on the other body areas remain intact.

Encouraged by the continual sagas of strange and unexpected cures, placebo effects, and a host of other examples, researchers have started to carry out systematic studies on the mind-immune connection. As already mentioned, the brain can easily produce chemical changes, such as increased steroid and neurotransmitter levels, that affect the efficiency of the immune system. The autonomic nervous system and the adrenal glands play an important role in this process and are very active in modulating the immune response. The sympathetic nervous system, part of the autonomic system, controls the adrenal glands and signals them to release cortisol, as we learned from our discussion of stress. Cortisol, one of our body's steroids, suppresses the immune response. (This suppression explains why steroids are given to people having an allergic reaction.) At the same time, the sympathetic nervous system is sending another signal, which orchestrates the secretion of epinephrine and norepinephrine by stimulating the adrenals. These substances, in turn, promote the production of lymphocytes, thereby enhancing the immune response. Also, the adrenal medulla secretes other steroids called mineralocorticoids, which serve to promote the immune system even more and inhibit the effects of the corticosteroids that inhibit the system! What is going on? Is there something for everybody in this mechanism, or does it make sense? As in most biological systems, there is a rationale. Every such system functions in dynamic equilibrium, and the mind-immune system is no different. In this particular instance the important details are still being worked out. Still, much is known.

Lymphocytes, the white blood cells that are the workhorse of the immune system, have alpha and beta receptors, and understanding their role serves as the key to how lymphocytes function. Much of the push-pull balancing act of the immune system works through these receptors. Certain chemicals called first messengers attach to these receptors. These are epinephrine and norepinephrine, the steroids, and also acetylcholine, which is secreted by the other arm of the autonomic nervous system—the parasympathetic system. What is important to remember is that if an alpha receptor is triggered, a specific chemical process within the lymphocyte is activated which produces the enzyme guanylate cyclase. This chemical is a "second messenger," and it tells the cell to produce an immune response. When the beta receptor is activated, another second messenger is triggered, the enzyme adenyl cyclase, and it promotes the opposite response, immune suppression. Thus, the alpha and beta receptors control the lymphocytes' capacity to respond to disease.

These are tangible mechanisms. Consequently, there is little problem seeing—at least in theory—how mind states, working through the autonomic nervous system, can influence the immune system. The serious issue is whether these known links actually play a useful role in altering the immune response to serious disease.

Mood and Disease

There is certainly good evidence that emotions can influence some immune processes. The herpes simplex virus, for example, lives in body tissues and causes cold sores, among other things. These sores blossom during times of emotional upheaval. Clearly, the balancing act the immune system performs between monitoring and attacking foreign elements can be disrupted and thereby can influence unwanted viral action. In short, if the herpes-carrying person is under stress, the immune system becomes depressed and the virus can take effect. But herpes is a relatively simple and tangible example of how the mind can affect the body. Whether the mind working through these same mechanisms can influence other, more complex diseases is the issue. Most highly experienced oncologists, many of whose patients display good will, good mood, good everything, do not accept the belief that mental states can affect the spread of cancer in any way. Both the good and the bad die when serious disease befalls them.

In a recent study from the University of Pennsylvania, Dr. Barrie Cassileth reported that in 359 cancer patients with severe malignancies, the death rate was 75 percent. There were no beneficial psychosocial factors that could change that unhappy fact. Her study, at one level, serves as an anchor for the discussion of healing. When certain dire processes are already at an advanced stage, positive mental health will do nothing to abate their course. This fact is extremely important, since quackery flourishes in the field of cancer. Some "medical practitioners," for instance, maintain that if seriously ill patients imagine how a treatment might affect a cancer cell, the efficacy of the treatment will improve. Although there are reports of remarkable remissions, there is as yet no reliably documented link between a positive mind state and a cancer cure. At the same time, most illness is not that dire. Consequently, the mind-health link in other diseases can be actively explored.

Spontaneous Remission, Learning, and the Immune System

As already noted, the vast majority of diseases have a spontaneous remission rate. The disease process simply stops. Why? Could fluctuating mental states and learning be involved? In other words, could memories or life experience play a role?

In the late 1970s, Robert Ader, a psychobiologist at the University of Rochester, conducted some intriguing studies. In his original set of experiments, Ader was trying to teach rats to

avoid saccharin-flavored water. He used the tried and true
method developed by John Garcia at UCLA. After the rats
drank some saccharin water, he injected them with cyclophosphamide, a drug that produces nausea. Animals commonly learn
to associate their sickness with the food they eat beforehand;
in this case, rats came to avoid their saccharin-flavored water
after the injection. What puzzled Ader, however, was that his
experimental rats kept dying even after he had stopped the
injections. In trying to determine why this should occur, he
found out that cyclophosphamide is also an immunosuppressant.
Could the rats have associated drinking saccharin water with
the effect that the drug had on their immune system? In short,
had they inadvertently learned to suppress their immune system
through the conditioning experience of pairing the saccharin
water with cyclophosphamide? Could the same kind of thing
go on unconsciously in humans? With their immune system
depressed, of course, the animals would be susceptible to disease
and die. It was a startling observation and well worth pursuing.

Ader took a strain of rats susceptible to that species's version
of lupus erythematosus, a so-called autoimmune disease, in
which the body's immune system becomes reactive and attacks
and destroys itself. If taste-aversion conditioning suppresses the
malfunctioning immune system, he reasoned, then rats with
lupus erythematosus should live longer following positive conditioning. And so they did.

Perceived Control
and Susceptibility to Illness

In discussing the effect of mental attitude on illness, one must
consider the role of perceived control. Conditioning experiments
built on the concept of "learned helplessness" demonstrated
that white blood cells were more listless in rats that had no
control over the delivery of shock as opposed to rats that were
able to prevent their shock. This paradigm, which we have

already discussed in our chapter on stress, suggests that experiencing a lack of control over the environment can increase stress, with the predictable effect of suppressing the immune system. Martin Seligman, who discovered the learned helplessness phenomenon, has done dozens of studies on how the body is adversely affected during stressful times. In animals he had conditioned into a helpless state, he injected cancer cells as his marker for disease spread. These animals developed tumors twice as often as control animals. The idea here is that mental states that look very similar to depression create a body chemistry that fosters disease.

A longitudinal study of "problem children" in Cambridge, Massachusetts, may be relevant here. That effort, a thirty-year follow-up assessment of adolescents who received psychological assistance during a period of juvenile delinquency, proved this group was far less physically healthy than another group that had not received outside psychological counseling. The untreated group may have perceived the world as more under their control than the group that was given assistance. One of the effects of outside psychological support may be to lessen patients' sense of control of life's events. It is as if they have adopted the idea that the counselor is taking care of their troubles, not they themselves. They are like the animals locked in the cage that cannot control the delivery of shocks. This attitude may in turn affect the immune system, with troublesome consequences for the patients' health. Recently, this possibility has been widely examined by several health psychologists, and their reports support this conclusion.

Bereavement is a seriously altered state of mind and body. The death of a loved one can be devastating, and public health scientists have noted for years that susceptibility to disease goes up during mourning. Clinicians often observe that when one spouse dies, frequently the survivor will die soon thereafter, even though he or she had been in perfect health. Are these "coincidences" related to mind-immune mechanisms? It is far too early to say. To date, the studies and observations are correlational, with little hard evidence of cause and effect, and as such must be regarded with great caution. With that caveat in place, let us examine the evidence.

As already noted, placebo effects produce real relief from pain. The body's own opiates, the endorphins, increase under such circumstances, and they trigger certain neural systems that modulate incoming pain messages from the body. John Liebskind, a talented psychologist at UCLA, has also discovered that endorphins have an immunosuppressant effect. For his studies, he implanted cancerous tumors in animals and placed them under a variety of behavioral conditions. For example, when one group of animals were given opiate-inducing shocks, the animals' cancer-fighting NK cells were less active than they were in a control group. In another study, animals that had been under stress also proved less able to cope with the tumors. In a more direct test of the role endorphins play in suppressing the immune system, animals were given opiate antagonists. Naloxone, the drug that blocks the action of self-produced opiates, was administered before a stress test that induced endorphin production. The naloxone appeared to block the usual immunosuppression that results from shocks. These naloxone-treated animals proved just as susceptible to disease as the normal, untrained animals. This experiment gives strong support to Liebskind's idea that endorphin mechanisms are an important link in the mind-health story.

These intriguing results, however, point up the complexity and possible pitfalls of this kind of research. If endorphins suppress the immune system, and if physical exertion such as jogging causes an overproduction of endorphins, then do people who exercise become more susceptible to disease? Then Winston Churchill's crack that he got his exercise serving as a pallbearer at funerals for friends who exercised seems not quite so far-fetched! No one seriously considers this line of reasoning valid, but it is no more correlational than the notions that have raised all of the possibilities we have been discussing. In that spirit, let us break some new speculative ground to illustrate how dangerous argument by correlation can be.

The person who exercises does so to feel better, to look good, or to allay fears of going physically slack. Exercise has an unquestionably beneficial effect on the entire cardiovascular system, making one tire less easily. Exercise supposedly leads to better overall health. In fact, what happens is that self-produced opiates reinforce exercise by blocking out pain in many of its forms. Thus, the activity produces an unforeseen reward. According to studies just reported, when one stops exercising, endorphin levels go down, and the body becomes more readily able to signal that certain disease processes may be active. However, with decreased exercise, one gets a negative feeling from the decreased production of opiates. This sense of vanished rewards in turn creates the impression that more exercise is needed. With that, the person commences the next round of exertion. The new exertion again produces the rewarding but masking narcotic effect of endorphins. While all seems well, the immune system may continue to be suppressed, leaving the body more susceptible to disease. This line of reasoning is the exact one used to explain why animals that produce opiates under stress grow one form of breast cancer faster than do animals not under stress. The only difference in the two cases is that in one, the opiates are considered the result of stress, a negative event, as opposed to the production of endorphins through exercise, a positive event. The perils of correlation are always with us. Sorting out the actual role of endorphins in health remains for future work.

Immune States Affecting Brain States

We have already seen that the mind can affect the immune system. Can the immune system govern brain processes? J. Edwin Blalock of the University of Texas at Galveston has made real advances in determining how the immune system is connected to the neurohumoral system, which has an effect on mental activity. He sees body and mind as totally intertwined. In one set of observations, he investigated the reason why children who suffered from a total pituitary deficiency that left them far shorter in height than average produced the normal increase in ACTH-positive leukocytes when they were put under stress. This normal reaction didn't make any sense, since the pituitary gland is the source for ACTH as well as growth hormone. Blalock, drawing from earlier experiments, deduced that ACTH might be coming from immune cells themselves. In order to make this observation, he had to do some clever *in vitro* experiments.

Since ACTH production is normally triggered by the secretion of corticotrophin releasing factor (CRF) from the hypothalamus into the pituitary, he studied the effects of introducing CRF directly into leukocytes placed in an experimental dish. Blalock discovered that the leukocytes made ACTH as well as beta-endorphins in response to the CRF. And he also discovered that this production of ACTH and endorphins could be suppressed when corticosteroids were introduced into the dish.

Recall that the hypothalamus secretes CRF, which passes to the pituitary. The pituitary in turn secretes ACTH, which stimulates the adrenal cortex. The adrenal cortex secretes corticoids, which among other things feed back and work to turn off the hypothalamus. The hypothalamus, in addition to secreting CRF, is activating the sympathetic nervous system, which stimulates the adrenal medulla to secrete epinephrine. Epinephrine stimulates bodily tissues for action and also feeds back to the hypothalamus and tells it to keep working.

This intricate, wholly neurohumoral system was modified by Blalock's work. He put one more loop in the control system. Leukocytes as well as the pituitary can respond to CRF, thereby allowing the immune system to play a role in the cycle just described. Leukocytes patrol the body to find what Blalock calls noncognitive signals, such as bacteria, viruses, and so on. When they come upon a disease process, they can alert the brain directly and activate it through their capacity to manufacture and secrete the brain-responsive chemicals ACTH and beta-endorphins. They can then stimulate the autonomic nervous system. With that system functioning, there is an inevitable expenditure of energy that leads, ultimately, to a feeling of fatigue. It is worth considering how this chain of events could affect the mind.

In the scenario just described, the state of fatigue is noted by the central brain's interpreter, and so there must follow some theory explaining why there is a tired feeling or malaise when no apparent physical exertion has taken place. A reasonable interpretation is that the thought of doing such and such is unsettling (felt as fatigue), which is why few activities are planned when the body is ill. If, however, the body is more or less chronically ill because of other, genetic considerations, there is the possibility that such a state could create a personality style approaching neurosis. In short, such body states compel certain mind states, which in turn can feed back on body states. The mind and body become delicate and intricate partners in health and personality.

With the connections that allow for central brain states to influence the immune system, and vice versa, clearly established, it is interesting to consider why people might vary in their capacity to control disease through mental attitude. One difference among individuals is the consistency with which each of our autonomic nervous systems responds to a signal. When several people are presented with an emotional stimulus, they will respond similarly but to a greater or lesser degree. However, any particular individual will have what is called an autonomic response stereotypy. In other words, he will always react in the same way. Such response patterns must be under rather tight genetic controls, since they are so little influenced by experience and training. (From a host of other studies, we know that it is virtually impossible to teach the autonomic nervous system anything.) Thus, how the autonomic system responds after being triggered by a mind state may vary tremendously from one person to another. And that variation should have an impact on those aspects of the immune response that are influenced by the nervous system.

Asthma and Unconscious Processes

Even more fascinating is how the unconscious might influence the autonomic nervous system. In modern psychological theory, unconscious processes have been demystified. They are looked upon as patterns of brain activity that can exist in parallel with those patterns supporting conscious action. They simply work outside the realm of conscious awareness. These patterns may support memories bearing associated emotional components. Further, these brain patterns can be activated by and can trigger the autonomic nervous system. If many of the stored memories that are part of the unconscious have disturbing emotional aspects, the autonomic system might well be in a chronic state of arousal, a condition that ought to affect the immune system. Consider the asthmatic attack.

Asthma is a disorder of the immune system that is characterized by distress in breathing, wheezing, and coughing. There may be a heightened secretion of mucus in the lungs; the airways themselves can become constricted, affecting the smooth muscle of the trachea and bronchi. An asthmatic attack is thought to be the result of the immune system's overreacting to a substance (allergen), and this overreaction is referred to as hypersensitivity. In this instance, an acquired immunity goes awry.

From prior exposure to a foreign substance, T-cells—sometimes called memory cells—have learned to "read" and react to the specific configuration of this substance. Over several exposure periods, the body builds up a hefty supply of T-cells that, when exposed again to this foreign substance, respond with a vengeance. (Studies have shown that T-cells remember the prior exposures of antigens up to twenty years later.) The normal antibody mechanism works to destroy the intruder, but with any new invasion, the T-cells secrete other substances that irritate tissues around the site of the intrusion. When this occurs in the lungs, the result is the common asthmatic attack. (If the attack occurs in the gut or stomach, there can be nausea or vomiting.) The substances that cause all this reaction are usually histamines, or any of several other chemicals. Yet many people argue that this somatic response has a huge psychological component.

Experiments have been carried out in which certain allergens were presented to animals along with another stimulus such as a particular odor. Exposure to the allergens was gradually built up, so that any new instance of it produced an allergic reaction. There was no mystery to that phenomenon. But experimenters demonstrated that when the odor only was presented, the animal still showed the allergic response. Corollary experiments with similar results have been done on humans. This suggests that a learned association was established between the stimulus and the allergic response, so that a neutral, biologically insignificant stimulus could trigger the hypersensitivity.

Asthma and other allergic attacks can happen any time, and they frequently occur outside the influence of a specific allergen. They tend to appear during periods of emotional upheaval, or they can be triggered mysteriously when there is not apparent psychological cause. One of the unconscious systems that we know to exist in brain networks may become activated and set off the full-blown asthmatic response.

The mind and body are like a mobile. Touch one aspect of it and the rest moves to adjust to the new disturbance. Working scientists tend to forget all the delicate reciprocal relationships among systems. At some level it is almost too much to consider. They look for big effects and usually find them; little effects are passed over. Yet little effects can add up, and it appears that after years of neglect, biomedical scientists are beginning to consider the mind-body interactions involved in healing.

A Final Word
The Good Life

Mind affects brain and brain affects mind. That is the message, and by accepting it you commit yourself to a special view of the world. It is a view that shows the limits of the genetic imperative on what we turn out to be, both intellectually and emotionally. It decrees that, while the secrets of our genes express themselves with force throughout our lives, the effect of that information on our bodies can be influenced by our psychological history and beliefs about the world. And, just as important, the other side of the same coin argues that what we construct in our minds as objective reality may simply be our interpretations of certain bodily states dictated by our genes and expressed through our physical brains and body. Put differently, various attributes of mind that seem to have a purely psychological origin are frequently a product of the brain's interpreter rationalizing genetically driven body states. Make no mistake about it: this two-sided view of mind-brain interactions, if adopted, has implications for the management of one's personal life.

To be explicit, the overall concept derived from scientific knowledge about the mind states of pain, love, anxiety, depression, stress, and so on is quite straightforward. Each of us is born with a genetic blueprint. The unfolding commands given by our genes to body chemistry are largely outside our control.

The genes unleash new information about our body throughout our life, always presenting it with surprises. The body responds to these changes, as does the mind. These commands can take the form of instructions to certain cells to secrete more or less of a specific chemical. Or the genes can tell cells to be more receptive to outside influences by changing the receptor mechanisms of the cells. Thus, our genes can intervene and wield power over our body and mind with impunity.

If the genetic influence were total, however, the story would be over quickly. There would be nothing to do but sit back and let life, as it was granted us, unfold. But it doesn't happen that way. Bodily events are triggered by our genes, but different consequences of those events are possible. Somehow, the state of mind and the mind itself, in combination, interpret the changes in bodily states. The interpretations can be individually inventive, since each of us has a differing psychological past. Yet the ideas, theories, and beliefs we conceive in our mind about our bodily and brain states then become part of our memory and our psychological history. This history is later drawn upon for other interpretations, and, quick as a flash, the relationship between body, mind, and our individual past becomes hopelessly and wonderfully intertwined. In short, mind and body are so linked that it becomes impossible to talk about one without the other.

My initial argument for this view of mind and brain grew out of the fact that each of us has an interpreting mechanism in our brain. This interpreter constructs theories about why we act and behave the way we do. Discovering the existence of the interpreter was made possible by studying patients who had had the two hemispheres of their brain divided, by examining how the left half brain dealt with actions recorded by the silent right half brain. The results were a compelling demonstration of the presence of something in our left brain that must interpret our bodily states. Those same studies also pointed up certain important features about how the brain is organized.

Results from split-brain experiments, as well as from other kinds of work, reveal that the brain has a modular organization. This means that thousands, if not millions, of activities go on relatively independently of one another and all outside the realm of conscious experience. These independent modules are capable of affecting things like bodily movement as well as more subtle events like mood shifts. Once the activities of these modules are expressed, the expressions become events that the conscious system takes note of and must explain. In the normal course of life, all of this works within reasonable bounds, creating some perceptions that are more true than others. The point at which the system breaks down is when one of the modules or groups of modules creates behaviors that are outside the normal; they are exaggerated states of bodily behavior, and the mind will adopt bizarre theories to explain them.

This view of mind finds much support from the observed phenomena of our mental lives reviewed in this book. The thorny problems of pain, memory, intelligence, and crazy thoughts all serve as examples of how the brain-mind system seems to be organized in this modular-interpreter way. Patients who suffer pain teach us that bodily states create images and memories of pain that can be as real as the initial pain experience, an experience more tightly connected to brain pathways and mechanisms. Studies on the perception of pain also show how cultural variables influence the personal perception of pain.

Mind-brain issues also involve what might be considered the "hard" operating characteristics of our mental life—memory and intelligence. Our capacity to remember changes with a changing brain state. This is best exemplified by observing the effects of brain lesions on memory capacity and how normal aging affects our memory. Adapting to changing capacity, the normally aging adult begins to adopt the view that the gist or big-picture aspect of a new experience is more important than the particular facts of the experience. Likewise, people with a poor memory for facts shy away from occupational activities that call upon this skill and frequently construct a theory of life that explains why they have adopted a less taxing job. The same scenario can be seen for people with a lower computational capacity—that is, analytical intelligence. Grand personal theories can develop as to why someone does what he does, but the truth is likely to be based on the fact that the interpreter is giving a reasonable theory to account for or rationalize a person's basic brain capacities and limitations.

The modular-interpretative view takes on special force as more emotion-laden states of mind are considered. The puzzling, seemingly opaque disease of schizophrenia becomes somewhat comprehensible when seen from this perspective. Faulty bio-chemical systems create changes in how information is evaluated. Probably the biggest distortion comes when information no longer triggers automatic rewards. The interpreter responds with strange theories of the world that gradually take on the status of confirmed delusions. When the biochemical system returns to normal, the residual delusions remain embedded, especially if they are long-standing.

And so it goes. In other emotional states such as depression, anxiety, love, or obsession, the same model seems to explain the main features of these states. The many modules of the brain, each of which has its own chemical dynamics, are capable of being influenced by mind states. Or the modules can influence felt states, which in turn are interpreted by the mind and fed into the mental outlook and theories of the perceiver. In depression, the felt state is so bleak that the interpreter's most likely response is to devalue all surrounding people, things, and events. When everything seems worthless, the felt state of depression follows naturally. If the depression is not treated, this view of the world becomes welded into the mind, and the hope for effective treatment diminishes. On the other side of the emo-tional coin are the states of arousal like passionate love. Person A triggers arousal in person B. The interpreter comes in and gives an explanation, and off the mind goes to construct a new and idealized image of the other person.

This interactive view of mind-brain and body having been laid out, the question then becomes: does it matter to know all of this? Does it help us live a better life? Or do we benefit equally well by following what our grandmother says? A friend of mine tells the story about his *buba* visiting him while he was in graduate school. He was enamored of the Minnesota Multiphasic Personality Inventory, a paper and pencil test that describes the personality. Upon her arrival he immediately gave her the test. He took the results and darted across campus to have the professor score and interpret the results. The professor told the young man that his grandmother's personality was such and such and she behaved so and so. My friend couldn't believe how accurate the professor was—and he hadn't even met *Buba!* He had only seen the test results. Full of the importance of this, he hurried back and said to his grandmother, "Look here, this man who has never met you is able to describe you perfectly by just scoring the test." *Buba* looked at her grandson, shrugged her shoulders, and said, "So? I tell him, he tells me." My friend never quite dismissed anything his grandmother said from then on. He also became a highly creative psychologist who made only counterintuitive discoveries!

The problem with folk wisdom and age-old insights is that if you think about them carefully, any one of them always has its opposite saying that's just as venerable. The whole objective of mind and brain science is to ascertain which views are truly correct about the nature of our species and which suggest important rules for our species to live by. To that end, we feel these very young sciences have made real progress. Our survey of a variety of states of mind and what is known about them at both a psychological and neurobiological level has revealed that mind and brain work in concert to mold our lives and ways.

This mind-brain game appears to be played out in full force when it comes to human disease. People respond differently to life's events, with some suffering stress at the drop of a hat and others treating most experiences as a challenge and thriving on adverse situations. It is not known for sure how an already established disease can be further influenced by stress and other mental states, but we have a tantalizing set of clues to follow. We do know that people vary tremendously in response to a common disease. Put another way, identical twins do not have a perfect or even a near-perfect correspondence in their response to disease. While their concordance rate is always higher than nontwin pairs, the variation in their response may well reflect different mind influences on the somatic response to genetic plans. The didactic power of the study of twins justifies one last story.

Examples of the similarity between identical twins who are reared apart are constantly used as evidence for the hereditary aspects of psychological and biological processes. These same cases can also be used to illustrate mind-brain interactions. Consider the lives of two identical twins, Stephanie and Sylvia. They were reared apart. One set of parents were academics and exacting. The other couple followed a policy of laissez-faire. The twins had come to each family through a bizarre series of events at the adoption agency. Neither set of parents knew anything about the biological parents of the two girls.

Stephanie was the bright stepchild of the two professors. They prided themselves on their rational approach to everything. They read *Consumer Reports* before buying a car or a VCR or a pair of binoculars. They wore seat belts everywhere. They read books about having a baby and about what you do when the baby arrives. When they remodeled their home, they bought a book on how to do it. They loved the written word and lived by it. They contributed to public television and bought Brio toys. They believed in constant surveillance. They corrected

Stephanie every time she made a speech error. They explained to her how toasters worked, how TVs worked, how everything worked. They were actually quite sure how the stock market worked. They were rewarded for all of this, because Stephanie is now grown and was accepted at Harvard.

Not surprisingly, Sylvia, who had identical genes, was also bright. Her luck of the draw found her being raised by a warm and generous family that took life as it came. Her adoptive parents were not quite as affluent, not quite as well educated, and not quite as interested in worldly concerns as the other pair. Their attitude about life was different. Achieving was not everything for them. If they had planned to work when an old friend showed up out of the blue, they abandoned their plans and spent the day with the friend. If Sylvia made a mistake in her speech, they laughed and hugged her. When the young Sylvia was being a nuisance, they told her to stop what she was doing—period. They didn't reason with her. When they wanted to fix up the house, they bought the supplies and paint, and through the sort of natural knowledge the nonanalytical pick up about the world, they were able to figure out things on their own as they went along. Sylvia turned out as successfully as her sister. She was accepted at Yale, but decided to spend a year in Paris before going to college.

Then came the news. Both twins had the most powerfully genetically linked disease—Huntington's. The gene for it had been identified and located, and in the case of their particular disease, it was known that each twin would have the exact same gene. Yet something very strange can happen with this disorder. Some victims experience a slowness of movement resembling a symptom of Parkinson's disease. For others it is just the opposite; their movements become rapid. As it happened, one twin became hyperkinetic and the other was Parkinsonian. How could this be?

Our idealized example of these two women points out the very real possibility that mind influences can well affect the genetic imperative. While the straight genetic view would tend to explain the variation in symptoms by citing a difference in the penetrance of the genes or the probability that several other genes had interacted in certain ways, it is just as likely that the mind states of the women were preparing their bodies to accept two different kinds of genetic information. In other genetically driven diseases, the concordance rate is nowhere near as high, thereby leaving even greater room for mind influences as well as other epigenetic influences. The suggestion here is that studies of twins reveal that the mind may be playing a major role in the response rates to disease.

But perhaps the most intriguing aspect of the model is the implication for society at large. All modern experimental work points to how important for good health is the perception that an individual is in charge of his own destiny. The massive amount of work on stress and its relation to disease argues for this view, as do other studies that suggest that outside psychological guidance frequently does more long-term harm than good in problems that range from addiction to fighting somatic disease. The argument that social structures, public authorities, and institutions should be more responsible for personal well-being than our own attitudes and actions may well be detrimental. In short, social structures that too easily offer psychological assistance can show how dangerous that help can be when the recipient begins to avoid personal responsibility in the belief that he is helpless.

Accepting the view of mind-brain interactions, therefore, means that relying solely on the good environment to improve life is an inadequate strategy, since it fails to acknowledge how each brain is unique in interpreting its interactions with the past and present world. And, just as important, this strategy has no sympathy for those who abandon others to find their own course in the world on the assumption that individuals can survive all challenges to right thinking, all perversions of reasonable behavior that might be foisted upon them. The inter-actionist view, in contrast, emphasizes the dynamic relationship that exists between structure and experience. Disturbing that equilibrium too strongly can destroy the balance that makes for the good life.

Suggested Reading

Introduction

There are available several excellent neuroscience texts that review much of what is discussed on the brain side of our story. For an advanced book, try *Principles of Neural Science,* 2nd edition, by Eric R. Kandel and James H. Schwartz (Elsevier, New York, 1985). A simpler but also excellent text is *The Brain* by Richard F. Thompson (W. H. Freeman and Co., San Francisco, 1985). The mind sciences also have many fine texts. Two of the better offerings are *The Society of Mind* by Marvin Minsky (Simon and Schuster, New York, 1987); and *The Science of the Mind* by Owen J. Flanagan, Jr. (MIT Press, Bradford Books, Cambridge, Mass., 1984). One of my own books describes in detail the evidence for the idea of the brain's interpreter: *The Social Brain: Discovering the Networks of Mind* (Basic Books, New York, 1985). Finally, a wonderful book that argues for a unified science of mind and brain is *Neurophilosophy* by Patricia Smith Churchland (MIT Press, Bradford Books, Cambridge, Mass., 1986).

Chapter 1

The classic general text on pain that is spellbinding is *The Challenge of Pain,* 2nd edition, by P. D. Wall and Ronald Melzack (Basic Books, New York, 1982). An excellent monograph that describes the brain side of the pain story in detail is *The Pain System* by W. D. Willis, Jr. (Karger, Basel, 1985). Frederick W. L. Kerr of the Mayo Clinic has also written a short book on pain: *The Pain Book* (Prentice-Hall, Englewood Cliffs, N.J., 1981). It gives an upbeat view of pain, suggesting there is more success to pain remedies than others would argue for. It is clearly written and very helpful. Another pertinent study is "Pain response in nepalese porters" by W. Crawford Clark and Susanne Bennet Clark (prepublication manuscript).

Chapter 2

A good new review of memory is to be found in Larry Squires's new book, *Brain and Memory* (Oxford University Press, New York, 1987). A review of recent work on brain aging by Robert Katzman and Robert Terry appears in the chapter titled "Normal aging of the nervous system," in *The Neurology of Aging* (*Contemporary Neurology Series*), edited by R. Katzman and R. Terry (F. A. Davis Company, Philadelphia, 1983). A good review on intellectual decline by Jack Botwinick is titled "Intellectual abilities," in *Handbook of the Psychology of Aging,* edited by J. E. Birren and K. W. Schaie (Van Nostrand, Reinhold, New York, 1977). More specific studies are "Learning and aging" by David Arenberg and Elizabeth A. Rogertson-Tchabo, in *Handbook of the Psychology of Aging,* edited by J. E. Birren and K. W. Schaie (Van Nostrand, Reinhold, New York, 1977); "Psychology of adult development and aging" by J. E. Birren, W. R. Cunningham, and K. Yamamoto (*Annual Review of Psychology* 34: 543–575, 1983); and "Nutrients that modify brain function" by R. J. Wurtman (*Scientific American* 246: 50–59, 1982). The following articles are to be found in *Trends in Neuroscience* (March 1980): "The anatomy of amnesia" by Larry Squires, and "Memory disorders" by Richard Wurtman. In the same journal: "Memory: A neuropsychological approach" by Freda Newcombe (July 1980); "Disorders of recent memory in humans" by Elliot D. Ross (May 1982); and "Neural and molecular mechanisms underlying information storage in aplysia: Implications for learning and memory" by John H. Byrne (November 1985).

Chapter 3

Raymond E. Fancher's *The Intelligence Men: Makers of the IQ Controversy* (W. W. Norton, New York, 1985) should not be missed. It is a superb account of the history and current status of the psychological story. Stephen J. Gould's *The Mismeasure of Man* (Norton, New York, 1981) is a fine account of zealots of the past. See also Howard Gardner's *Frames of Mind* (Basic Books, New York, 1983). More specific studies are "Human brain glucose utilization and cognitive function in relation to age" by R. Duara et al. (*Annals of Neurology* 16: 702–713, 1984); "Wechsler adult intelligence scale performance" by T. N. Chase et al. (*Archives of Neurology* 41: 1244–1247, 1984); and "Education policy and the heritability of educational attainment" by A. C. Heath et al. (*Nature* 314: 734–736, 1984); "Heredity and familial environment in intelligence and educational level: A sibling study" by T. W. Teasdale and D. R. Owen (*Nature* 309: 620–622, 1984).

Chapter 4

Schizophrenia has been written about by hundreds of psychiatrists, psychologists, and neuroscientists. A very good description of the brain side of the story is to be found in the Kandel and Schwartz book listed under "Introduction." Jonathan H. Pincus and Gary J. Tucker have a good discussion in their *Behavioral Neurology*, 3rd edition (Oxford University Press, New York, 1985). A broad overview of the clinical side is *Schizophrenia: Symptoms, Causes, Treatments* by Kayla F. Bernheim and Richard R. J. Lewine (W. W. Norton, New York and London, 1979). Also see *Schizophrenia, Its Difference and Pathology: Stereotypes of Sexuality, Race, and Madness* by Sander L. Gilman (Cornell University Press, Ithaca and London, 1985). More specific works are "Concomitant obsessive-compulsive disorder and schizotypal personality disorder" by M. A. Jenike et al., and "The prognostic significance of obsessive-compulsive symptoms in schizophrenia" by W. S. Fenton and T. H. McGlashan (both in *American Journal of Psychiatry* 143: 530–532 and 437–441 respectively, 1986). The following articles are found in the *Journal of Abnormal Psychology* 94, 1985: "Are schizophrenics' behaviors schizophrenic? What medically versus psychosocially oriented therapists attribute to schizophrenic persons" by V. Shoham-Salomon, pp. 443–453; "Neuropsychological performance and positive and negative symptoms in schizophrenia" by M. Green and E. Walker, pp. 460–469. Also of interest is "Biological markers in schizotypal personality disorder" by L. J. Siever (*Schizophrenia Bulletin* 11: 564–575, 1985).

Chapter 5

Donald W. Goodwin's book *Anxiety* (Oxford University Press, New York, 1986) is exemplary. It is one of the finest pieces of biomedical writing, reviewing, and reporting that I have seen in a long time. All of the topics dealt with in this chapter are discussed in far more detail in this excellent book. Richard Goodwin's fine book *The Anxiety Disease* (Scribners, New York, 1983) is also most informative. He is an expert in treating anxiety and has detailed in his book much of what is commonly done for the anxious patient. More detailed works include "Biological constraints on conditioning" by J. Garcia, B. K. McGowan and K. F. Green, in *Classical Conditioning: II. Current Theory and Research,* edited by A. H. Block and W. F. Prokasy (Appleton-Century-Crofts, New York, 1972); and "Hormonal influences on memory" by J. L. McGaugh (*Annual Review of Psychology* 34: 297–324, 1983).

Chapter 6

The biochemical issues in depression are nicely discussed in the Kandel and Schwartz book listed under "Introduction." Psychological issues are convincingly argued in *Helplessness: On Depression, Development and Death* by M. E. P. Seligman (W. H. Freeman, San Francisco, 1975). Other studies are "Lithium and mania" by D. C. Tosteson (*Scientific American* 244: 164–173, 1981); "Endorphins and the psychiatrist" by A. V. Mackay (*Trends in Neuroscience,* May 1981); and "Life events and depression: A psychiatric view" by E. S. Paykel and J. A. Hollyman (*Trends in Neuroscience,* December 1984).

Chapter 7

Several texts give excellent descriptions of obsessions and compulsions: *The Abnormal Personality* by R. White and N. Watt (Wiley and Sons, New York, 1984); *Elements of Psychology* by D. Krech, S. Crutchfield, and N. Livson (Knopf, New York, 1974); and *New Perspectives in Abnormal Psychology,* edited by Kazdin, Bellack, and Hersen (Oxford University Press, New York, 1980). Notable articles are "Obsessive-compulsive disorders" by T. R. Insel (*Symposium on Anxiety Disorders* 8: Psychiatric Clinics of North America, 1985); "Biological factors in obsessive-compulsive disorders" by S. M. Turner, D. C. Beidel, and R. S. Nathan (*Psychological Bulletin* 97: 430–450, 1985); "Clomipra-mine in obsessive-compulsive disorder: A review" by J. Ananth (*Psy-chosomatics* 24: 723–727, 1983); "The obsessive-compulsive neurosis: Review of research findings" by D. I. Templer (*Comprehensive Psychia-try* 13: 375–383, 1972); "Obsessive-compulsive disorder: A question of neurologic lesion" by M. A. Jenike (*Comprehensive Psychiatry* 25: 298–304, 1984); and "Obsessional states" by John Pollitt (*British Journal of Psychiatry* 9: 133–140, 1975).

Chapter 8

Two general discussions on drug addiction and abuse can be found in *Coping and Substance Use,* edited by Saul Shiffman and Thomas Ashby Wills (Academic Press, New York, 1985); and *Drug and Alcohol Abuse: A Clinical Guide to Diagnosis and Treatment* by Marc A. Schuckit (Plenum, New York, 1984). More specific studies are "Encyclopedic handbook of alcoholism" by E. M. Pattison and E. Kaufman, and also "A physician's view of alcoholism" by J. J. Newton, both found in *Alcoholism: Treatment and Recovery,* edited by M. J. Goby (Catholic Health Association of U.S., St. Louis, 1984); "Smoking as a coping strategy" by A. D. Revell, D. M. Warburton, and K. Wesnes (*Addictive Behaviors* 10: 209–224, 1985); "Cocaine: An overview of current issues" by J. Grabowski and S. I. Dworkin (*International Journal of the Addictions* 206: 1065–1088, 1985); "The self-medication hypothesis of addictive disorders: Focus on heroin and cocaine dependence" by E. J. Khantzian (*American Journal of Psychiatry* 142: 1259–1264, 1985); "The central nervous system and chromosomes in narcotic addiction" by L. Roizin, J. C. Liu, and H. K. Fischman (*Trends in Neuroscience,* March 1980); "Multiple opiate receptors" by K. J. Chang, E. Hazum, and P. Cuatre-casas (*Trends in Neuroscience,* July 1980); also "Learning and the develop-ment of alcohol-tolerance and dependence: The role of vasopressin-like peptides" by John C. Crabbe and Henk Rigter (*Trends in Neurosci-ence,* January 1980). Additional pertinent articles: "Autoradiographic localization of drug and neurotransmitter receptors in the brain" by M. J. Kuhar (*Trends in Neuroscience,* March 1981); "Marihuana in man: Three years later" by Leo E. Hollister (*Science* 172: 21–29, 1971); "Limit setting on drug abuse in methadone maintenance patients" by J. J. McCarthy and O. T. Borders (*American Journal of Psychiatry* 142: 1419–1423, 1985); "Cocaine" by C. Van Dyke and R. Byck (*Scientific Ameri-*

can 246: 128–137, 1982); "Longitudinal study of marijuana effects" by J. A. Halikas et al. (*International Journal of the Addictions* 20: 701–711, 1985); and "Carry-over effects of marijuana intoxication on aircraft pilot performance: A preliminary report" by J. A. Yesavage et al. (*American Journal of Psychiatry* 142: 1325–1329, 1985).

Chapter 9

The benchmark book on the topic is the lively and engaging *A New Look at Love* by E. Walster and G. Walster (Addison-Wesley, Reading, Mass., 1978). Notable studies are "The development of infant-mother interaction among the Ganda" by M. D. S. Ainsworth, in *Determinants of Infant Behavior*, vol. 2, edited by B. M. Foss (Wiley, New York, 1963); "Platonic love, transference love, and love in real life" by Martin S. Bergman (*Journal of American Psychoanalytical Association* 30: 61–87, 1982); "Delusional loving" by Mary V. Seeman (*Archives of General Psychiatry* 35: 1265–1267, 1978); "Barriers to being in love" by Otto Kernberg (*Journal of American Psychoanalytical Association* 22: 486–511, 1974); "Elements of pathological love relationships" by John M. Curtis (*Psychological Reports* 53: 83–92, 1983); "Love: addiction or road to self-realization, A second look" by Jane Simon (*American Journal of Psychoanalysis* 42: 253–263, 1982); "Learning to love" by H. Harlow (*American Psychologist* 25: 161–168, 1970); "The nature of love—simplified" by H. Harlow and M. Harlow (*American Scientist* 54: 244–272, 1966); "Case report of de Clerembault syndrome, bipolar affective disorder, and response to lithium" by Gary Remington and Howard Book (*American Journal of Psychiatry* 141: 1285–1287, 1984); and "Sensation seeking: A comparative approach to a human trait" by Marvin Zuckerman (*Behavioral and Brain Sciences* 7: 413–471, 1984).

Chapter 10

The brain side of sleep is reviewed nicely in the Kandel and Schwartz text listed under "Introduction." The American Medical Association has produced an excellent book with the advice of three leaders in sleep research, W. C. Dement, S. H. Frazier, and E. D. Weitzman, called *Guide to Better Sleep* by L. Lamberg (Random House, New York, 1985). A book on dream research is *Handbook of Dreams*, edited by Benjamin B. Wolman (Van Nostrand, Reinhold, New York, 1979).

Additional works include: *Clinical Aspects of Sleep and Sleep Disturbances,* edited by T. L. Riley (Butterworth, London, 1985); *The Functions of Sleep,* edited by R. Drucker-Colin, M. Shkurovich, and M. B. Sterman (Academic Press, New York, 1979); "Endogenous sleep-promoting factors" by S. Matthysse and K. K. Kidd, and also "New perspectives in sleep research" by M. H. Chase (both in *Trends in Neuroscience,* July 1982); "Sleep: A neurobiological window on affective disorders" by J. C. Gillin and A. A. Borbely (*Trends in Neuroscience,* December 1985); and "Emotional stress, mood state sleep" by R. J. G. Cluydts and P. Visser, in *Fifth European Congress on Sleep Research* (Karger, Basel, 1981).

Chapter 11

The classic book on stress is by Hans Seyle and is called *The Stress of Life* (McGraw-Hill, New York, 1976). Other studies are *Seyle's Guide to Stress Research,* edited by Hans Seyle (Scientific and Academic Editions, New York, 1983); *Stress, Attitudes, Decisions* by Irving L. Janis (Prayer Publishers, New York, 1982); *The Philosophy of Stress* by Mary Asterita (Human Services Press, New York, 1985); "Thought processes, consciousness and stress" by George Mandler, in *Human Stress and Cognition: An Information Processing Approach,* edited by V. Hamilton and D. W. Warburton (Wiley, New York, 1979).

Chapter 12

An excellent book that deals with the topic of healing is *The Healer Within* by Steven Locke and Douglas Colligan (Dutton, New York, 1986). While this book is heavily committed to the notion that mind states can influence health states, it does point up many interesting facts on the topic. A superb book is *Body and Self* by George Block (William Kaufmann, Los Altos, Calif., 1985). This book was brought out as an undergraduate text. It is much more, however, being a good source for specifics on anything that deals with mind and health. Another is "Peptide hormones shared by the neuroendocrine and immunologic systems" by J. E. Blalock, D. Harbour-McMenamin, and E. M. Smith (*Journal of Immunology* 135: 858s–861s, 1985).

Index